THE TRAILER SAILER OWNER'S MANUAL

BUY—OUTFIT—TRAIL—MAINTAIN

BY

GREGG NESTOR

Copyright ©2008 Gregory Nestor

All rights reserved. No part of this book may be used or reproduced in any manner whatsoever without written permission, except in the case of brief quotations embedded in critical articles and reviews. For information, contact the publisher.

Cover design by Rob Johnson, www.johnsondesign.org
Editing and book design by Linda Morehouse, www.webuildbooks.com

Printed in the United States of America
First Edition
ISBN 978-0-939837-82-X

Published by
Paradise Cay Publications, Inc.
P. O. Box 29
Arcata, CA 95518-0029
800-736-4509
707-822-9163 Fax
www.paracay.com
paracay@humboldt1.com

FOR JOHN AND KEVIN

PREFACE

Almost 30 years ago I stepped aboard a sailboat for the first time. It was a friend's 14-foot daysailer; we spent the afternoon lazily cruising a small inland lake. On this initial adventure my wife-to-be, Joyce, said, "What a great place to clear the cobwebs from your mind." And so it all began. Four boats (all trailerable sailboats) and numerous sailing grounds later, my fascination with the sport has not diminished.

Through the years, I've performed my own maintenance and upgrades and have developed several novel approaches to common sailing dilemmas. What you hold in your hand, *The Trailer Sailer Owner's Guide,* is much of what I've learned. It's a book dedicated to trailerable sailboats—trailer sailers. In it you'll see how to choose a boat that fits the type of sailing and the sailing grounds that you're interested in. You'll also see how to outfit it, maintain it, and most of all, enjoy it.

Two things that you won't find in the following pages are how-to-sail instructions or a sales pitch for a specific brand or type of boat. What you will find is a discussion much like a conversation with a fellow sailor . . . relaxed, informative, thought-provoking, and hopefully entertaining.

CONTENTS

Preface — iv
Introduction — 1

SECTION I
SEARCHING FOR THE RIGHT FIT — 3

1. Choosing the Right Trailerable Sailboat — 5
2. Sailboat Searching — 13
3. Deciphering the Classifieds — 20
4. Selling Your Boat — 27
5. The Anatomy of a Sailboat — 33

SECTION II
TRAILERS AND TRAILERING — 39

6. Trailer Sailer Begins With "Trailer" — 40
7. Buying a Used Sailboat Trailer — 53
8. How Much Are You Towing? — 64
9. The Tow Vehicle — 66
10. On the Road — 70

SECTION III
OUTFITTING YOUR TRAILER SAILER   73

11. Fitting Out   74
12. Safety   78
13. Customizing for Comfort and Safety   83

SECTION IV
TAKING CARE OF YOUR BOAT'S SYSTEMS
AND HER CREW   99

14. The (Infamous 2-Cycle) Outboard Motor   100
15. Care and Feeding of the Trailer Sailer's Battery   110
16. Reducing Electrical Noise Interference   120
17. Sail Management   131
18. The Trailer Sailor's Galley   141

SECTION V
SNAKE OILS AND ELIXIRS TO KEEP YOUR BOAT
HEALTHY AND HAPPY   151

19. Sealants and Adhesives   152
20. Engine Lubricants   166
21. Engine Coolants   172
22. Simply Clean   177
23. Choosing the Right Antifouling Paint   185
24. Applying Bottom Paints   192
25. Restoring Luster to Your Deck   195

SECTION VI
MARLINESPIKE SEAMANSHIP — 199

26. Cordage — 200
27. Knots — 210
28. Whipping and Splicing — 224
29. Tackle — 231
30. A Handy Heaving Line — 238
31. Rope Mats — 241

SECTION VII
YOUR TRAILER SAILER AT REST — 251

32. Anchors — 252
33. Anchor Rode Bag — 261
34. Marking the Anchor Rode — 264
35. North Coast Pick-Up Buoy — 266

SECTION VIII
LAUNCHING AND RETRIEVAL — 269

36. Launching and Retrieval — 270
37. KISS: Keep it Simple, Sailor! — 273

SECTION IX
DON'T OVERLOOK THE DETAILS — 285

38. Weather 101 — 286
39. A Proper Winter Cover — 308
40. Passing Safely Beneath — 311
41. Checklists — 313

Appendix — 325

ACKNOWLEDGMENTS

No book is written entirely alone. While the actual combining of words and putting them to paper is a solitary pursuit, many people have contributed towards the production of this manuscript, either with the sharing of knowledge and experience or with their encouragement and support.

First of all, my sincere thanks go to all those trailersailors who generously responded to my questions. It was their input that led to each of these chapters.

I'm also indebted to those non-sailors who spent time explaining their particular fields of expertise and reviewing select parts of this manuscript.

My special appreciation goes to Joyce, my wife, who listened endlessly to my ideas, offered suggestions, acted as my personal editor, and was a constant supporter.

INTRODUCTION

The versatility, simplicity, and economics of a trailerable sailboat can't be beat. No longer must you be limited to one sailing area. Having the ability to go to windward at 55 mph broadens your horizons. In a single season you can enjoy the different scenery and sailing conditions that only distant and diverse sailing grounds can offer. Just hitch up the trailer, drive to the water, step the mast, float the boat, and you're sailing! Also, unlike a non-trailerable, you have the option of driving out of an inclement weather system. Northern sailors can become "snow birds" during the winter and travel south to warmer sailing grounds. And on the way, they can use their boats as land yachts and save the cost of a motel room.

The rigging and systems on board a trailerable are usually simple and easy to maintain with minimal effort. For example, most trailer sailers rely on outboard motors as their auxiliary engine. These are far easier to maintain than their inboard counterparts. And because they can be removed and transported to a mechanic, major repairs tend to be less expensive and don't eliminate the use of the boat. This equates to more time on the water and less time devoted to long hours of boat maintenance.

Trailer sailers, including their trailers, are less expensive to buy and maintain than their larger non-trailerable cousins. While less than a gallon of anti-fouling paint may adequately cover the bottom of a 22-foot trailerable sailboat, its larger cousins will need considerably more and at a correspondingly greater cost. Also, with a trailer sailer you'll eliminate dockage, storage, and seasonal haul-out fees. Your trailer sailer can be stored on its trailer in your backyard, where it awaits your next sailing adventure.

If it's challenges and excitement that you want, trailersailing offers that too. Nothing beats the "feel" of the helm and the instant feedback that comes from sailing a small boat. It's a great platform on which to learn and hone your sailing skills. A trailerable sailboat has it all. It just comes in a smaller package.

SECTION I

SEARCHING FOR THE RIGHT FIT

All trailerable sailboats must meet a principal design criterion: They must be able to be launched and retrieved from a ramp. From this point on, hull form, draft, ballast, rig, interior layout, etc. differ from one trailer sailer to another not unlike snowflakes in the Rockies. No one configuration or design is best. It all depends upon the type of sailing and the sailing grounds that interest you. Add to this mix aesthetics and just plain old personal preference and things can get pretty interesting. A good approach is to develop a "dream sheet" to help you define and put on paper your preferences and prejudices. This will enable you to ask the right questions, look at the right features, and quickly eliminate boats that don't meet with the criteria you have established.

IF YOU'RE INTERESTED IN A CLOSE-TO-WATER EXPERIENCE
OR THE SIMPLICITY OF OFF-THE-BEACH SAILING,
A BOARDBOAT LIKE THIS AMF MINIFISH MAY BE THE BOAT FOR YOU.

CHAPTER 1

CHOOSING THE RIGHT TRAILERABLE SAILBOAT

So, you're in the market for a trailerable sailboat. Great! There are approximately 50 new trailerables currently in production, ranging in size from 14 to 25 feet. The number of models on the used sailboat market is probably close to six times that. Which sailboat should you buy? Good question. Since selection is not a problem, you'll need to define your requirements, wants, expectations, likes, etc. in order to narrow the field down to just a handful of candidates. How do you do that? One way is to ask yourself the following How, Where, When, and Why questions. Answer them, in as much detail as possible, before you open your checkbook. After having done this, you'll have a clearer picture of what that "right" trailerable sailboat might be.

HOW DO YOU PLAN ON USING YOUR BOAT?

Are you new to sailing and do you want to learn to sail? Or are you a novice sailor who desires to build a solid foundation of sailing skills for racing? Or maybe you're interested in the close-to-the-water experience or the simplicity of off-the-beach sailing. If so, consider a dinghy, boardboat, or even a small multihull. These types of boats afford a close cause-and-effect relationship with wind and water, which is an ideal platform for learning how to sail or for building solid sailing skills for racing. These boats, which are usually simple to rig and launch/retrieve, are easiest on the pocketbook.

If you want a drier boat that will accommodate you and two or three others plus some gear for a day's sail, consider the bigger, more stable daysailer. These boats traditionally have larger cockpits with little or no cabin space. If there is a small cabin or cuddy, it is useful for storing sails, extra gear, and that picnic lunch. A daysailer is the perfect boat on which to take the family out for a day's cruise or to hone your sailing skills. Daysailers include both centerboarders and keelboats. While launching and retrieval are relatively easy, rigging can range from the simple to the more complex, with cost directly related to size and complexity.

DINGHY-TYPE DAYSAILERS SUCH AS THIS JESTER ARE DRIER THAN THEIR BOARDBOAT COUSINS AND WILL ACCOMMODATE A CREW OF TWO OR THREE.

1. CHOOSING THE RIGHT TRAILERABLE SAILBOAT

If your goal is to spend weekends or vacations aboard, you'll need berths, a galley, a head, and a dining area. To accomplish this adequately, you'll want a pocket cruiser, starting around 22 feet.

THIS O'DAY 19 OFFERS SOME LIVEABOARD CREATURE COMFORTS FOR THOSE WHO WOULD LIKE TO STAY OUT OVERNIGHT.

These are generally keelboats, either fixed, swing, or incorporating a centerboard. Although you'll spend more time rigging the boat, this type of craft affords liveaboard creature comforts and also allows you to entertain dockside. As is the case with daysailers, the amount of money you'll spend on a pocket cruiser is a direct reflection of the boat's size and complexity.

THIS SHARK IS A PERFORMANCE-ORIENTED POCKET CRUISER.

So you may have your eye on that Wednesday night race trophy, but your family has other ideas. They want to cruise the coast during next year's summer vacation. Don't worry, a performance cruiser may be just what you need. Several pocket cruisers have been designed for this dual role. They may carry a generous amount of sail, sport more aggressive keels, have a longer waterline, and exhibit less wetted surface. While they offer many of the amenities of the pocket cruiser, be prepared to make some sacrifices in comfort (headroom, for one). Since this can be considered a variation of the pocket cruiser, your outlay of time and money will be similar.

1. CHOOSING THE RIGHT TRAILERABLE SAILBOAT

THIS CHRYSLER 22 IS MEANT FOR CRUISING RATHER THAN RACING.

With racing in your blood, speed will be your highest priority. Since speed comes in different sizes, check with your local sailing clubs to determine if there are any one-design fleets, or what type of boats are being raced locally. Consider matching boat type with the majority of local racers. You don't want to be the "one of" boat. If you're really serious, look at the one-designs that can lead to national competitions. As a dedicated racer, prepare to spend time and money tuning and tricking out your boat.

WHERE ARE YOU GOING TO SAIL YOUR BOAT?

If your sailing grounds are the Great Lakes or coastal areas where sailing conditions can be challenging, boat construction quality and size will be of great importance. Boardboats and daysailers are only acceptable close to shore. Larger boats will be more comfortable farther from shore. However, the vast majority of even the largest trailerables are not blue-water boats. Regardless of boat size, pay close attention to unusual weather and water conditions. Make sure that your boat's sails can be reefed. Also, prepare your craft with a greater level of safety equipment. Backups for VHF and GPS are a good idea. Having charts and knowing how to use them is essential.

Many sailors sail only on a specific inland lake. In relatively protected bodies of water such as these, most any trailerable sailboat will work fine. Knowing the water depth, the shoreline configuration, and the facilities available will aid you in your selection process. Since you may be tacking more often, consider a smaller boat, which requires less effort. Bear in mind that small lakes frequently exhibit changing winds, caused by trees and other shoreline obstructions. Such a phenomenon makes these bodies of water great places on which to learn.

If you're a purist and want to be a true "trailer sailor," make sure that the boat you select is easily launched, retrieved, and trailered. Consider a boat of around 22 feet as being the max for these conditions. Also, the type of keel will play a big role here. Stay away from deep, fixed keels. Swing keels, shoal drafts with or without centerboards, and centerboard boats go a long way in making launching and retrieval easier. They also offer the best versatility when it comes to thin-water sailing, beaching, and contending with underwater obstructions. How much time you're willing to spend on rigging is something you'll also want to address before you buy. If you're not quite sure what to do, you may want to select a boat based on the body of water you will sail on most, while keeping in mind some of the other sailing destinations you're interested in.

WHEN DO YOU PLAN ON TRAILERING YOUR BOAT?

One of the main reasons to own a trailerable sailboat is that it gives you the ability to experience a variety of sailing destinations with relative ease. If you intend on sailing different lakes for days or a

1. CHOOSING THE RIGHT TRAILERABLE SAILBOAT

week at a time, rigging time may be less important than the size of the boat and the creature comforts it has to offer. On the other hand, if your plans are to daysail different lakes, the amount of time spent rigging should be kept at a minimum. Also, you may want to consider a small boat, which will allow you access to shallower bodies of water.

Many trailerable sailboats are only trailered twice a year, once to the mooring or slip and once back for storage. If this is your plan, rigging may be the least of your concerns; you may want to move up to the maximum size trailerable.

WHY DO YOU WANT A TRAILERABLE SAILBOAT?

As is quite apparent, the previous three questions deal specifically with the more tangible aspects associated with how you plan on using a trailerable sailboat. This last question addresses those subjective, yet common reasons why a trailerable craft is desired.

If your motivation is to avoid paying slip or mooring fees, look for a boat that is quickly rigged, launched, and retrieved. If your boat lacks these qualities, you won't use it as often and it now becomes an expensive liability rather than an enjoyable asset.

You want to save on storage costs. True, a trailerable can be stored on its trailer. However, do you have the space to keep boat and trailer at your home? If not, will you need to rent space at a boat yard or self-store facility?

Yes, you can trailer your boat almost everywhere. Do you have a tow vehicle capable of pulling a large, heavy boat? If not, you'll need to either get a larger tow vehicle or set your sights on a smaller trailerable sailboat.

If you think trailerables are less expensive than non-trailerables, think again. A sailboat is a sailboat, regardless of whether it is trailerable or not, and new ones are more expensive than older ones.

So, it's all been decided?

You've answered the questions, there's storage space next to the garage, your SUV can pull a Sherman tank, and you and your family have mapped out sailing destinations for the next two years. Sounds like a plan. But before you start touring the boat yards and dealers with checkbook in hand, you might want to give a little thought to a few personal preferences, such as: new boat vs. used, wood vs. fiberglass, sloop vs. cutter vs. catboat vs. yawl, etc., masthead vs. fractional rig, motor vs. no motor, 2 cycle vs. 4 cycle vs. diesel, lots of bright work vs. minimal bright work, traditional vs. leading edge... Ahhh, decisions, decisions. So many boats and so little time!

CHAPTER 2

SAILBOAT SEARCHING

When Joyce and I made the conscious decision (maybe more conscious on my part than hers) to again upgrade boats, this time from a daysailer to a trailerable cruiser, it became readily apparent that we needed to establish some sort of selection guidelines. I had a litany of ideas as to what constituted the perfect boat; however, I soon discovered that Joyce was viewing this from an entirely different perspective.

SETTING THE STAGE

While I cloistered myself in the den with Jimmy Buffet and pored over my collection of sailing books and magazines, Joyce made herself a cup of tea. This respite gave her the opportunity to review what she liked and disliked about daysailing and to formulate what she wanted cruising to be for us and how to enhance the likes while minimizing the dislikes.

    First, allow me to back up just a bit to the decision point of upgrading from a daysailer to a trailerable cruiser. Both Joyce and I agreed that our primary interest was to see new and different places within the country. True, this could easily be done with our daysailer, but we also liked the idea of having a cabin with amenities to spend the weekend nights in. She also didn't want a very large boat because trailering, launching, retrieving, and mast stepping would be more difficult. In addition to seeing our country by sailing on its inland lakes, Joyce personally liked the idea of the relative safety and security afforded by these sheltered waters when compared to blue water or even Great Lakes sailing. Joyce had no desire to race, and I knew that she would much rather prefer to spend a leisurely afternoon gunkholing or tacking back and forth.

She'd told me that she felt comfortable with my technical and analytical abilities, but that sometimes she felt my feet are not planted on firm enough ground for her comfort (figuratively speaking…I hope). So, with our primary interest defined, I began to evaluate more information.

BIGGER IS NOT BETTER

My research in the den provided me with many more questions than answers. However, I quickly came to the conclusion that I couldn't take a 40-something-foot blue-water cruiser, with all its amenities and systems, and shrink it down to trailer size. Also, to be truly trailerable, bigger is not better. So, after comparing notes with Joyce, our first consideration became size.

In order to get the most into the smallest, I established a size range of 19 to 23 feet. This encompassed such trailer sailers as the Com Pac 19 and the O'Day 23. I knew quite well that there would be exceptions, but regardless of which way I went, up or down, the trade-offs would increase dramatically. To us, a cruiser meant spending weekends aboard or possibly even longer. We, especially Joyce, weren't willing to settle for some type of aquatic backpack camping.

I also didn't want to mess around with any special type of hitch. After consulting the manufacturer's specifications for our ½ ton pickup, I targeted the weight at around 3,000 pounds (so much for a Marshall 22).

2. SAILBOAT SEARCHING

NEW VS. USED

We began reviewing the classified ads and sail publications while also visiting marinas, boat shows, and the occasional dealer. Early on in our quest we looked at a shiny new Precision 23 with a galvanized trailer; this craft had a mast stepping system and was priced at around $25,000. While Joyce and I were still discussing (Joyce called it negotiating) the finer points of our potential new boat, we became unanimous that it wasn't going to be a *brand* new boat. It was to be an experienced craft, for sure. That one decision concentrated our field of selection on a variety of boats, many of which were no longer in production.

While many would tend to shy away from boats no longer being made, it didn't bother us. Sailboats aren't like cars; they have only about two dozen moving parts, all of which can be either repaired or replaced with the aid of a decent chandlery. Anyway, I'm pretty handy and enjoy tinkering around. As a plus, Joyce thought that many of these experienced boats had greater eye appeal, since they possessed what she calls that "traditional sailboat look." And from a practical standpoint, she knows that they float (they have been floating for several years already) and that they cost less than a new boat.

Unlike a new boat, many used boats often come outfitted with extras such as PFDs, additional sails, fenders, ground tackle, electronics, and even galleyware. For example, friends of ours recently purchased a cruiser for what was a very reasonable price. When they added in the almost $5,000 worth of extras, many of which were new and had never been used, the price was better than bargain basement.

While Joyce enjoys the warmth of hardwood floors and wooden antique furniture, wood is not something that she wanted our new boat to be made of, teak trim topside and wood accents below notwithstanding. Likewise, as the contractor who sided our house said, "Ma'am, vinyl is final." Fiberglass was to be the material of choice.

KEEPING IT SIMPLE

Since Joyce and I would be a crew of two, the stepping and unstepping of the mast needed to be quick and easy. Also, we felt that the rigging should be simple and uncomplicated, much as with our previous daysailers, both of which were fractional rig sloops. Therefore, we eliminated boats with multiple spars, including gaff rigs, club-footed headsails, and cutters. With this decision, the Nimble Bay Hen and a couple others didn't make the cut.

Our love of gunkholing and desire to travel to different sailing areas, most of which are uncharted, dictated a boat with a shallow draft. Launching and retrieval would also be easier with a shallow draft sailboat. Therefore, we eliminated boats with fixed keels measuring 3 feet or longer (goodbye, Ranger 23) and looked at boats with shoal keels, swing keels, centerboards, and combination keels. The water ballast/centerboard combination, while it has obvious advantages, was eliminated, thus striking some Santanas and MacGregors from our list. Joyce felt that water should only be on the outside of the boat and I tended to agree with her.

CREATURE COMFORTS

While I concerned myself with the spars and rigging, there were a number of creature comforts that Joyce was definitely interested in. First of all, she wanted a cabin with berths for 3—4 in a pinch. We have two grown sons, one of who would be with us most of the time. Since both my son and I are taller than 6 feet, she wanted full sitting headroom in the cabin, maybe even with a pop-up arrangement. A galley of sorts would be nice, with a space for a cooler, a small stove, and a sink. It would be nice to not always have to brown-bag our lunch or grill on-shore. We couldn't forget the port-a-potty area. That would definitely be a plus for Joyce in upgrading from a daysailer!

Even with all of that in the cabin, she wanted as much stowage space as possible. We've lived in quite a number of different houses, and we're both well aware that there is never enough closet space. In any event, this would mean looking for a sailboat with an outboard engine. Not too tall an order for the boat length range we were interested in.

Also, what's the point of spending a summer night on the lake without portlights and hatches that open to allow for as much ventilation as possible? Last, but definitely not least, Joyce wanted our new boat to have as big a cockpit as possible. Maybe this is a holdover from our daysailing days, or maybe she knows how cramped it can be hanging out in close quarters with a couple of guys over 6 feet tall.

THE BOTTOM LINE

Now that we had our "dream sheet," all we needed was to find the boat and hopefully a deal. Not so quick! True, we did a lot of preselection on paper; however, when we began to look in earnest, another set of factors impacted the selection process. How long were we willing to spend looking? We had sold our daysailer and were now boatless. How far were we willing to travel in pursuit of our goal? Living on the boat-rich shore of Lake Erie, we felt that long-distance travel was not warranted. How much were we willing to spend? We had the money from the sale of our daysailer and to that we added some savings, thus establishing our top dollar.

Developing our dream sheet helped us to define and put on paper our preferences and prejudices. This enabled us to ask the right questions, look at the right things, quickly eliminate boats that didn't appeal to us, and make intelligent comparisons.

How many boats did we look at? A lot. We crawled over, around, and through what seemed like an endless array of sailing vessels, in an endless array of conditions. A partial list included: West Wight

Potter 19; Rhodes 22; Chrysler 22; San Juan 21; O'Day 22, 222, & 23; Tanzer 22; Columbia 23; and the ubiquitous Catalina 22.

WE CRAWLED OVER, AROUND, AND THROUGH
WHAT SEEMED LIKE AN ENDLESS ARRAY OF SAILING VESSELS.

While all of them fit our dream sheet, one way or another the field narrowed quickly based on condition, value, and first impression. (Remember, there's only one opportunity to make a good first impression).

In the end, we purchased a 1984 O'Day 222. While it fits our specifications closely, it doesn't exactly have what Joyce earlier referred to as that traditional sailboat look. However, the large

2. SAILBOAT SEARCHING

THERE'S ONLY ONE OPPORTUNITY TO MAKE A GOOD FIRST IMPRESSION.
THIS O'DAY 222 NOT ONLY DID THAT,
BUT FIT OUR SPECS AND POCKETBOOK AS WELL

cockpit, attention to detail topside and below, and the near-showroom condition made up for it many times over. By the way, it did come with many extras, including a set of wineglasses still in the unopened package. It doesn't get any better than that.

CHAPTER 3

DECIPHERING THE CLASSIFIEDS

Over the years, I have found that the classifieds of the various sailing publications can be both informative and entertaining. While I'm not actively looking for another sailboat, I do like to keep current with the used sailboat market. That's what I've told my wife, Joyce. Also, I just plain enjoy reading about sailboats.

Having spent many years in a corporate marketing department, I've had my share of experience in accentuating the positive while downplaying, if not ignoring, the negative. If it weren't for us wordsmiths, many products would have never been sold. I'm not saying that we out and out fibbed; we just worded things in a more favorable way.

With that said, let's get back to the subject at hand, the classifieds. I'm sure you have noticed ads peppered with all sorts of abbreviations and terms unique to sailboats. Once you've figured out what S/D, R/F, GPS, and RDF are, to name a few, you'll be well on your way to deciphering the classifieds, right? Wrong. It's those easily understood, plain English phrases that can sometimes throw you off.

To demonstrate what I mean as well as to possibly help you in your perusal of the classifieds, I offer the following phrases as potential "misspeak" candidates. All of these were taken from actual ads.

If it's a board boat like a Sunfish, a daysailer, or maybe even a small keelboat like a Catalina 22, the phrase "good starter boat" may be taken literally. However, when attached to something over 30 feet, you can bet it's long in the tooth, has been sailed hard, and is pretty tired inside and out. I heard this phrase uttered by a broker in conjunction with almost every boat on his lot. I suspect he was trying to upgrade the sale or at least get me ready for that next boat, even though I hadn't bought the first one yet.

"Lots of sails" or "large sail inventory" is often noted in ads for boats with racing pedigrees. Most cruising boats don't usually emphasize this point. (If anything, ads for cruising boats may list specific sails.) Sometimes the sail inventory is nothing more than the working sails and a set of worn-out originals. An acquaintance of mine once looked at a boat that advertised a nine-sail inventory. After going over a few of the sails and asking repeated questions, it was determined that only two sails were for the boat. The other seven sails were from other boats and would require loft work before or even if they could be used.

It is not unusual to see ads for older boats with the phrase "freshly painted." I still would want to know why, with what, and by whom. A newer boat that has been repainted is suspect and a candidate for many questions and a close examination. I know of a two-year-old boat that was painted red just because the owner liked the color. He's a fireman. Unfortunately, he and his three kids did the job. Kinda like Tom Sawyer whitewashing the fence. It looks good from a distance...a long distance. The owner of a five-year-old ketch said he had the boat painted to improve it cosmetically. A survey revealed that the cosmetic treatment was his way of saying "extensive hull repair work."

"Ten layer epoxy bottom." Wow! Couldn't they get it right the previous 9 other times? Was the blistering problem that bad? Maybe the owner/seller is just supercautious. Unless you're just curious, it might be best to pass this one by.

Every time I see the words "customized interior" I recall a boat that I briefly looked at three years ago: Rainbow-colored shag carpeting throughout (sole, walls, and overhead), plaid cushions, a beaded curtain dividing the cabin from the v-berth, and to finish things off, an eight track complete with over fifty tapes! Jimmy Hendrix would have felt right at home. The point to remember here is that not everyone's carpentry skills or decorative tastes are first rate or match your style.

There are many valid reasons why an owner may elect to have his boat "professionally maintained"—lack of time, lack of ability, uniqueness of the craft, absentee ownership are but a few. This is not unusual with larger sailboats. However, it is a little unique when the boat is much smaller, say a 20-year-old trailer sailer. I once talked with the owner who was selling his 1979 Paceship. To him, professionally maintained meant that at the beginning of the season the marina painted the bottom and launched the boat. At the season's end they hauled it out, pressure-washed the bottom, and covered it with a tarp. Anything else that needed attention was done with the help of his fellow club members or was jotted down on a to-do list (that came with the boat). A boat that has been truly professionally maintained and comes with a documented maintenance history is a real plus, both for the buyer and the seller.

To a saltwater sailor, the phrase "fresh water boat" may not mean too much. However, the fact remains that a fresh water boat will usually command a slightly better price than its saltwater identical twin. A Great Lakes sailor might assume that all locally advertised boats are fresh water boats. Not so. The various interconnecting waterways coupled with today's mobile society can mean the Bahamas in the winter and Lake Champlain in the summer.

3. DECIPHERING THE CLASSIFIEDS

LET'S TALK PRICE AND CONDITION

It seems to me that there are four classic ways a seller addresses price in his ad:

- *$XXXX.XX FIRM*

    More often than not there's no negotiating room here. Unless you uncover something which can adversely affect the price, this is the seller's bottom dollar.

- *ASKING $XXXX.XX*

    Usually, this means there's some negotiating room here. An acquaintance of ours just bought an S-2 8.0 for close to half the asking price.

- *MUST SELL/ANXIOUS TO SELL*

    While you may think that there's plenty of negotiating room here, the seller may just be trying to entice you. Then again, a divorce, job relocation, illness, or some other circumstance may be responsible. One of the members at the sailing club got his boat for close to one quarter of her value just because the seller's wife was tired of looking at it in the backyard.

- (no price listed)

    Either the boat is expensive, overpriced, or the seller thinks that once you call he can make the sale. I don't know about you, but unless I'm interested in that model boat and like the rest of the ad, I just move on down the page. It's a buyer's market.

Here is how you may see boat conditions described:

COMPLETELY RESTORED

Unless the boat is some type of vintage classic, this phrase has very little positive sales impact. While some plain old, everyday, garden-variety sailboat has been lovingly put back to better-than-showroom condition, restoration will not significantly increase the selling price. Looking at it from another angle, how do you define restoration? A cosmetic coating of bottom paint over an untreated blistered hull? Applications of sail tape where a sewing machine is more appropriate?

MANY UPGRADES AND AMENITIES

The key word here is amenities. See *Customized Interior.*

MANY SPARE PARTS

Did the seller forget to put whatever he was working on back together? Are these bona fide spares or just a collection of leftovers from a prior job? Was something replaced and this is the old one? The spare parts that came with my friend's boat were a combination of old, worn-out parts, a coffee can of stainless steel nuts and bolts, and a brand new set of lazy jacks complete with hardware.

GOOD LOOKER

While life may be too short to sail an ugly boat, beauty is only skin deep. Look past that new paint job or coat of wax. Take her out for a sail. If she sails as good as she looks, have her surveyed.

GOOD PROJECT BOAT

Unless you're real handy, have lots of time and maybe even lots of money, or Don Casey's a friend of yours, steer clear of this one. My son almost bought a $500 wooden runabout until he discovered that it was going to take close to $2,000 to replace much of the structural wooden members, after which he'd have a $1,000 wooden runabout.

BOAT IS WELL-BUILT, BUT NEEDS SOME TLC

This is maybe one step up from *Good Project Boat*. In any event, if you have the skills, and most of all enjoy the challenge, you might uncover a gem in the rough. Tread carefully here, and before you open your checkbook get a professional opinion.

A CLASSIC

I believe that if a sailboat is truly a classic you don't need to include these words in the ad. Anyone interested in buying a boat of this type will know what he's/she's looking at. Old boats, good and otherwise, are often advertised as classics.

NEWER ELECTRONICS

Don't confuse this with new electronics. It is often difficult, if not impossible, to get service, replacement parts, or even operation manuals for *newer* electronics. This is the voice of experience speaking.

CLASSIC INTERIOR

This has a lot in common with *A Classic*, but mostly it means narrow, dated décor, possibly well worn, and for sure old.

In a recent local sailing publication I found this gem of a sales pitch: *Sail Away Condition, Well Maintained, Overall Good Condition, A Few Cosmetic Minor Nicks and Scrapes, Some TLC Required.* The seller has a strong beginning but winds up buying back everything by the time he reaches the end.

Now that you know how to decipher the classifieds, the next time you read one, remember, "I know you believe you understand what you think was said, but I'm not sure you realize that what you read is not what was meant."

CHAPTER 4

SELLING YOUR BOAT

I know, this section of the book is entitled "Searching for the right fit" and that's what you're doing. But believe me, the information contained in this chapter is going to come in handy no matter whether you're buying or selling.

The boat of your dreams became available and you bought it, you've decided to go larger, or scale down, or you're changing gears and considering the "terminal trawler." Whatever the reason, there comes a time in every sailor's life when he/she is faced with the task of selling his/her current sailboat. While this can often be an emotional undertaking, common sense and a well thought out and executed plan can minimize this awkward period and result in a reasonably quick and profitable sale.

Bear in mind that it's the little things that make a big difference when selling a boat. Most potential, serious buyers will make a decision within the first few minutes of stepping aboard. After that decision has been made, they look for confirmation. This confirmation may be in the form of a well-documented maintenance log; a dry, odor-free bilge; or freshly varnished brightwork.

FIRST THINGS FIRST

In preparing to sell, first remove all of your personal gear. Once this has been accomplished, begin removing any excess gear. This includes junk, cleaning supplies, old parts, etc., in addition to any items that you can use on your new boat. However, be mindful not to strip the boat. Don't leave obvious voids or cause damage to the craft. Do leave any gear that is Coast Guard required, as well as a basic gear inventory. This includes such items as working sails, anchor and rode, life preservers, three to four fenders, dock lines, signaling gear and the like. Nothing is more frustrating or deal-squelching than for a prospect to see a fully outfitted craft, only to learn that this and this and that and that don't go with the boat.

While it may be true that extra gear may enhance the boat's marketability, this will only yield pennies on the dollar. Also, it will take an astute buyer to fully appreciate these extras. In any event, make sure that what they see is what they get.

REPAIR AND CLEAN

Now is not the time to spend big bucks and make those upgrades and postponed replacements. Rather, attention should be directed towards those relatively inexpensive and obvious repairs and maintenance issues. Make sure that the engine starts and that the oil and filter are changed, stuffing's not bulging out of the cushions, and that the sails aren't torn.

While age and normal wear and tear are areas you can do nothing or very little about, you do have total control over cleanliness. This is the single most important factor in how well a boat shows. If you haven't been doing it all along, now's the time to work on it in earnest. Often a sale is made in the mind of a potential buyer with that first impression. This translates into a spotless deck, hull, and cockpit. Start with a wash and wax followed by freshly maintained brightwork.

Below, make a special effort in cleaning and deodorizing the galley and head. A musty-smelling icebox or, even worse, head odors have killed more than one sale. In addition to employing cleaning/disinfecting products, it may be necessary to replace those odorous head hoses. Don't forget to air out lockers and keep an open box of baking soda in the icebox or refrigerator to keep things smelling fresh. Remember, the "nose knows." Don't overlook any nook or cranny. A dry and deodorized bilge and a clean engine are indicators of overall condition and suggest that the boat was cared for and not abused.

A clean, organized boat will generally fetch 10-15 percent more—not too bad for a bit of elbow grease.

ORGANIZE YOUR RECORDS

By assembling all pertinent paperwork in one place, you'll be better able to establish your price, develop a "sales brochure," and give potential buyers the impression that the boat has been well cared for. This includes the boat's legal documentation, brochures/instructions for any installed gear, maintenance records, and owner's manuals. I personally know of two deals that were sealed when the buyer was presented with a binder containing an organized collection of all the boat's records.

ESTABLISH A PRICE

This is often the hardest part of selling your own sailboat. There is a tendency to allow one's emotional involvement to overshadow reason, which usually results in an unrealistic asking price. To avoid this pitfall you need to develop a price range, including a high, low, and average price. You can do this by reviewing the classified ads of several marine publications or consulting the major boating websites. Look for sister ships or comparable boats. Consult the *Used Boat Price Guide* (often referred to as the blue book) and see how your boat has fared in the marketplace. You may also elect to have the boat surveyed or appraised. Any and all of these tools will help you in establishing the boat's value.

Several factors can affect the selling price, both positively and negatively. Some of the major ones include: the reputation of the builder, the reputation of the designer, whether or not the builder is still in business, the overall quality/condition of the boat, how the boat's equipped, and any repairs or upgrades needed. Market conditions, local popularity, an active class association, and your need to sell are more subjective factors, but nonetheless should also be considered when pricing the boat.

Often overlooked are those hidden costs, both direct and indirect, that can erode the price you finally receive when the boat is sold. All the while the boat is on the market, your out-of-pocket direct costs are insurance, maintenance, mooring, and advertisement. You also have money tied up and no interest being generated. Time is also money; time spent showing, negotiating, checking on the boat, and maintaining it in showable condition are a few of the indirect costs that you'll incur. The longer it takes to sell your boat the greater the negative impact of these hidden costs. Over a year's time, they may easily eat up 10-15 percent of the final selling price. You may want to consider pricing your boat for a quick sale. This approach minimizes the negative impact of the hidden costs and maximizes the amount of time you can spend sailing your new boat.

Timing is another factor to consider. Spring and summer are prime times to sell. Buyers will get immediate gratification. Fall can also be potentially a good time. Many buyers are looking for a good deal, and if you've priced your boat right, it'll sell quickly. A fall sale will save you winter storage/moorage and maintenance costs.

MARKETING

There are two items key to a good marketing approach: a concise, informative ad, and a fact sheet or brochure. The ad is your initial

4. SELLING YOUR BOAT

contact point and should include year, length, make, model, one or two important/outstanding features, price, and a means of contacting you. The fact sheet or brochure comes into play once you've been contacted. Use it as a reference piece and as a handout to delineate the boat's specifications; list all gear included with the boat, depict a diagram or two, or maybe even include a photo.

Once these two paper tools are ready, it's time to get the word out, and there's no quicker way than the shotgun approach. Get your ad in club newsletters, on bulletin boards at marinas and chandleries, in the Sunday paper, local sailing magazines, listing services, and so forth. You get the idea. Don't forget the Internet and word of mouth (maybe offer a finder's fee); a For Sale sign won't hurt, either.

Be available to respond to inquiries and to show the boat. Make it easy for the prospect to find you/the boat. Be prepared for no-shows. Use your fact sheet/brochure to assist in answering your prospect's questions. Accentuate the positive, don't go anywhere near the negative. If you don't know the answer to a question, say that you don't know; don't make something up. Don't talk too much.

To sweeten the deal you may elect to:
- Offer X amount of consultation time on how all the systems work.
- Offer X number of sailing lessons.
- Offer a conditional guarantee for X period of time.
- Arrange for delivery or transport of the boat.

EBay is another approach you might want to consider. If cyberspace selling appeals to you, do your homework carefully. EBay gets paid by the auction, by the seller, and by the service. These costs can add up quickly. For a boat, there's a $40 listing fee. With a winning bid there's a $40 transaction fee. Add to these fees the final transaction fee, which would be 5.25 percent of the initial $25 ($1.31), plus 3 percent of the initial $25 to $1,000 ($29.25), plus 1.50 percent of the remaining balance above $1000.01. For example, if the boat sells for $10,000.00, the eBay fee would be $40.00 + $40.00 + $1.31 + $29.25

+ $135.00, for a grand total of $375.25. If the boat does not sell, there's no fee, with the exception of the initial $40.00 listing fee. Log on to www.ebay.com and check it out.

THE SALE

If there is interest on the part of the prospect, be prepared to bargain—offer and counter offer. Once a price has been reached, obtain a deposit of 10-20 percent. This holds the boat for usually no more than two weeks, during which time the buyer can have a survey conducted or make a sea trial. Remember, no sea trial without a deposit. Also, all costs associated with a survey or sea trial, including any damage that may occur, are the responsibility of the buyer.

Spend a few dollars and have a sales agreement drawn up by an attorney. It should delineate all aspects of the sale, leaving nothing to chance. Both parties should sign it and retain copies.

If the deal is simple and straightforward or you'd rather eliminate the involvement of an attorney, log onto www.lawdepot.com. Here you'll find an excellent do-it-yourself sales agreement. Just fill in the blanks and hit Print.

If any problems are discovered as a result of the survey, be prepared to enter into new negotiations or possibly cancel the sale. On the other hand, should the buyer back out of the sale for no good reason, you are legally entitled to keep a portion of the earnest money that reflects your direct losses associated with removing the boat from the market. Remember, you want to sell the boat, not joust with a former prospect; be reasonable.

Assuming all goes well, the deal is closed by your receipt of a money order or cashier's check for the balance of the agreed-upon selling price and the surrendering of the boat to the new owner. You can now notify your insurance company and the appropriate titling and registering agency of the sale. Don't forget to keep copies of all paperwork associated with the sale. Good luck.

CHAPTER 5

THE ANATOMY OF A SAILBOAT

Sailboats are classified by the placement of their mast or masts, their mast height(s), and the sail plan that they carry. Four of the most common types include the sloop, the yawl, the ketch, and the schooner. However, most of today's small sailboats, a category in which trailer sailers are included, are single-masted boats rigged as sloops. A sloop consists of a triangular-shaped mainsail and a triangular headsail or jib. This jib-headed sail plan is often referred to as a Bermudian rig, since it was first encountered in Bermuda.

A picture being worth a thousand words, refer to the figure on the following page, which illustrates the basic components of a typical sloop.

THE BOAT

The actual body of the sailboat, excluding its superstructure, spars, rigging, and rudder, is called the HULL. That portion of the hull above the waterline is referred to as the TOPSIDES. The foreword part or "pointy end" of the boat is called the BOW, while the aft or back of the boat is the STERN.

Below the water, there is an appendage extending down that provides transverse stability and resists leeway. If affixed to the hull it is called a KEEL. An appendage that swings up and down on a pivot is a centerboard, and one that knifes up and down is called a

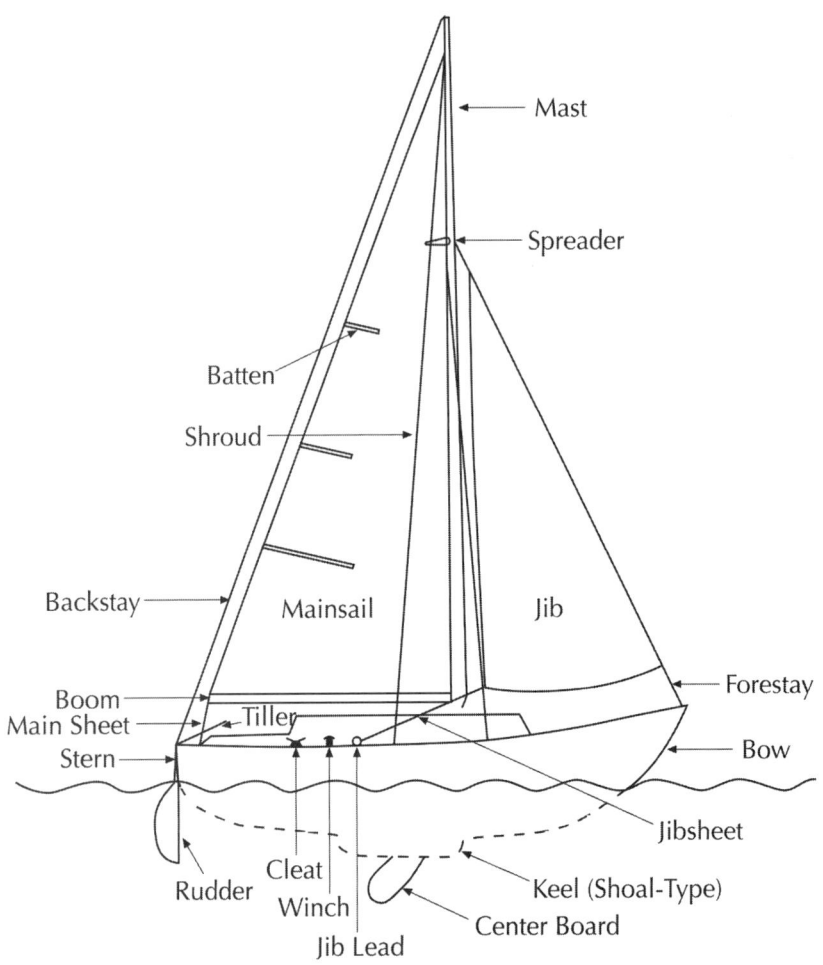

PARTS OF A TYPICAL SAILBOAT

daggerboard. The RUDDER, which is typically mounted to the boat's stern, is another underwater appendage that extends downward. The pressure of the rudder on the water when moved by the TILLER is what causes the boat to turn.

SPARS

A spar is a general term for all of the poles and supports used on board. On a sloop, these consist of the MAST and the BOOM.

The MAST is the most important spar, without which no sail can be set. It is that tall pole extending skyward from the boat. It is typically made of wood or a light aluminum alloy extrusion. On a trailer sailer, it is usually stepped (connected to the boat) on deck. It may be flexible and is subject to shock and compression loads. Standing rigging supports the mast.

The BOOM is attached to the mast by a universal joint called a GOOSENECK, from which it extends aft. Most booms are made of aluminum or wood. This spar allows for the lateral movement of the mainsail.

STANDING RIGGING

Standing rigging is the wire rope that supports the mast and does not control the sails. It is comprised of shrouds and stays.

On a sloop, there is typically a combination of upper and lower SHROUDS, always in pairs, supporting the mast laterally. The upper or cap shrouds pass through SPREADERS, which position the upper shrouds for good alignment. The lower shrouds are attached to the mast beneath the spreaders, usually two-thirds of the mast's height. One pair of lower shrouds runs slightly foreword of the mast, and another slightly abaft it for maximum support.

The FORESTAY and BACKSTAY support the mast upright against halyard tensions. The forestay is also an attachment point for the jib. Many backstays are adjustable while under way. This provides tension control over forestay sag and over forward mast rake.

RUNNING RIGGING

All the moving cordage that hoists, trims, lowers, and controls sails and gear is termed running rigging.

HALYARDS are lines that hoist up and tension sails. Each is named after the sail or object that it serves, *e.g.* main, jib, and flag halyard. Halyards are often fed onto a WINCH for mechanical advantage and then belayed to a CLEAT.

SHEETS, oftentimes rigged as tackle, control the lateral movement of the sails. Like halyards, they too are named for the sail that they control, i.e. mainsheet and jib sheet.

On the mainsail, one end of the mainsheet tackle is connected to the boom and the other end is often attached to a traveler. The traveler exactly positions the boom athwartships, thus giving fine control to the mainsail's shape.

The jib sheets, one port and one starboard, are attached to the jib's clew. Each sheet is led aft through a LEAD, onto a winch, and then cleated. The leads, usually on a sliding track, adjust the angle of the sheets for optimum sail shape.

SAILS

On a sloop, the mainsail is the primary driving sail. The Bermudian mainsail is long, narrow, and triangular in shape. It is easily handled and possesses excellent "on the wind" ability. Its leading edge or LUFF is attached to the aft edge of the mast by means a luff rope or mast track slides, sometimes called slugs. A single halyard attached to the HEAD of the sail is the only line required to raise and tension it. The sail's lower edge or FOOT is attached to the boom in much the same way that its luff is attached to the mast. While the lower

5. THE ANATOMY OF A SAILBOAT 37

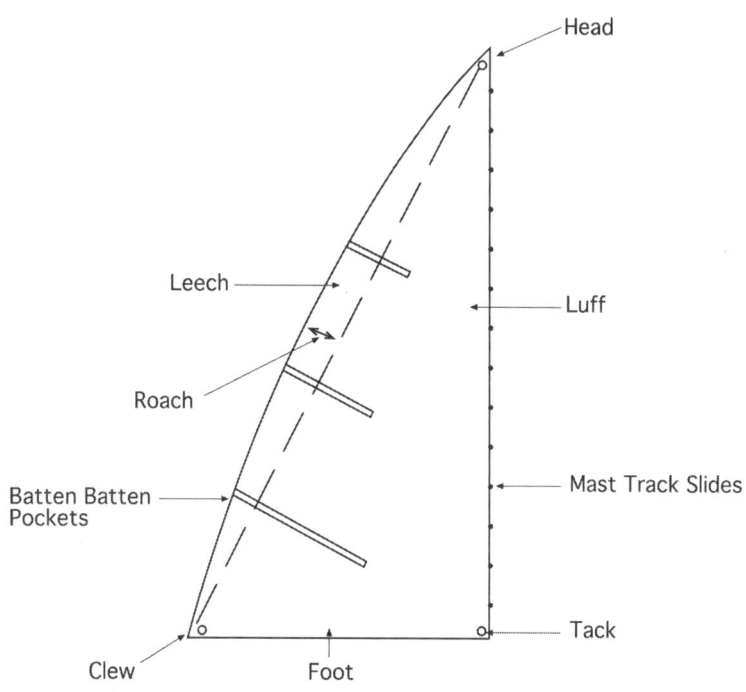

THE BERMUDIAN MAINSAIL IS LONG, NARROW, AND TRIANGULAR.
ITS POPULARITY IS DUE TO ITS EASE OF HANDLING
AND ITS EXCELLENT "ON THE WIND" ABILITY.

leading corner or TACK is fixed to the boom, the CLEW, or trailing aft corner, is attached to an adjustable line. This OUTHAUL line tensions the sail's foot. The trailing edge of the sail is called the LEECH. Often it is cut in a long curve, from head to clew, that allows for greater fullness. This extra material, which gives extra drive to the sail when reaching or running, is called the ROACH. This roach tends to sag or flap in the wind. To avoid these conditions, stiff, narrow slats called BATTENS are inserted into pockets to help the sail hold its shape.

The purpose of the jib is threefold: to smooth and balance the wind flow, to create a driving force, and to assist in steering the boat.

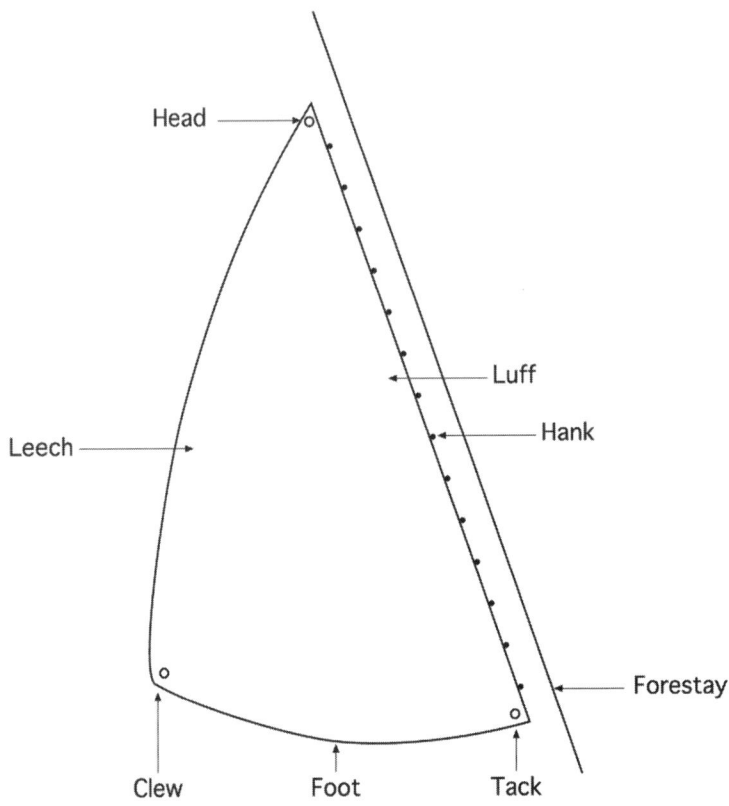

THE JIB AIDS IN SMOOTHING OUT THE FLOW OF WIND,
AS WELL AS BALANCING OUT THE FORCES ACTING ON THE SAILS.

Like the Bermudian mainsail, the jib is triangular in shape and its parts are named exactly the same. Its position on the boat is between the forestay and the mast. Its tack is attached to the deck, while the luff is affixed to the forestay by means of snaphooks or HANKS. While a single halyard is used to raise and tension the jib, a pair of sheets, one port and one starboard, is connected to the sail's clew.

SECTION II

TRAILERS AND TRAILERING

Going to windward at 55 miles per hour has its obvious advantages... simplicity, variety, and flexibility, to name but a few. Just hitch up your trailer sailer to the old SUV and head out for those distant shores. While sailing may be the primary focus of your attention, the trailering portion of your adventure is something that should not be taken lightly. Towing a heavy load at highway speeds is fraught with potential hazards. Also, while a boat typically receives considerable attention, its trailer is often neglected. True, most trailers don't require much in the way of maintenance; however, they do require some maintenance. If the trailering and trailer maintenance weren't enough, add a tow vehicle—now we've really spiced up the mix. Got your attention? Good.

CHAPTER 6

TRAILER SAILER BEGINS WITH "TRAILER"

One of the biggest advantages to trailer sailing is that you are not limited to one sailing area in a single sailing season, but rather can experience a cornucopia of sailing destinations, compliments of our extensive highway system.

While much attention is spent selecting, outfitting, and maintaining a seaworthy trailerable craft, less attention is often paid to that contraption which allows trailer sailors to achieve this enviable versatility, the trailer.

As seen below, a trailer's systems are few and relatively simple. However, if neglected they can be a continual source of unwelcome distractions. Therefore, with a little bit of care and understanding, you can make the trailering portion of every trip uneventful and the sailing eventful.

TIRES AND WHEEL BEARINGS

Tires and wheel bearings are the most critical items on your boat trailer. If they are not cared for properly, much of your sailing may take place on the side of the road. Therefore, a little special attention throughout the season is required.

First of all, make sure that the tires are rated for trailer service and that they are both the correct size and type. Unlike passenger vehicle tires, trailer tires are subject to greater flex, weight, and heat stresses. While trailer tires do not outwardly appear to be different from passenger vehicle tires, they possess a much higher load range rating: typically a load range rating of C or D, which is approximately 1,000 to 2,500 pounds, in contrast to the A or B range ratings of 850 pounds or less. This increase in load range is mostly due to the increased number of plies used in the construction of the tire, especially in its sidewalls. Typical passenger vehicle tires generally have 2-ply sidewalls, whereas trailer tires often have as many as 8 plies and usually no fewer than 6.

MAKE SURE THAT YOUR TRAILER'S TIRES ARE RATED FOR "TRAILER USE".

While trailer tires are still available in both bias and radial ply configurations, the overwhelming trend is towards radial ply tires. Bias ply tires have plies that crisscross the tire diagonally from bead to bead. Less expensive than radials, they are therefore the affordable choice for lighter loads. The plies of radial tires run at a 90-degree angle from bead to bead. Radials dissipate heat better than bias ply tires and are the tire of choice for long distance travel or heavier loads.

Regardless of what type of trailer tire you select, do not mix radials with bias ply tires, since they exhibit very different handling characteristics, which will result in severe sway and tracking problems. Also, never use a tube in either of these tubeless tires. A tube increases heat development and retards heat dissipation.

Next, check tire pressure often and make sure that the tires are properly inflated. Follow the tire manufacturer's recommendations. Proper tire pressure reduces premature tire death due to overheating. In the off-season when storing your trailer with your boat onboard, raise it up onto blocks. This takes the load off of not only the tires, but also the springs, axles, and wheel bearings. Also, shade the tires from sunlight, since UV rays dry out the oil in the tire's rubber. Lastly, be on the lookout for cracking on the sidewalls. This is a sign of old age and indicates it's time to replace the tires.

In the normal course of launching and retrieving your boat, the trailer's tires along with their wheel bearings are routinely immersed in water. If the bearings are cool and the hubs are filled with grease, this is not too much of a problem. However, when traveling down the highway, even well lubricated bearings warm up and, depending upon conditions, can even get hot. Then, when immersed in cold water, a vacuum is created and water is drawn into the wheel hubs. This condition can cause the bearings to seize up and render them useless. Salt water aggravates this condition tenfold.

To protect your wheel bearings, try to keep your hubs out of the water when launching and retrieving your boat. If this is not possible, install bearing protectors on each wheel hub. These are spring-loaded devices that maintain a slight pressure on the grease packing in the hub, which helps prevent water intrusion when the trailer wheels are submerged. Since bearing protectors incorporate a zerk (grease) fitting, they make lubricating wheel hubs dramatically easier.

On an annual basis, inspect and repack your wheel bearings, making sure to fill the wheel hub completely with marine grade wheel bearing grease. Unlike standard wheel bearing grease used on passenger vehicles, marine grade wheel bearing grease is formulated especially for the severe operating conditions of the marine environment. In addition to its lubricating properties, marine grade wheel bearing grease is water-insoluble and contains corrosion inhibitors and antioxidants. It affords corrosion protection against moist/wet conditions, especially the highly corrosive environment of salt water. Marine grade wheel bearing grease won't soften, break down, or wash out in water. It maintains its stability and lubricity under the high heat conditions resulting from pressure and high rpms.

BRAKES

Depending upon the gross weight the trailer is designed for and/or the state in which it is registered, trailer brakes may be required.

There are two types of legal braking systems: electric and surge (hydraulic). Electric brakes function by sending a voltage to the trailer via an electric brake controller that is located in the tow vehicle. This voltage activates the trailer's brakes when the tow vehicle's brakes are applied. Surge brakes work from the trailer's momentum. When the tow vehicle's brakes are applied, the trailer surges forward and applies its brakes through a closed hydraulic system, self-contained on the trailer. Most modern boat trailers use surge braking systems.

Regardless of the type, trailer brakes are designed to activate in conjunction with the tow vehicle's brakes and should continue to operate even if the trailer is accidentally separated. Be sure that the emergency breakaway cable leading from the trailer to the tow vehicle is shorter than the safety chains. It is this brake cable that sets the brakes should the trailer break loose.

After immersion, the brakes temporarily lose a significant portion of their breaking power. Allow them to drain before heading out. Also, for the first quarter-mile or so you can maintain slight pressure on your brake pedal to generate some heat, which in turn will evaporate any water remaining between the brake drum and lining.

As is the case with most metallic components, immersion in water can result in corrosion, and salt water corrodes most aggressively. While performing your annual repacking of the wheel bearings, inspect the condition of your brakes. If you suspect anything amiss, have a qualified brake technician take a closer look.

LIGHTS

Lights on boat trailers experience rougher treatment than lights on passenger vehicles. No lighting system can tolerate repeated immersion, even those rated "waterproof." Salt water is especially aggravating.

Having the trailer lights removable or mounted high enough so that they do not get immersed, goes a long way in reducing premature lighting failures. However, if this cannot be done, disconnect them from the tow vehicle prior to backing down the launch ramp. This can be accomplished simply by manually unplugging the electrical connector, which is typically located between the tow vehicle and the trailer at the hitch juncture. Remember, heated bulbs can crack when touched by cold water. Be sure to allow bulbs enough time to cool down before they are immersed.

If the lights do not operate and the bulbs appear to be good, you may need to polish the bulb terminals with fine sandpaper or steel wool. A small amount of corrosion will keep them from making good electrical contact. Corrosion on the electrical connector between the tow vehicle and trailer can also be removed by sanding. The most frequent cause of trailer light failure is a faulty ground, which creates an open or poor circuit. The ground is normally identified as a white wire. Make sure it is bonded to both the trailer frame and the tow vehicle.

Lastly, you may want to consider adding additional lights and/or reflectors beyond those required by law, especially to the trailer's sides. This substantially increases night safety. Also install a heavy-duty flasher in the tow vehicle to handle the increased lighting load, and routinely check the operation of all trailer lights before heading out.

HITCH

Trailer hitches, or more correctly that portion permanently attached to the tow vehicle, are classified based on GTW (gross trailer weight) and TW (tongue weight). GTW is the combined weight of the trailer, boat, and gear, while TW is the weight the loaded trailer places on the towing hitch.

Hitch class	GTW	TW*
1	up to 2,000 pounds	200 pounds
2	2,000-3,500 pounds	350 pounds
3	3,500-5,000 pounds	500 pounds
4	>5,000 pounds	>500 pounds

*Ideally, the TW should be 7-10 percent of the GTW. Too much tongue weight will result in "tail dragging" of the tow vehicle, while too little will cause the trailer to sway excessively while being towed.

Unfortunately, there are no rules-of-thumb guidelines or relationships between the tow vehicle and trailer. The manufacturer of the tow vehicle has the first and last word in setting the towing specifications. Check the owner's manual before hitching up. Assuming that the tow vehicle can adequately handle the load, match the hitch to the load. When in doubt, move up to the next higher rated hitch.

There are two types of trailer hitches commonly used with boat trailers: weight-carrying and weight-distributing. Both of these are bolted to the tow vehicle's frame. Weight-carrying hitches come in all classes and as the name implies, bear the entire trailer's tongue weight. They are most commonly used in class 1, 2, and 3 configurations. Rather than supporting the tongue weight, weight-distributing hitches apply leverage between the tow vehicle and trailer by means of a spring bar or bars. This causes the tongue weight to be borne by all axles of the tow vehicle and trailer. Typically, weight-distributing hitches are used with heavier loads (class 4 and larger).

To connect the tow vehicle to the trailer, attach the coupler located on the trailer's tongue to the ball on the tow vehicle's hitch. These balls come in several sizes. Make sure that you are using the correct size ball for your coupler. Too small a ball can cause the coupler to come loose; too large a one will bind and the trailer will not track the tow vehicle correctly.

Prior to connecting the trailer to the tow vehicle, grease the ball slightly. This makes for smoother movement of the hitch.

Trailer couplings can be screw type or latch type. If yours is latch type, secure it with a pin or lock. This will keep it from coming loose.

Associated with the hitch are safety chains, which are permanently attached to the trailer's tongue and secured to the tow vehicle with a hook or shackle. Don't allow the chains to drag on the road surface. They only need to be long enough to allow free turning of the hitch. When connecting them to the tow vehicle, cross the chains under the hitch, thus forming a cradle. Should the coupling fail, the cradle will prevent the trailer tongue from hitting the pavement and digging in.

6. TRAILER SAILER BEGINS WITH "TRAILER" 47

EXAMPLE OF A SCREW-TYPE COUPLER.
NOTE THE EMERGENCY BREAKAWAY CABLE.
ALONG WITH THE SAFETY CHAINS, THIS CABLE SHOULD BE ATTACHED
TO THE TOW VEHICLE. SHOULD THE TRAILER ACCIDENTALLY
BECOME SEPARATED FROM THE TOW VEHICLE, THIS CABLE
WILL AUTOMATICALLY SET THE TRAILER BRAKES.

DON'T TRUST YOUR BOAT'S SECURITY SOLELY
TO THE TRAILER WINCH'S LOCKING MECHANISM.
USE A SHORT LENGTH OF CABLE OR CHAIN
TO SECURE THE BOW EYE TO THE WINCH'S BASE.

A COUPLER WITH AN INTEGRATED TONGUE EXTENDER (SECURED POSITION).

WINCH AND TIE DOWNS

The primary point of attachment of a sailboat to the trailer is the bow eye to which the trailer winch is connected. The winch line is usually steel cable or can be polypropylene rope or strapping. While cable may rust over time and eventually need to be replaced, synthetics will deteriorate more rapidly because of the UV rays in sunlight. Inspect the winch line annually and replace the synthetics if degradation is suspected. Do not use nylon for winch line, since it stretches too much.

Be sure that the winch has an anti-reverse lock and that it is in working order, but don't rely on it totally. Use a short length of cable—or better yet, chain—and secure the bow eye to the base of the winch. Also fasten a cable from the bow eye to the tongue of the trailer. This provides anti-surge protection (of the boat), should you need to stop abruptly.

The boat needs to be firmly secured to the trailer. While the bow is held in place by means of the winch cable, etc., tie-downs should be fastened at or near the stern of the boat. A gunwale tie-down stretching across the boat and hooked to either side of the trailer, or transom tie-downs connected to lifting rings and to the trailer, will accomplish this. The larger the boat, the larger and the more tie-downs required.

Remember, if you need to stop in a hurry, you want your boat to stay on the trailer and stop when you do!

LAUNCHING

The single most important thing to do before launching is make sure that the water at the launch ramp is deep enough to accept your boat. Some ramps are marked. If not, check with the marina or ramp operator or other sailors, or if all else fails, get wet. If you determine that achieving adequate water depth requires that your trailer be extended far out, you may need to employ a tongue extender. Many sailboat trailers incorporate them as part of their design. Some marina and launch ramps have them available for use, either free or for a fee. If none of these are the case, you'll need to locate a deepwater ramp. Under no circumstances should you allow the rear wheels of the tow vehicle to go past the water's edge.

The following is a list of other items to consider when launching your sailboat, *prior* to backing down the ramp:

- Remove all tie-downs, but *do not* disconnect the winch line from the bow eye.

- Raise and lock anything that may snag on the trailer or in shallow water. This includes the outboard motor, rudder, and centerboard or swing keel.
- Insert drain plug(s), if so equipped.
- Attach bow and stern lines to maintain control of the boat and to help ease it off the trailer.
- If you can, remain in the tow vehicle. Leave the engine on, keep your foot on the brake, and put the transmission in park (if auto) or first gear (if manual).
- If you must get out of the tow vehicle to assist, turn off the engine, set the parking brake, put the transmission in park (if auto) or first gear (if manual), and chock both rear wheels.

LEGAL CONSIDERATIONS

One of the few absolutes in trailering a boat is its width. The widest boat you can legally tow on most state roads is eight feet. Anything greater requires a special permit. On interstates, some access roads, and on federally funded highways having 12-foot-wide lanes, the maximum width is eight feet six inches. These widths include both the boat and the trailer. However, regulations are continually changing and differ from state to state. Consult your state police and your bureau of motor vehicles to obtain the most current regulations.

TRAILER GEAR

Regardless of how diligent you are in maintaining your trailer, sooner or later a breakdown will occur. Make the following items part of your trailer gear inventory:

- Mounted spare trailer tire inflated to the proper pressure
- Trailer jack or scissors jack and handle
- Lug wrench sized to fit the trailer's lug nuts

- Spare wheel bearings and wheel bearing grease
- Spare light bulbs
- Tools to replace wheel bearings and make minor repairs

With the above items, the majority of trailer breakdowns can be easily and quickly remedied. This is especially important on those hot Sunday afternoons when you are driving through the middle of nowhere.

CHAPTER 7

BUYING A USED SAILBOAT TRAILER

For the most part, sailboat trailers are semi-custom, owing to the fact that each must be designed and built to accommodate a specific sailboat model's hull/keel configuration. This one factor alone makes them very expensive. For example, a new trailer capable of hauling, launching, and retrieving a typical 25-foot trailer sailer with a shoal draft keel/centerboard and weighing around 5,000 pounds can range in price from $4,500 to $8,000. A comparable used trailer, on the other hand, may cost from 10 to 90 percent less than a new one. This significant variation in price is dependent upon the trailer's age, model, and most of all, condition.

    You'll achieve the best results in locating the right used trailer to fit your trailer sailer if you become an educated consumer. The first step in the process is to contact the sailboat's manufacturer and obtain their recommendations. After all, who else would best know the sailboat's hull/keel configuration? However, if, as with many good old boats, the manufacturer is no longer in business, check out the owner's association. Ask several members what make and type trailers they use. Also talk with other sailors who have the same or similar boats. Various boat trailer manufacturers are another source of specifications. Armed with this newly acquired information, you're ready to search the used trailer market.

WHERE TO LOOK

Unfortunately, I know of no used sailboat trailer store, therefore you'll need to get creative in your search and leave no stone unturned. Places to look for used sailboat trailers include the local *Boat Trader* publication, marinas, boat dealers/brokers, local chandlery bulletin boards, and the Internet. The classified section of your local newspaper will probably be the best source of leads. You will find that used powerboat trailers are more common and cheaper, but don't despair. Sailboat trailers are around.

At this juncture, let's digress a moment. Why not obtain a powerboat trailer and modify it, you ask? While this may sound simple, it isn't. First of all, most powerboat trailers have their axles located too far back to make for a good conversion. Secondly, the rated capacity of the powerboat trailer will most probably be too low. Powerboats don't have a weighted keel as sailboats do. Lastly, in order to properly make a safe conversion on which to secure your sailboat, one needs to possess significant mechanical/engineering skills and possibly access to tools and equipment often beyond what a typical homeowner may have. Obviously, there are easier ways, but if you're still interested in pursuing this avenue, good luck.

WHAT TO LOOK FOR

When checking out a used sailboat trailer, the first item to note is its rated capacity. This information is listed on the manufacturer's identification plate, which is located on the trailer's tongue. Remember that the capacity is not just the base weight of your boat, but the combined weight of the boat, motor, fuel, water, provisions, anchor and rode, plus all accessories and personal gear you have or might have on board. Adding all these together plus a safety factor of perhaps 10 percent yields a trailer weight capacity. Make sure that the trailer you're considering has that capacity or a bit more. Don't skimp or go borderline. On the other side of the coin, don't get way more capacity than you need. The stiff ride resulting from the heavier suspension could damage your sailboat's hull.

In addition to being able to bear the load of boat, motor, gear, etc., the trailer needs to conform to the shape of your sailboat's hull/keel configuration. While most trailers have multiple adjustment points, even the most adjustable trailer cannot be properly fitted for every sailboat. In determining whether or not a given trailer will fit your sailboat, the most important area to check out is the support system. The supports should be located at reinforced or structural areas of your boat, such as the bulkheads, along lifting strakes, and the keel. There should be enough supports on both sides, beneath the hull, and at the bow to distribute the weight. The support arrangement should avoid excessive pressure at any one point, as well as inhibit lateral and forward movement of the craft during transport. Lastly, the supports should be situated in such a way as to carry the boat as low as possible; this keeps the center of gravity close to the road. This also makes for easier ramp launching and retrieval. If the supports are properly arranged, during launch and retrieval the boat's hull will be constantly centered on the trailer and will not scrape along any unpadded parts of the trailer.

PERSONAL PREFERENCES

As with sailboats, so with sailboat trailers—some things are givens, some are negotiable, while others fall into the category of personal preference. While trailer weight capacity and the matching of its supports to the sailboat's hull are givens and non-negotiable, such things as bunks vs. rollers, painted frame vs. galvanized, and single axle vs. tandems fall into both of the latter categories.

Bunk-type trailers have carpeted rails or "bunks" from which shallow draft boats are floated on and off and deeper draft boats are slid on and off. They are designed for relatively steep/deep launching ramps, where the trailer is immersed over the top of its fenders. The principle advantages of bunk-type trailers is that, with

A GALVANIZED, TANDEM-AXLE, BUNK-TYPE TRAILER.
ITS A-FRAME CONSTRUCTION CAN HANDLE HEAVY LOADS.

proper adjustment, there is continuous fore and aft hull support, which equates to minimum risk of damage to the hull from jolts and bounces when being transported. Also, bunk-type trailers can be as much as 25 percent cheaper than roller-type trailers.

EXAMPLE OF A PAINTED, SINGLE-AXLE, ROLLER-TYPE TRAILER.
ITS POLE-TONGUE CONSTRUCTION IS BOLTED TOGETHER
AND AFFORDS MULTIPLE ADJUSTMENT POINTS.

Roller-type trailers employ low-friction rubber or synthetic rollers mounted on adjustable brackets to make launching and retrieval easier. Since bunk-type trailers do not allow boats to slide on and off without some difficulty, roller-type trailers can be used on less steep launching ramps. On steep ramps, it is easier to winch a heavier boat onto a roller-type trailer than it is to skid it onto a bunk-type trailer. The extra hardware involved on a roller-type trailer justifies its higher cost.

If you're sailing in salt water, a galvanized trailer is superior to one that is painted. It will also be more expensive. Painted trailers, if judiciously fresh-water rinsed after each and every immersion in salt water, plus if care is taken to touch up any nicks with rust preventative paint, will stand up to many years of salt water service.

THE BUNKS OF THIS SINGLE-AXLE TRAILER PROVIDE
CONTINUOUS FORE-AND-AFT SUPPORT.

7. BUYING A USED SAILBOAT TRAILER

A tandem axle trailer (two or three axles) generally can carry more load than a single axle trailer, simply because the load is dispersed over more tires, springs, and the like. Compared to single axle trailers, tandem axle trailers give a smoother ride; however, maneuverability is impaired because of a tandem axle trailer's tendency to track in a straight line. Should you get a blowout with a tandem axle trailer, you might be able to limp along on three or more tires; on a single axle trailer, you'd best have a spare, jack, and the tools to make the change.

TANDEM-AXLE TRAILERS GENERALLY CAN CARRY MORE LOAD THAN A SINGLE-AXLE TRAILER, SIMPLY BECAUSE THE WEIGHT IS DISTRIBUTED OVER MORE TIRES AND SPRINGS.

THERE'S MORE

With the trailer's capacity and support configuration properly matched to that of your sailboat, attention should be directed towards the trailer's condition. Condition easily equates to money saved or spent and/or negotiating room.

TIRES

After years of occasional use, the tread of trailer tires may still be adequate. However, long term exposure to the sun's UV rays may have resulted in the deterioration of the sidewalls, characterized by numerous small cracks. If this is found to be the case, the tires will need to be replaced. When doing so, make sure that the capacity of the new tires, which can be found on the tire's sidewall, is equal to or greater than the load being carried divided by the number of tires on the trailer.

In other words, if the load being carried is 3,600 pounds, each tire on a single axle trailer must be rated to be at least 1,800 pound capacity. If the tires appear to be in good shape, confirm that they are of the proper capacity. Also, the tires must be of the same size and type (bias or radial). Do not mix bias and radial tires. Their construction and performance characteristics are significantly different and can result in severe trailering difficulties.

WHEEL BEARINGS

The most critical areas on a boat trailer are the wheel bearings. Why? It's simple. When the trailer is immersed in water, rapid cooling takes place, which causes the grease and any trapped air in the wheel hubs to shrink. The resulting vacuum draws water into the hubs and can cause corrosion and bearing failure. Pull the hubs and check the condition of the bearings, even if they have bearing protectors

7. BUYING A USED SAILBOAT TRAILER

installed. Make certain that the bearings are in good condition and that the hubs are filled with grease.

SUSPENSION

Inspect the springs to make sure that they both have the same number of leaves and that none are broken. Since the springs are usually unpainted, don't be too concerned about surface rust. However, if the rusting appears to be excessive, a closer look is warranted, especially if the trailer has seen saltwater service. Leaf springs are generally attached to the trailer frame by means of shackles, which are held in place by bolts. Over time and use, these bolts wear to the point that they need to be replaced. A visual inspection will generally reveal what, if anything, needs to be done.

LIGHTS

Make sure that the trailer lights work. Water and electricity do not mix well. When warm bulbs hit cold water, while the trailer is immersed at the launch ramp, the bulbs often break. Check them first. Also, light sockets can corrode, which makes for a poor electrical connection. More often than not, a poor ground is the culprit with lights that don't work. The ground wire is usually white. If the lights are still not functioning properly, suspect a short. You now have a bit of negotiating room.

BRAKES

If the trailer is equipped with brakes, inspect them when you are checking out the condition of the wheel bearings. Excessive corrosion of the braking components may indicate that the brakes are seized. In addition to corrosion, note the thickness of the pads or shoes. If possible, activate the brakes slowly and determine if they work. With surge brakes, applying reverse pressure on the hitch, which in turn activates the master cylinder, can do this. Lightly press the lever on the actuator if the brakes are electric.

RUST

Technically speaking, rust is the end product of the oxidation of iron, which occurs when steel comes in contact with water. If salt is present, the process is accelerated dramatically. On a boat trailer, unchecked corrosion can eat away exposed steel surfaces. This can result in a gradual thinning and eventually failure of a trailer frame component. A good visual inspection, along with a bit of hammer tapping and screwdriver poking/scraping, will tell you a lot.

STRUCTURAL INTEGRITY

This is not difficult and can even be a bit of fun. Look at the frame components carefully. Make sure they are not bent. Wiggle everything and test all of the bolts and nuts for tightness. Check any welds or bends for cracks and crevice corrosion. When in doubt, give the questionable area a love tap with your handy three-pound sledge hammer. If the noise produced is not a clang but a dull thunk, some repair work may be needed.

ALL THAT'S LEFT: WITH EVERYTHING ELSE BEING A GO...

Examine the winch and make sure that it operates and is not rusted to the point of being frozen inoperable. Test operate the brake/locking mechanism. Confirm that it works in both directions. It is this small device that prevents the crank from spinning out of control. Winch line is usually galvanized or stainless steel or can be synthetic web strapping or even rope. While cable may rust or its strands break over time, causing weakness and ultimately resulting in failure, the synthetics will deteriorate more rapidly because of sunlight UV degradation. Pay out the entire line and examine it closely.

Inspect the hitch and work the locking mechanism to determine that it is operable. It is this latch or screw-type mechanism that will keep the coupled trailer and tow vehicle from coming loose. Safety chains should be present and permanently attached to the trailer's tongue.

With roller-type trailers, make sure that all of the rollers are present and that they turn freely. Broken or severely cracked rollers will need to be replaced. Rock all roller assemblies back and forth and side to side, confirming that their pivot points move easily.

Check the undersides of the carpeted rails on bunk-type trailers. Broken, badly cracked, or rotten wooden rails need to be replaced. Slide your hands over the carpeted areas. Make sure that none of the fasteners holding the carpeting down are protruding. These can gouge or even puncture the sailboat's hull.

FINAL THOUGHT

While searching for a suitable used sailboat trailer may appear to be an overwhelming undertaking, keep in mind that trailersailing has never looked better. Slip rentals and winter storage fees continue to go up at an alarming rate, and mooring space is virtually nonexistent in many areas. These are inconveniences that do not plague the trailer sailer. Depending upon your homeport, you could experience the thrill of a freshwater regatta today and enjoy saltwater cruising tomorrow. Unlike its waterbound cousins, the range of the trailer sailer is unlimited.

CHAPTER 8

HOW MUCH ARE YOU TOWING?

As a trailersailor, it's important to know how much weight you're towing behind the old SUV.

One way to get this information is to load your boat with all of your gear and provisions (remembering to fill your fuel tank and potable water tank) and tow it over to a weigh station. (Hint: Places that sell gravel, topsoil, or bulk mulch, such as a landscaping supply company, usually have scales or can direct you to someone that does.)

If you would rather not drive your boat and trailer all around the neighborhood, another equally accurate way to determine how much you're towing can be carried out without leaving your own backyard. Use your bathroom scale as follows:

1. Load your boat with all of your gear and provisions.
2. Place a bathroom scale under the trailer's dolly wheel.
3. Chock the trailer's wheels and level the trailer.
4. Measure and record the distance (in inches) from the center of the trailer's wheel hub to that of the dolly wheel's. This is "D".
5. Note and record the weight (in pounds) indicated on the bathroom scale. This is "W".
6. Without moving the trailer, move the boat back a short distance. (Hint: To help accomplish this, connect a line to the boat's towing eye, then run it along the starboard side and around a block located aft on the trailer's starboard corner. Bring the line

8. HOW MUCH ARE YOU TOWING?

forward and connect it to the trailer's winch. Repeat this on the port side. Now, when the winch is engaged, the boat will be pulled straight back.)

7. Measure and record the distance (in inches) that the boat was moved. This is "d". (Hint: Before moving the boat, stick a piece of masking tape on the boat and align another piece opposite on the trailer. After the boat has been moved, stick another piece on the trailer opposite the piece on the boat. The distance between the two pieces of tape on the trailer is "d".)
8. Note and record the new weight (in pounds) indicated on the bathroom scale. This is "w".
9. The boat and its contents = (D / d) x (W - w).
10. Total towing weight is equal to the weight of the boat and its contents (#9) plus the weight of the trailer (from capacity plate).

Example: D=136 inches
           d=5.5 inches
           W=168 pounds
           w=72 pounds

           (136 / 5.5) x (168 – 72)
           = 24.73 x 96
           = 2374 pounds

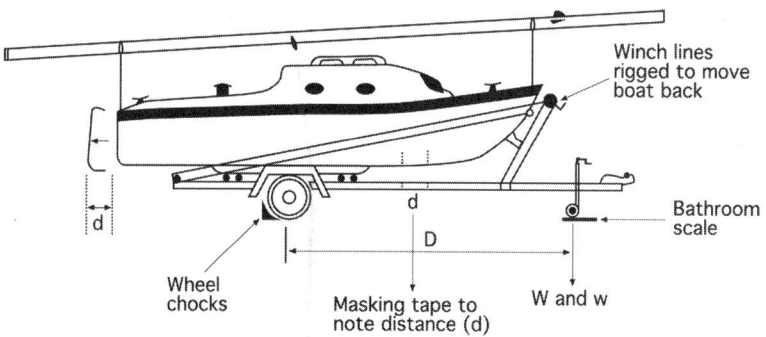

CHAPTER 9

THE TOW VEHICLE

Trailering is not something to be taken lightly. Combining highway speeds and a heavily laden trailer is an activity fraught with potential hazards. A mismatch between trailer and tow vehicle can have severe, even devastating consequences. Therefore, before you attach your trailer sailer to your SUV or walk into a showroom to begin that search for a new tow vehicle, you need to know a few things.

How much weight will you be towing? This may sound like an easy question, but you'd be surprised how many sailors don't know the answer. In determining this, it's important to consider the combined weights of the trailer, the boat, and all the gear including fuel, water, and provisions. Once you know the weight that's going to be pulled, you should check it against the towing capacity of your current vehicle. If your current vehicle is not up to the job, you'll need to begin a search for a new tow vehicle.

When searching for that tow vehicle (or even when examining your current vehicle), you'll come across several ratings; it's important that you know what each of them means. The gross vehicle weight rating (GVWR) is the measurement of how much the total vehicle can weigh. This number includes the vehicle, passengers, cargo, and a full tank of fuel. The trailer weight allowance (TWA) is the maximum amount a loaded trailer can weigh and still be towed. Combining the GVWR and the TWA yields the gross combined weight rating (GCWR). This is the total package: boat, trailer, cargo, tow vehicle, fuel, passengers, and everything else. It's a very important numerical value. Exceeding this number will almost certainly lead to serious problems.

Once you have this information in hand, you can begin the selection process. Selecting a vehicle or two is the easy part. Picking the right features from among the many can complicate the process. Most vehicle manufacturers offer trailering packages. This is a good option to consider; it usually consists of a larger radiator, oil and/or transmission cooler, and a hitch and wire harness. Other features to consider include:

ALL WHEEL DRIVE (AWD)

This feature is designed for slippery surface driving (wet, snow, or icy roadways). It will work well on slippery launch ramps. AWD is always engaged and will automatically transfer power and torque from one set of wheels to the other as needed. AWD will not improve towing on dry pavement.

FOUR WHEEL DRIVE (4WD)

The trailering capacity for 4WD vehicles is usually less than their rear wheel two-wheel-drive counterparts. This is due to the added weight of the four-wheel-drive components. However, like AWD, the extra traction of 4WD can help out on a slippery launch ramp. Also, the 4WD's low-range gears are great for pulling a boat out of the water. Unlike AWD, 4WD is part time and must be engaged manually. If this option is to your liking, you'll also need to select between manual and automatic locking hubs.

TWO WHEEL DRIVE (REAR WHEEL VARIETY)

While the towing weight is correctly situated on the rear wheels, if they begin to spin or if the ramp is steep, trouble could be in the offing. Two-wheel-drive with a locking differential will offset this problem.

FRONT WHEEL DRIVE (FWD)

This is the least towing-capable configuration and should be avoided.

TRANSMISSION

All manufacturers specify an automatic transmission for towing. Why would I say otherwise?

AXLES

Limited slip axles transfer power from a spinning wheel to the wheel directly across from it. Hopefully that wheel isn't also spinning. Locking differentials increase traction by locking both rear wheels when the right wheel is spinning. When it comes to selecting an axle ratio for towing, a high number is better; however, the higher the number, the lower the gas mileage.

DIESEL VS. GASOLINE

Diesels cost more initially, usually afford better fuel mileage, last longer, and have better torque for pulling a trailer. You'll need to do the math on this one.

Other options to consider include larger side mirrors, heavy-duty suspension, dual rear wheels, special tires, electrical connections, and a hitch.

9. THE TOW VEHICLE

Now that I've taken what initially appeared to be a straightforward task and muddied the waters, there is help out there. The SUV Owners of America have developed a guide to help buyers choose the right vehicle to suit their towing needs. The guide lists all major manufacturers in one place. It gives the towing capacities for each of the models offered and for each variation within those models. Included are such items as engine options, axle ratios, and hitch configurations. The site is keyword searchable; to make it even easier, if you enter the weight of what you wish to tow, the site will respond with a list of every vehicle with an equal or greater towing capacity. To access this list go to their website http://www.suvoa.com.

CHAPTER 10

ON THE ROAD

According to *BoatUS Trailering* magazine, the top three reasons for roadside breakdowns are: flat tires (43%), bearing failures (20%), and tow vehicle problems (15%). In order to avoid these pitfalls, driving with a trailer requires extra care and some specific strategies.

PREDEPARTURE

Before heading out, make certain that the boat is well secured to the trailer. This includes straps round the boat's beam and at the transom, and a safety chain in addition to the trailer winch. Many trailersailors don't want to be inconvenienced with stern tie-downs. Unfortunately, rounding a corner too quickly or swerving to avoid a collision could easily cause an unrestrained boat to part from its trailer. Also, never depend solely on a winch strap or cable to prevent the boat from accidentally sliding off or riding up its trailer.

The mast and rigging must also be securely tied down. Close all ports and hatches. Lastly, make sure that everything is properly stowed, including dodgers and biminis, and that nothing is left on deck or in the cockpit. Traveling at highway speeds is nothing short of subjecting your trailer sailer to hours of gale-force winds.

With the boat properly secured, attention should be focused on the trailer. Make sure that the tires are properly inflated. This includes the spare. Check the pressure rating embossed on the tire sidewall.

Insure that wheel hubs are packed with grease to reduce friction and to keep water out. If they're equipped with bearing protectors, give each a shot or two of fresh grease. Make sure that your trailer brakes are working properly. If they're fitted with surge brakes, keep the brake fluid reservoir full.

Check to insure that the hitch is properly connected to the tow vehicle. The safety chains should be crossed and attached to the tow vehicle. Connect the electrical harness and check the operation of the trailer lights.

HITTING THE ROAD

Towing a trailer significantly increases your stopping distance. Follow at a safe distance and don't tailgate. Maintain at least a 3-second interval between you and the vehicle in front of you. If traffic stops abruptly, you'll need the extra space and time to react. Keep in mind that wet pavement can be slippery and necessitates traveling at slower speeds and having more distance between vehicles.

Employ a steady hand on the steering wheel and a gentle foot on the brakes. Avoid making quick steering maneuvers and never step hard on the brakes while turning. This can cause you to jackknife and possibly roll over.

Avoid lane changes unless you can do it safely. Use your mirrors and turn signals. If you occasionally hold up traffic, don't feel guilty. If you're on a two-lane highway and vehicles can't pass, find a safe place to pull over and let them by.

Never exceed the maximum posted speed limit. Staying with the traffic is fine, if your rig can keep up safely. On an interstate highway, limit your maximum speed to 55 miles per hour.

During periods of reduced visibility, such as dawn, dusk, and periods of rain, always turn on your headlights. Don't drive with just your parking lights on. In many states, driving with just parking lights on can get you a traffic citation.

Keep to the right lane, particularly when going downhill. Pay attention to your driving. Check your rearview mirrors often. Be aware of traffic all around you. Always be ready for an emergency and have an alternative plan ready to go.

To ensure that all is going as planned, while on the road, make periodic stops to check all connections, tie-downs, the tires, and wheel bearings. A good plan is to stop after 10 miles for the first check and every 100 miles or so after that. Tug on the tie-downs, feel the tires and wheel hubs, and make sure the rigging is secure.

Even if you're a seasoned trailersailor, using a checklist will avoid most common pitfalls and help ensure that you arrive at your destination safely and with enough time to launch your boat.

SECTION III

OUTFITTING YOUR TRAILER SAILER

You've asked questions, conducted research, read dozens of articles, talked to all those "experts" at the launch ramp, and looked at more boats than you can count. Now, based on your wants, needs, and comfort level, you've bought a trailer sailer. Whether it's fresh from the manufacturer's molds or has a few miles beneath its keel, it's a "new" boat to you and you can hardly wait to get under way. However, before you add water, there are some things that you'll need to do. Initially, this will involve such items as establishing legal ownership (registrations) and confirming that the required safety equipment is on board. As the miles pass beneath your boat's keel, you'll begin to personalize your trailer sailer to best suit the type of sailing you do.

CHAPTER 11

FITTING OUT

No matter whether you buy new or used, the supposed "sailaway" or "fully equipped" boat will always require a little something before you're able to release the docking lines and set out.

REGISTRATION

Hopefully, as part of the purchasing process, the transfer of the boat's registration from the seller to you, the new owner, was done. If not, a quick check with your state's Department of Watercraft will provide you with the necessary application. In addition to transferring the boat's registration, don't forget to transfer the trailer's registration. A call or visit to the Department of Motor Vehicles will quickly set this straight. Depending upon the state, there may be sales or personal property tax due. Be prepared to pay this, along with any registration fees, prior to obtaining the new registrations.

SAFETY

Many states require that you provide evidence of having completed a safe boating course. Even if this is not a requirement, it's a good idea. In addition to the Department of Watercraft, the U.S. Power Squadron and the U.S. Coast Guard Auxiliary, to name but a few, regularly offer safe boating courses. Cost of these courses is nominal and worth every penny.

11. FITTING OUT

The state in which your boat is registered regulates the recreational watercraft of that state and dictates what safety equipment is required. The exact type and number of safety devices is predicated on the size and type of boat. This information is usually provided as part of your registration package. Items that are considered required equipment include: life jackets, fire extinguishers, visual distress signals, sound signaling devices, anchor and line, lights, and registration and numbers.

While it's not a mandatory piece of equipment, consider including a VHF radio. Many sailing grounds afford only spotty cell phone coverage.

CHART(S)

With the development of GPS, many recreational boaters have given up on paper charts and rely solely on electronic positioning technology. This is unwise—batteries fail and systems routinely malfunction. As a backup or as your primary navigation aid, one of the first purchases you should make is a current chart of the waters that you'll be sailing in. Add to this, information about local sailing conditions obtained from knowledgeable sailors and you'll be good to go.

SPARES

Go over your boat from stem to stern and make a list of some simple parts you should carry on board. This includes such items as: cotter pins (both straight and ring), fuses, light bulbs, and assorted fasteners. Also include spark plugs and oil for the engine, as well as a general-purpose lubricant for turnbuckles, cables, and hinges. A gallon or so of fuel in an approved container is also a good idea. Don't forget an all-purpose cleaner and rags for wiping up spills. An oil absorbent pad is invaluable in catching any fuel or oil that may spill. Toss in a roll of self-adhesive sail repair tape, needle and polyester thread, a spare batten, and some spare line. Don't forget to include a basic toolkit. Without it, your spares will be just about useless.

BOAT GEAR

Carry at least two fenders to protect your boat's topsides from piers and other vessels. It seems that you can never have enough docking lines. Four is the minimum, with six being better. Make sure they are of the proper diameter for your boat's length and that they are long enough (as long as your boat). Don't forget a boat hook and an anchor and rode selected for the type of bottom encountered in your sailing grounds. Manuals for the boat, the engine, and any installed gear should be read in depth and kept on board.

PERSONAL GEAR

Sailing is no different than other hobbies or sports. It has its own vocabulary and its own gear. Don't spend a lot of money on highly specialized "technical" sailing gear. Use common sense and select those items that will enhance your comfort and safety while sailing.

To help you maintain sure footing and keep you on the boat, nonskid, non-marking (usually white soled) boat shoes are a must. A good hat and a pair of polarized sunglasses will not only protect you from the sun's harsh rays, but will also enable you to see better. Don't forget a clip for the hat and a lanyard for the sunglasses. These two simple tethers will help keep your hat and sunglasses from going overboard. Select breathable fabric clothes, including some foul weather gear for those times you get caught out in the rain. Lastly, invest in a pair of good sailing gloves. They'll improve your grip and protect your hands from rope burns.

11. FITTING OUT

PRESAIL CHECK

Before casting off for that inaugural voyage, familiarize yourself with the boat's various systems. All sailboats are not created equal; they may have different arrangements for sheeting, reefing, vangs, and so forth. Practice raising and lowering the sails, reef and unreef the main, adjust the boom vang, and raise and lower the centerboard (if so equipped). Become familiar with the operation of the boat's auxiliary motor. This is where the boat's manuals are invaluable. Read them. Investing a little time at the dock will result in a less stressful inaugural sail.

After a few sails you will soon realize that fitting out is not a simple one-time exercise, it's an ongoing process. As your knowledge grows and your sailing horizons expand, so will your needs. While extra gear adds fun, improves operation, and enhances safety, it also adds cost. Always keep in mind that what you need depends on how and where you use the boat.

CHAPTER 12

SAFETY

A sailor must be aware of a multitude of things, but none is more important than the safety and well being of his/her ship and crew. Every year the U.S. Coast Guard answers more than 60,000 distress calls and saves more than 6,000 lives. Unfortunately, there are nearly 1,000 lives lost because of boating mishaps. Before setting sail, make sure that you are familiar with your boat, your crew, and your safety equipment. If your boat capsizes, it's too late to get the life jackets out of their plastic wrappers!

The goal of almost all boater education courses is to provide a basic understanding of safe boating practices as well as state and federal laws relating to recreational boating. It has been proven that the application of this knowledge helps reduce or manage on-the-water risk. Since all of these courses are "introductory" and general in nature, it is strongly advised that a serious sailor continue his/her education by contacting one or more of the following organizations. In doing so, one will obtain area-specific competency training/certification.

    U.S. Coast Guard Auxiliary
    U.S. Power Squadron
    American Sailing Association
    U.S. Sailing Association
    American Red Cross
    BOAT/U.S.

Competency training/certification(s) involving both written and on-the-water examinations will result in not only a safer and more competent sailor, but also a more enjoyable time under sail. Joyce and I are always learning and enjoy the process. We have taken courses and hold certificates with all of the above-cited organizations.

THE FLOAT PLAN

Before setting sail, file a float plan. Even a casual day sail can be adversely affected by bad weather, an equipment breakdown, or an injury. File your plan with a relative or friend (not the Coast Guard). In general, the plan tells them where you are going, the route you plan to take, when you plan on returning, and whom to call if you don't return on time. (Most often, you'll ask that the Coast Guard or appropriate search and rescue personnel be notified if you're overdue.)

As a trailersailor, leave a copy of your float plan under the windshield wiper of your tow vehicle. Police, park rangers, marina personnel, etc. will find it, usually soon after dark. This simple act could be a lifesaver.

Don't forget to cancel your float plan when you return. The person with whom you left it may not know that you have returned safely. The last thing you want is to be responsible for someone initiating a needless search.

Like everything else in this world, the type and number of float plan forms are countless. Over the years, I've found that the U.S. Coast Guard has developed the most comprehensive version(s). The first version, or what I call the long form, works best for long cruises that involve multiple destinations. It comes with a Boating Emergency Guide that can be used with either float plan. For daysails and weekend trips, I use the second or "shorty" version.

If you don't like any of these, do a web search for "float plan" and you'll have a variety of others to choose from. It doesn't matter

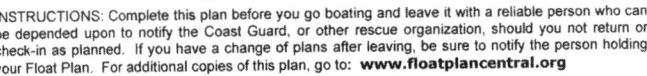

INSTRUCTIONS: Complete this plan before you go boating and leave it with a reliable person who can be depended upon to notify the Coast Guard, or other rescue organization, should you not return or check-in as planned. If you have a change of plans after leaving, be sure to notify the person holding your Float Plan. For additional copies of this plan, go to: **www.floatplancentral.org**

nws.cgaux.org — **Do NOT file this plan with the U.S. Coast Guard** — www.uscgboating.org

VESSEL

IDENTIFICATION:
Name & Home Port _____
Doc/Registration No. _____
Year & Make _____
Length _____ (ft/M) Type PWR Draft _____ (In/CM) Hull Mat Fiber
Hull Color(s) _____
Prominent Features _____

TELECOMMUNICATIONS:
Radio Call Sign _____
DSC MMSI No. _____
Radio-1: Type none Ch./Freq. Monitored _____
Radio-2: Type none Ch./Freq. Monitored _____
Cell Phone No. _____
Pager No. _____

NAVIGATION: (Check all on board)
☐ Maps ☐ Charts ☐ Compass ☐ GPS / DGPS
☐ Radar ☐ Loran C ☐ Sounder ☐ _____

PROPULSION:
Primary - Type Gas IO No. Eng. ____ Fuel Capacity _____ (gal/L)
Auxiliary -Type none No. Eng. ____ Fuel Capacity _____ (gal/L)

SAFETY & SURVIVAL

VISUAL DISTRESS SIGNALS:
☐ Day Only type
☐ Night Only type
☐ Day & Night type

PFDs: (Do not count Type IV devices)
Quantity On Board _____

AUDIBLE DISTRESS SIGNALS:
☐ Horn / Whistle
☐ Bell
☐ _____

GROUND TACKLE:
☐ Anchor: Line Length _____ (ft/M)

OTHER GEAR:
☐ Life boat / Life raft   ☐ Flashlight / Searchlight
☐ Dinghy / Skiff   ☐ Signal Mirror
☐ Food & Water   ☐ Drogue / Sea Anchor
☐ EPIRB none   ☐ _____
☐ Foul Weather Gear   ☐

PERSONS ON BOARD

OPERATOR:
Name _____   Age ____ M/F ____ Notes (Special medical condition, Can't swim, etc.)
Address _____   Has experience: w/Boat ☐ w/Area ☐
City _____ State ____ Zip Code ____ Home phone: _____
Vehicle (Year, Make & Model) _____ Vehicle License No.: _____
Trailer will be parked at: _____   Trailer License No.: _____

PASSENGERS/CREW: Name & Address   Age M/F Notes (Special medical condition, Can't swim, etc.)
1. _____
2. _____
3. _____
4. _____
5. _____

Attach "Supplemental Passenger List" if additional passengers or crew on board.

ITINERARY

	DATE	TIME	LOCATION	MODE OF TRAVEL	REASON FOR STOP	CHECK-IN TIME
Depart						
Arrive						
Depart						
Arrive						
Depart						
Arrive						
Depart						
Arrive						
Depart						
Arrive						
Depart						
Arrive						

Attach "Supplemental Itinerary" if space for additional destinations is needed.

Contact 1: _____ Phone Number _____
Contact 2: _____ Phone Number _____

If you have a genuine concern for the safety or welfare of any persons on board the Vessel described above, who have not returned or checked-in in a reasonable amount of time, then follow step-by-step instructions on the **Boating Emergency Guide™** included with this plan, or on the World Wide Web at:

www.floatplancentral.org/help/BoatingEmergencyGuide.htm

Rev 2007.05.11   Copyright 2001-2007 Float Plan Central. All rights reserved.

FLOAT PLAN WITH BOATING EMERGENCY GUIDE ON BACK

12. SAFETY

 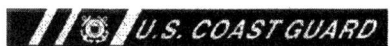

FLOAT PLAN

Complete this page before going boating. Leave it with a reliable person who can be depended upon to notify the Coast Guard or other rescue organization, should you not return as scheduled. **Do Not file this plan with the Coast Guard.**

Name of person filing:		Phone number:	

Description of Vessel

Type:		Color:		Trim:	
Registration No:		Document No:		Length:	
Vessel Name:		Make:		Other info:	
Engine Type:		Horsepower:			
No. Of Engines:		Fuel Capacity:			

Survival Equipment
(check as appropriate)

PFDs		Flares / Type:		Mirror		Smoke Signals	
Flashlight		Food		Paddles		Water	
Anchor		Raft / Type:		Dinghy		EPIRB / Type:	
Other:							

Communication / Navigation Equipment

Radio		VHF-FM		MF		HF		Other:	
DSC		VHF-FM		MF		HF		MMSI:	
Cellular phone / Number:									
LORAN C		GPS		RADAR					

Automobile / Trailer

Auto license No. / State:		Auto make / model:	
Auto color:		Auto year:	
Trailer type:		Trailer license No:	
Where parked:			

Persons On Board (#   )
(list additional persons on back)

Name	Age	Address & Telephone No.

Do you or any of the persons on board have a medical problem?		Yes		No	
If yes, what?					

Trip Expectations

Leave at:		From:		Going to:	
via:		via:		via:	
Expected to arrive / return by:		(time)	and not later than:		(time)

FLOAT PLAN (SHORT VERSION SUITABLE FOR DAYSAILING AND SHORT CRUISES) which one you use...just use one! By the way, I have found that copies of float plans make excellent additions to the ship's log, both from a historical and legal perspective.

CHAPTER 13

CUSTOMIZING FOR COMFORT AND SAFETY

I'm not a shipwright, nor am I a rigger, carpenter, or any type of tradesman. I'm the skipper of a trailer sailer and I'm responsible for my boat's two Us: upkeep and upgrade. While routine maintenance is a necessary evil, it's the little extras (my wife calls it "make work") that I enjoy doing. Some of the little make-work gems that have improved life aboard are described in this section.

COCKPIT NIGHT LIGHT

The sailing club that we belong to has limited dock space. Therefore, the majority of us have our boats on moorings. This is normally not a problem; however, with the bay being small and filled with boats, rowing out to our mooring on a moonless night can be challenging.

I decided that some type of light on my boat would make night identification and boarding much easier. Having only one battery and relying solely on my motor (which I use infrequently) for charging, I didn't want the added battery drain. Therefore, to add night illumination to my cockpit without any wiring or battery load, it had to be solar powered.

A quick trip to our local discount store (not marine store) provided what we needed: a solar powered garden accent light. There were literally a dozen models to choose from, but a hanging model, along with a double snap hook, made installation instantaneous.

SOLAR POWERED COCKPIT NIGHT-LIGHT

The unit is designed for outdoors and is weatherproof. Sunlight charges the replaceable AA NiCad battery during the day, while the LED (light emitting diode) turns on automatically at night, by means of a built-in photoelectric cell.

Compared to standard solar lights, the new LED technology in these units provides longer run time. Our unit has multiple LEDs, which afford brighter light output. It also has a defractor lens that disperses the light evenly.

While sailing we clip our light to a lifeline, where the sunlight charges the battery. Once at our mooring, we clip it to the end of our boom (more specifically to a grommet in our sail cover), where it's ready to do its work.

13. CUSTOMIZING FOR COMFORT AND SAFETY

With the addition of our new solar light, night identification and boarding of our sailboat is easy; as an added bonus, when staying aboard at night we have a cockpit "night light" for under $25.00.

HARD BODY WINCH COVER

Like most sailors, I take pride in ownership and this is directly reflected in how I maintain my sailboat. In addition to routine washings and waxings and touching up the occasional ding, every item not in use is stowed in its proper place and anything with a cover is covered. In other words, "shipshape and Bristol fashion." It is because of this attention to detail that *Splash,* my O'Day 222, routinely receives unsolicited compliments from other sailors.

Also, if there is a repair or upgrade that I can perform on the boat, I would gladly rather do it myself, than surrender her to the hands of a stranger.

Being the owner, skipper, and maintenance chief, I'm aware of the costs associated with boat ownership and am always on the lookout for ways to save money, which brings me to the topic at hand.

I recently had a need for a couple of winch covers. Wanting something more substantial than the conventional cloth covers, I paid a visit to the local home improvement store, where I obtained a pair of 4" PVC end caps and a 13" scrap piece of 4" PVC pipe. With a minimal amount of work these would be transformed into a pair of hard body winch covers.

Fabricating the covers was a snap. I cut the scrap length of pipe to match the height of the winch. All cut ends and any rough spots I sanded smooth. Using PVC cement, I then glued the pipe into the end cap. To finish off the winch cover, I drilled a small hole into the side of the end cap and attached a short lanyard of ⅛" line.

PVC end caps come in many sizes; however, the ones best used for making winch covers are 4", 5", and 6". All of these have IDs (inside diameters) ½" larger; even when a short piece of PVC pipe is inserted to accommodate for winch height, the ID is still greater than the nominal pipe size. Measure the diameter and height of the winch before purchasing the materials.

Not only do the hard body winch covers afford protection and look good, but when turned over they are also convenient receptacles for storing springs, prawns, and associated parts for servicing the winch.

HARD-BODY WINCH COVER WITH LANYARD

GPS BRACKET

While checking out the goodies offered for sale at a neighborhood flea market, I came across a used, handheld GPS. The unit came complete with batteries, external power cord, and owner's manual. After a cursory check of its operation, a little negotiation with the seller, and the exchange of a crisp new Alexander Hamilton, the palm-sized 21st century technology was all mine.

Now that I owned this little handheld marvel, I not only needed to learn how to operate it, but I also needed to find a convenient and secure place for it on my boat. The learning part was relatively easy; however, locating a proper mounting place on the boat was a bit more challenging.

I decided to purchase a readily available GPS mounting bracket, of which there are several to choose from. A quick check of the marine catalogs ended that line of thought. The bracket would cost more than twice the price of the GPS. True, not a fortune, but it's the principle. So, back to the drawing board. I figured I could build a custom bracket for next to nothing. And that's what I did.

With bulkhead space being a premium (taken up with coiled lines, compass, depth and knot meters, and cup holders, not to mention a backrest for the First Mate's sunbathing activities) the only available area was the companionway. True, it was visible from all reaches of the cockpit, but there was nothing there...at least not yet.

Necessity being the mother of invention, I rooted around my workshop and located a piece of ¼" plywood roughly the size of my lower hatch board. A few simple cuts and it slid perfectly down the companionway slides. Out of ¼" scrapes I fashioned a simple open-sided boxed shelf into which I could slide the GPS. The box was glued and assembled with stainless steel screws and mounted in the center of the new pen board. Four coats of marine spar varnish completed the project.

To use my GPS bracket board, I simply slide it into place, add the GPS, and depress the ON button. The centralized location and open side allows access to all the function buttons as well as an unrestricted view of the screen.

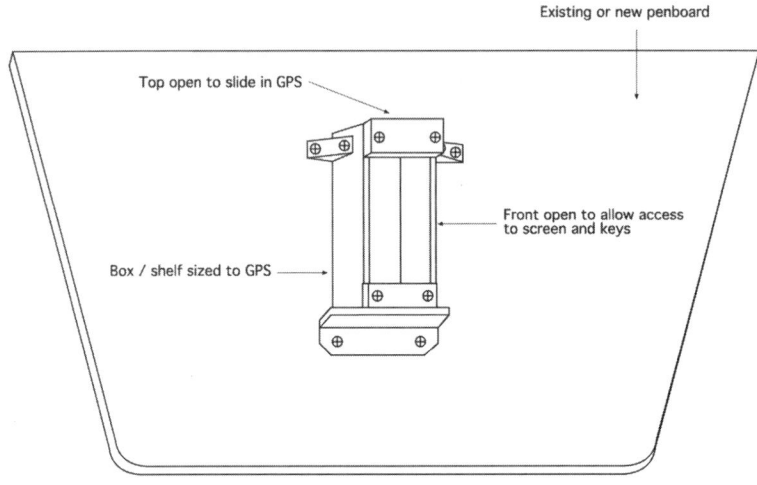

PENBOARD-MOUNTED GPS BRACKET

HEADSAIL DOWNHAUL

I learned long ago that having three dozen or so brightly colored lines with three dozen or so purposes not only did *not* impress the First Mate, but also complicated what should have been a simple and relaxing sailing experience. Now, when I get that itch to add some nice-to-have gear, I run it by the First Mate to help determine if it will make our sailing easier, safer, or more enjoyable.

With trailer sailers, ease of set-up and takedown are areas often negatively impacted by the addition of nice-to-have gear. Roller furling, while very popular, is one of those systems that can not only

13. CUSTOMIZING FOR COMFORT AND SAFETY   89

complicate the setup/takedown, but also requires additional time and care when stowing/securing it for highway travel.

A BOWLINE TIED TO THE HEAD OF THE JIB,
USING LIGHTWEIGHT DACRON LINE

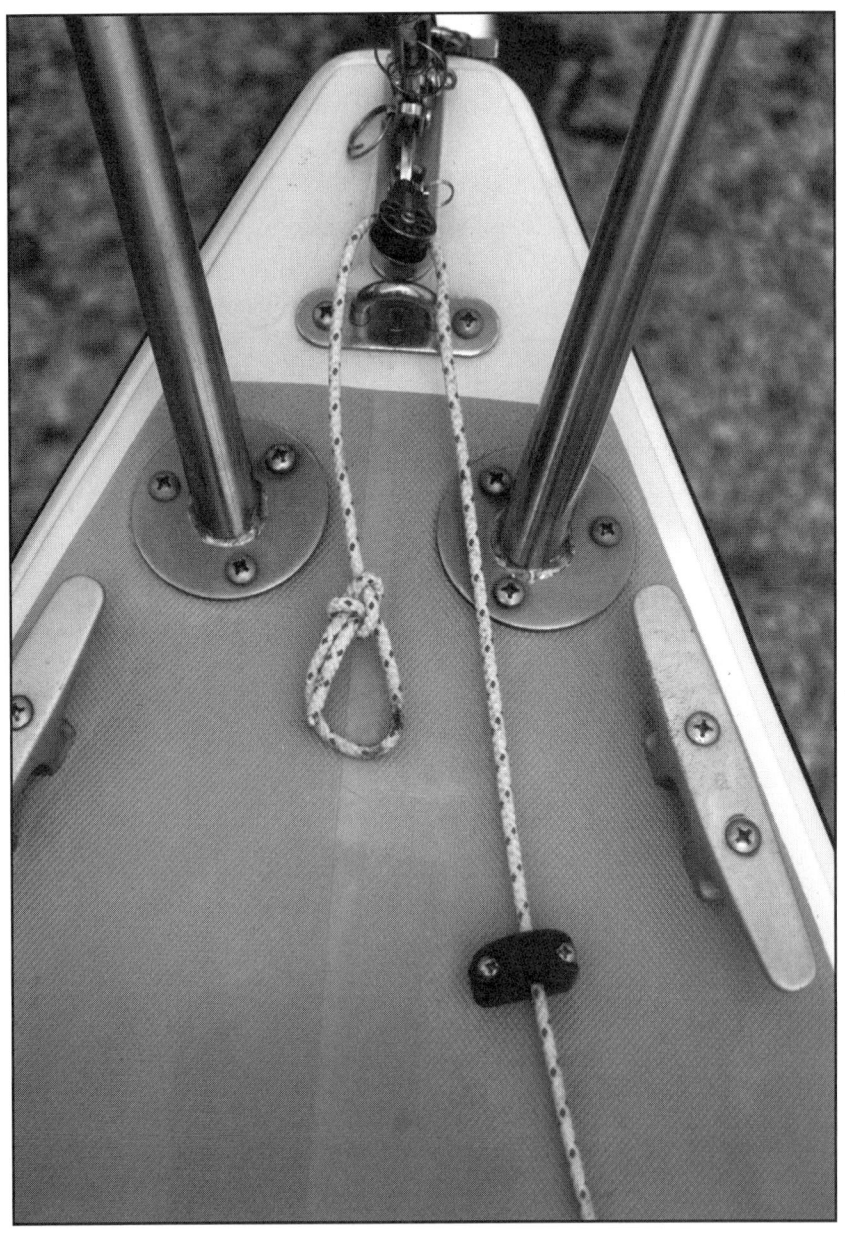

THE LINE FROM THE JIB'S HEAD IS LED THROUGH A BLOCK AT THE STEMHEAD FITTING AND BACK TO THE COCKPIT.

In addition to keeping things simple while also avoiding incurring the cost of the furling hardware and the associated sail modifications, we elected to install a simple headsail downhaul. We installed one of these on our first boat over twenty years ago, and according to the current owners, it still works well.

I tied a bowline in the end of a light Dacron line and attached it to the head of the headsail. From there the line is led down through a block located at the stemhead fitting, then back to the cockpit via fairleads, where it is cleated off.

When hoisting the headsail, the downhaul is freed and fed out as the halyard is pulled. To douse the headsail, the process is reversed. Either one of these tasks can be done singlehandedly. If there are others aboard, a crewmember can gather the sail on deck and either stuff it under the downhaul line or bundle it with shock cords. This not only temporarily secures the headsail out of the way, but also clears the foredeck for docking or anchoring.

A CURE FOR MAST RATTLE

A while back, we had the occasion to spend the night aboard our boat at an unfamiliar marina. The wind was freshening and the water was stirring in the bay, causing the boat to do some rocking. About 2 A.M. (why is it always the middle of the night when things happen?) I was awakened by the sound of something banging on the mast. Knowing that my halyards, topping lift, and EZ jacks are all external to the mast, I quickly surmised that I had forgotten to properly secure them away from the mast, thus creating such a cacophony. I shook my head clear of sleep, zipped my windbreaker up over my PJs, grabbed a flashlight, and headed up the companionway. I discovered that all of the lines had been properly secured. In spite of this, the noise continued. Pressing my ear to the mast, I determined that the sound was coming from inside. The wiring from my anchor light, steaming light, and antenna was dangling about the inside of the mast and causing the rattling sound. This had to be corrected, but not in the middle of the night.

Later, with the mast down, I saw the loose wires that were responsible for the noise. Since I've wanted to install a foredeck light for some time, I used this opportunity to also eliminate the mast rattle. I fastened a messenger line to the wires at the top of the mast and pulled them out through the base of the mast. I added a pair of wires for the foredeck light and bound all the wires together using cable ties. The cable ties were placed at 12–14 inch intervals, their tails were left long, and each was offset approximately 120 degrees from the other. After using the messenger line to pull the wires back into the mast, I made the appropriate connections. Looking inside, I saw that the wire ties, with the tails attached, held all the wiring essentially in the center of the mast. It's been quite some time since I performed this fix and I'm happy to report that my mast is rattle-free.

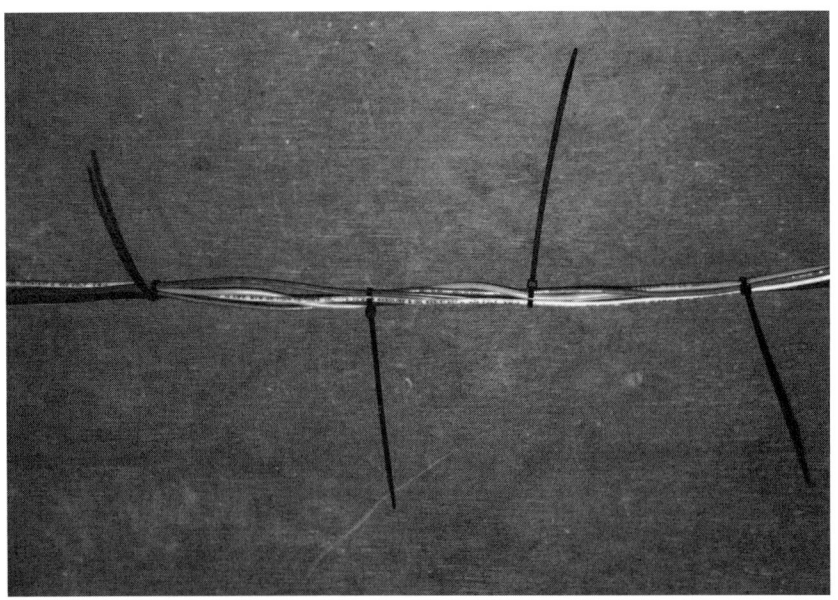

CABLE TIES KEEP THE WIRING IN THE MAST CENTERED
SO THAT THEY DON'T RATTLE.

13. CUSTOMIZING FOR COMFORT AND SAFETY

THE 39-CENT COVER-UP

An acquaintance of mine wanted to make his sailboat more conducive to single-handed sailing. By installing a deck organizer, he discovered that he could run his main halyard, boom vang, and the single reefing line back to the cockpit. Along with his Genoa sheets, already located on the cockpit coamings, and the main sheet, situated on the bridge deck, this simple rerouting would bring all of the boat's key lines within easy reach of the helm. Great. However, he postponed this simple modification for almost two years. Why? Because his boat had a fiberglass headliner, and he and his First Mate didn't want any unsightly holes in the cabin's overhead.

For several months he tried unsuccessfully to locate some type of cap, plug, or suitable cover that could be used to hide the holes he needed to make when installing the deck organizer. The boat's manufacturer went out of business in the 1980s, other dealers were of no help, and the local chandler just shrugged his shoulders. Since my acquaintance didn't want to tackle a fiberglass patching and painting project, he figured that his last chance was the local home improvement store.

In the electrical aisle he picked up a pair of blank, duplex outlet covers. Once on board, what had appeared in the store to be a close size and color match turned out in fact to be a near perfect match. After drilling small access holes in the overhead liner, he quickly installed the deck organizer and rerouted the lines aft. Then, using the screws that came with the cover plates, along with a dab of silicone to aid in securing them, he fitted the blank electrical plates over the holes. Not only does this installation offer easy access, but it also looks like a factory job, and the First Mate is pleased as well. Best of all, you can't beat the price: 39 cents! Now if only he could find a similar deal on three rope clutches.

BEFORE AND AFTER THE COVER UP

KEEPING MY LIBRARY ON THE SHELF

I'm a strong advocate of the maxim, a place for everything and everything in its place. This is especially true when stowing things aboard our boat, where space is at a premium.

A few years back, after a particularly rough passage I was distressed to find the cabin sole littered with just about every book and item that had been neatly stowed on the starboard bookshelf. Considering that the shelf is nearly six feet long, that was quite a few items. Despite the fact that the shelf is fiddled, the gyrations and excessive heeling experienced during the trip overcame the restraints of the fiddles. Fortunately, there was no damage except to my organizational pride.

13. CUSTOMIZING FOR COMFORT AND SAFETY   95

Not wanting a repeat performance, once we were in port I set about to remedy the situation and make the bookshelf more secure.

At the local chandlery I purchased a wooden boat cover bow and a pair of surface mount bow sockets. On each of the two bulkheads that flank the bookshelf, I installed one of the sockets.

BRACKET WITH WOODEN BOW BOAT-COVER BOW IN PLACE

I located the sockets approximately 4 inches above and directly in line with the existing fiddle. I cut the bow to match the length of the bookshelf and snapped it into the sockets. The boat's chainplate is situated almost midway along the shelf's length; by sliding the bow behind it, I have a convenient restraining point for the bow. This insures that the bow doesn't spring out from the weight of shifting books. On a shorter shelf, this three-point configuration probably isn't necessary, especially if the bow is cut an inch or so longer and when installed arcs slightly inward towards the books.

I had a choice of either a hardwood or a fiberglass bow. Even though the fiberglass bow was more substantial, I chose the wooden one. Somehow, I think the bright orange fiberglass bow might have clashed a bit with the boat's interior. After a coat of penetrating stain and two coats of satin varnish, the tulip poplar bow closely matches my varnished teak interior, and best of all, it works great. Cost of the project was about $20.00.

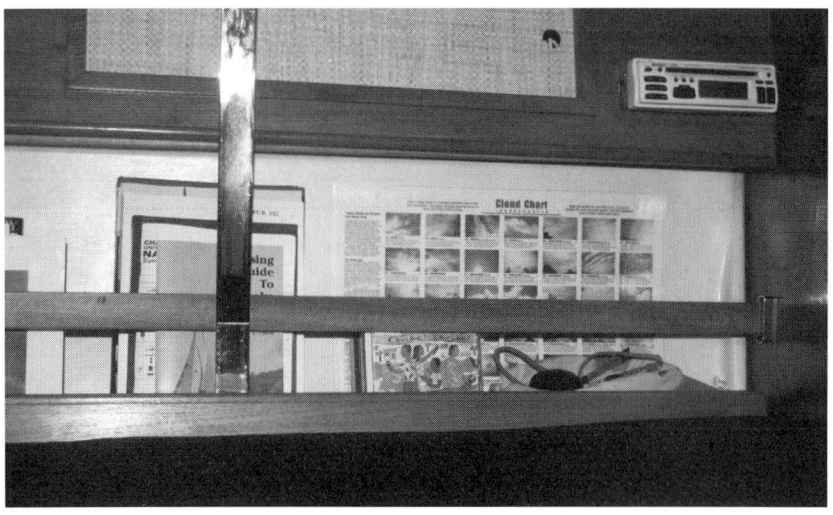

FINISHED SHELF RESTRAINT

13. CUSTOMIZING FOR COMFORT AND SAFETY

MAINTENANCE-FREE BRIGHTWORK

While I appreciate brightwork on a sailboat's deck, I'm not one who enjoys the annual maintenance that usually accompanies such esthetics. Our O'Day 222 has about the right amount of teak brightwork to enhance its sand-colored deck without presenting a heavy maintenance burden. As is the case with all sailboats, there is that one exception. Our exception is the wooden rungs on the swim/boarding ladder. I'm sure that at one time they were all made of teak, were properly secured with rustproof fasteners, and were judiciously maintained. However, years of use/abuse had taken their toll and after being treated as stepchildren (no pun intended), they needed attention.

Rather than reconditioning the rungs, we opted for replacing them. I checked around and found that for about $100 I could replace the six rungs with new teak milled for a custom fit. The price was not a king's ransom, but we would also be buying future maintenance. There had to be another way.

A visit to the boat show uncovered marine lumber made from recycled plastic milk jugs (polyethylene)—PlasTeak. The stuff's UV stabilized and is colored throughout. It won't rot or stain and is resistant to salt water and most chemicals. For about the same cost as teak, I had wider rungs fabricated and milled out of the PlasTeak. I mounted them using conventional stainless steel wood screws and, in a few minutes, the project was history and so was its future maintenance.

How does it look? From about six feet away and without careful scrutiny, it's awfully hard to tell the difference between the PlasTeak and real teak. In fact, the First Mate is thinking about replacing our current teak toerail.

FAUX TEAK LESSENS ANNUAL MAINTENANCE
TO THE SWIM LADDER'S RUNGS.

SECTION IV

TAKING CARE OF YOUR BOAT'S SYSTEMS AND HER CREW

One of the appealing things about a trailer sailer is that it is a relatively uncomplicated craft. In most instances, this degree of simplicity extends to the boat's various systems. For example, while the boat may have an auxiliary engine, it is probably an outboard motor; its electrical system may be nothing more than a 12-volt battery and a few lights, and its galley, a simple camping-type stove. Uncomplicated as this may sound, these systems need to be understood and maintained in order to provide carefree service. One guess as to who's the first maintenance tech in line?

CHAPTER 14

THE (INFAMOUS 2-CYCLE) OUTBOARD MOTOR

Since the main power plant on a sailboat is its sails, and rightfully so, the engine on a sailboat is correctly described as an auxiliary. When compared to a powerboat of similar size, a sailboat has a very small engine.

Just as the in-the-water sailor has slip rent and crane fees, the freedom and versatility enjoyed by the trailer sailor has its price—the trailer, and to a much greater extent, the infamous 2-cycle outboard motor.

Most engine-equipped trailerable sailboats, those up to about 28 feet, rely on outboard motors as their auxiliaries. However, not just any outboard motor will do. Most standard outboards are designed for the high-speed operation required by powerboats. *We sailors know this all too well!* Outboards specifically designed for sailboat applications have slower-turning, high torque propellers. Also, they often have longer shafts that enable them to reach the proper water depth. When correctly matched to the sailboat, an outboard can easily move a displacement sailboat at hull speed.

Outboard motors are mounted on sailboats in one of two fashions: on the transom, either directly or by means of an adjustable bracket, or in a motor well. Transom mounted outboards are the most common. They offer the advantage of being able to be tilted out of the way, thus eliminating prop drag when under sail. As on a typical powerboat, they can be easily steered. Also, since they are totally exposed, access for repairs/maintenance is excellent.

14. THE (INFAMOUS 2-CYCLE) OUTBOARD MOTOR

THIS TWO-CYCLE SAILMASTER OUTBOARD
IS SPECIFICALLY DESIGNED FOR SAILBOAT APPLICATIONS.
IT HAS A SLOWER TURNING HIGH-TORQUE PROPELLER AND A LONG SHAFT.

Outboards mounted in wells are less common but afford a better overall appearance to the sailboat than transom mounted units. Being always in a fixed position, their lower portions are always in the water ready to apply power. However, being in the water can create drag when under sail. One common problem associated with outboards mounted in wells is their tendency to become starved for air while under load. In some instances, the motor will choke on its own exhaust.

Today's outboard motors are much more reliable than their predecessors of even a few years ago. Computerized ignitions, oil injection and, of course, the crème de la crème 4-cycle outboards have eclipsed the earlier 2-cycle outboards, which seemed to work on the "internal destruction principle."

TODAY'S OUTBOARDS ARE MUCH MORE RELIABLE
THAN THEIR PREDECESSORS OF EVEN A FEW YEARS AGO.
THIS TWO-CYCLE UNIT BY SUZUKI HAS BOTH
A COMPUTERIZED IGNITION AND OIL INJECTION

14. THE (INFAMOUS 2-CYCLE) OUTBOARD MOTOR

However, even advances in technology cannot overcome the problems associated with typical sailboat auxiliary operation—namely, infrequent, slow-speed use. Here are a few things that you can do to minimize these problems.

SIZE IT RIGHT

Outboards are designed to operate best at three-quarter throttle or better. Therefore, it is important to size the outboard so that the sailboat can achieve hull speed at three-quarter throttle. The tendency to overhorsepower is common. Bigger is not better. Overhorsepowering often results in the sailboat reaching hull speed at half throttle. Operating for extended periods at half throttle or less invites spark plug fouling. Leaning out the air-fuel mixture may help, but some degree of fouling is inevitable and this tinkering with the ratio can adversely affect engine temperature as well as high and/or low speed operation.

QUALITY FUEL

The fuel of a 2-cycle outboard serves the dual function of producing ignition and distributing lubrication. This is accomplished by mixing 2-cycle oil with gasoline, either directly in the fuel tank in a fairly precise ratio, or by means of an oil injection system. In operation, the fuel-oil mixture enters the carburetor and is mixed with air. From here it is drawn into the crankcase, where some of the oily mist settles out, lubricating the crankshaft and lower end of the connecting rods. The rest of the mixture enters the combustion chamber to lubricate the piston, rings, and cylinder wall. The fuel-oil-air mixture is then burned during the combustion process.

Using less than the specified amount of 2-cycle oil can result in poor lubrication and excessive engine wear. Using too much 2-cycle oil causes spark plug fouling, excessive smoking, and erratic carburetion.

THE COMBINATION OF A FIXED BRACKET AND A SHORT SHAFT
OFTEN PRODUCES A CONDITION KNOWN AS CAVITATION.
A PARTIAL VACUUM IS CREATED IF THE PROPELLER IS
NOT DEEP ENOUGH IN THE WATER.
SINCE THE PROPELLER DOES NOT GET A GOOD "BITE" ON THE WATER,
THE MOTOR OVER-REVS. THIS CAN DAMAGE THE ENGINE
AND/OR RESULT IN PITTING THE PROPELLER BLADES.

14. THE (INFAMOUS 2-CYCLE) OUTBOARD MOTOR

Most 2-cycle outboard motors utilize a 50:1 fuel-oil mixture (16 ounces of 2-cycle oil to 6 gallons of gasoline). However, there are many exceptions, so follow the engine manufacturer's mixing instructions to obtain the recommended fuel-oil mixture.

In addition to a proper fuel-oil ratio, fuel quality is another key factor. Even the smallest particle of dirt can result in carburetor problems. Cleanliness is of prime importance. Always use fresh gasoline. Gasoline that has been stored for more than 60 days, even under ideal conditions, begins to form gum and varnish. This sour fuel can form restrictive/plugging deposits and can also be a source of spark plug fouling.

ANNUAL MAINTENANCE

Routine annual maintenance will increase dependability, maintain good performance, and extend the life of the outboard. Frequently, more problems will occur or begin to develop while during the off-season than when the engine is being used—that is, unless a few simple steps are taken. The precise maintenance steps are usually detailed in the outboard owner's manual. While some maintenance procedures for a particular make of outboard motor may be different, the following is a standard routine for preparing the average 2-cycle outboard motor for the off-season.

1. Prepare a batch of storage fuel as follows:
    a. 1 gallon of gasoline/2-cycle oil mixture
    b. 1 ounce of fuel conditioner/stabilizer
    c. 4 ounces of fogging oil
2. Start the outboard (operate the motor while in the water) and allow it to warm up and circulate the stabilized fuel throughout the engine.
3. Stop the outboard after approximately 5 minutes of running time.

4. Remove the spark plugs and discard them or set them aside if they are to be reused.
5. Spray a liberal amount of fogging oil into each cylinder via the spark plug holes.
6. Rotate the flywheel clockwise several rotations. This distributes the fogging oil throughout the cylinder.
7. Remove the outboard motor from the water, keep it vertical, and rotate the flywheel clockwise several more rotations. This will drain the water from the water pump.
    a. If the outboard motor is used in salt water, this is the time to flush it with fresh water.
    Also wash the exterior of the outboard motor with fresh water.
8. Clean and regap or replace the spark plugs.
9. Drain the fuel from the tank.
10. Drain and refill the lower unit with gear oil lubricant.
11. Lubricate the following with marine grade grease:
    a. Tilt-lock mechanism
    b. Throttle-to-shaft gears
    c. Carburetor linkage
    d. Magneto linkage
    e. Swivel bracket
    f. Motor cover latch
12. Remove and check the condition of the propeller. Clean and lubricate the propeller shaft. Reinstall the propeller using a new cotter pin.
13. Clean all external surfaces with an all-purpose marine cleaner. Allow the engine to dry thoroughly.
14. Paint over any nicks and scratches. Do not paint over sacrificial anodes.
15. Inspect sacrificial anodes; replace any that are less than two-thirds their original size.
16. Apply a good quality marine polish.

17. Store the outboard in an upright position, in a dry, well-ventilated area.

The major consideration in preparing an outboard motor for storage is twofold:

(1) to protect it from corrosion and
(2) to have it ready for next season's operation.

TROUBLESHOOTING

Proper fuel, lubrication, and maintenance will reduce the need for troubleshooting. However, even with the best of care a 2-cycle outboard motor is prone to problems and will eventually require troubleshooting. The following section lists some typical starting, fuel, and ignition system problems along with probable causes and solutions.

ENGINE WON'T START

Tip: Fuel system troubleshooting should start at the fuel tank and work through the system, reserving the carburetor as the final point.

- Fuel tank is empty
- Fuel tank vent is closed/clogged
- Fuel line fittings are not properly connected to the tank and/or engine
- Engine is not primed
- Engine is flooded (look for fuel overflow)
- Clogged fuel filter or fuel line
- Spark plug wires are disconnected or reversed
- Spark plug gap is too wide

LOSS OF POWER

Tip: Don't automatically assume that the carburetor is at fault when the outboard does not run properly. While fuel systems problems are not uncommon, carburetor adjustment is seldom the answer. Unnecessary carburetor adjustments will only compound the problem.

- Too much oil in the fuel mix
- Fuel hose kinked
- Slight blockage in the fuel line or fuel filter
- Fouled propeller
- Fuel/air mix too rich

STARTER MOTOR WON'T WORK (ELECTRIC START ONLY)

Tip: If the outboard motor is equipped with electric start, keep in mind that the electrical system is the weakest link in the operational chain. More problems result from electrical malfunction than from any other source.

- Gear shift not in neutral
- Defective starter switch
- Battery low or dead
- Battery connections loose or dirty

OUTBOARD MISFIRES

Tip: If misfiring occurs only while under heavy load, as when accelerating, it is usually the result of a defective spark plug. Operate the engine at night to check for spark leaks along the plug wires.

14. THE (INFAMOUS 2-CYCLE) OUTBOARD MOTOR

- Spark plug damaged
- Spark plug loose
- Plug wires broken
- Spark plug incorrect
- Poor quality fuel
- Fuel/air mixture too lean (outboard backfires)

While some repairs may require a trained mechanic, it's surprising how often a little knowledgeable investigating will uncover the nature of the problem and get the outboard motor quickly back into operation.

Even though today's outboard motors are much more reliable than their predecessors, nothing can substitute for using quality fuel and performing timely maintenance. These two simple acts will go a long way in assuring that the auxiliary will be ready to perform when needed.

CHAPTER 15

CARE AND FEEDING OF THE TRAILER SAILER'S BATTERY

The battery onboard a trailer sailer is the closest thing to an aquatic indentured servant as one can find. It is often forgotten and forced to spend most of its life in some dark, cramped, damp recess of the boat's bowels. It's usually cared for poorly and often subsists on meager rations. However, when called upon it is expected to perform unparalleled electrical feats; that is, until Mr. Murphy's Second Law kicks in: *When left to themselves, things always go from bad to worse.*

Understanding how a marine battery works and responding to its needs go a long way toward nurturing it into healthy old age. It's not rocket science, but rather a combination of routine maintenance and proper charging—in other words, care and feeding.

TECH TALK

Electrically speaking, marine batteries are technically known as accumulators (storage batteries). They are made up of a series of several "secondary" galvanic cells. Secondary cells can be recharged by passing an electrical current through them so that their electrodes are regenerated. Cells in which the electrodes cannot be recharged and are consumed during discharge are called "primary" cells. Disposable flashlight batteries are an example of primary cells. Typically, the electrodes of a storage battery are comprised of alternating negative (lead) and positive (lead dioxide) electrodes or plates suspended in an electrolyte of dilute sulfuric acid. In operation, the electrodes, together with the electrolyte, convert chemical energy into electrical energy. During this discharge, lead sulfate and water are formed. Recharging reverses this process.

TYPES AND KINDS

Currently, there are three battery chemistries or varieties of marine storage batteries on the market. They are the wet or flooded cell, the gel-cell, and the AGM (absorbed glass mat). The flooded cell, the least expensive of the three, requires periodic inspection and topping off with distilled water; the gel-cell, a sealed no-maintenance battery, is a bit more costly than the flooded cell; and the AGM, another sealed no-maintenance battery, is roughly twice the cost of a comparable flooded cell battery.

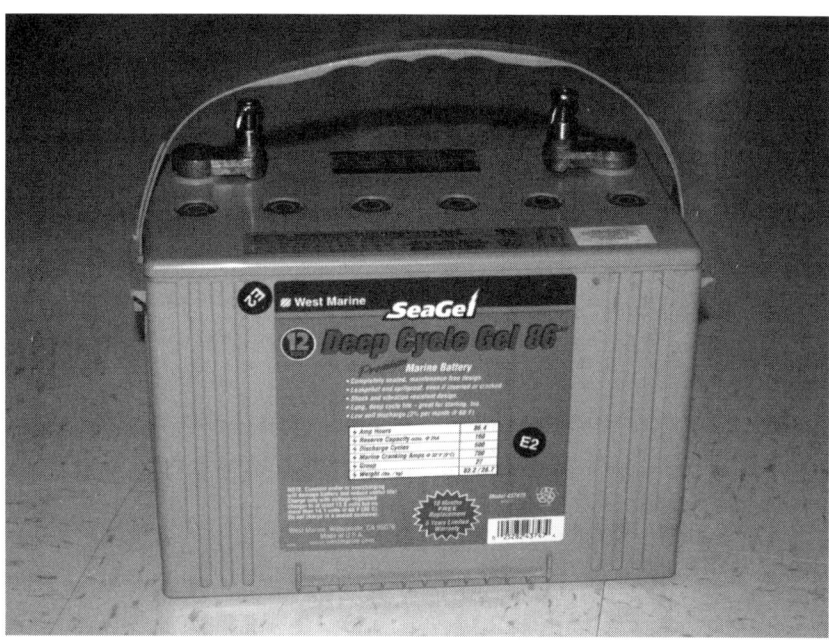

THIS GEL-CELL IS A NO-MAINTENANCE, SEALED BATTERY THAT'S A BIT MORE COSTLY THAN ITS FLOODED CELL COUSIN

There are pros and cons to each type of marine storage battery, some significant and some moot. As long as you purchase a quality product, it will work well. Follow the manufacturer's maintenance and charging recommendations. If you have a multiple battery system, do not mix types.

In addition to the three chemistry types, marine batteries are available in the following configurations: deep cycle, starting, and dual-purpose.

Deep Cycle Batteries are designed with thick electrode plates that enable them to be deeply discharged repeatedly without incurring damage. The combination of one discharge and one recharge is termed a cycle. The number of 100 percent discharge cycles that can be produced over a battery's life is how the battery's longevity is measured. 300 to 500 cycles are typical. Deep cycle batteries are best suited as house batteries to power lights, electronics, and other onboard electrical accessories.

Compared to deep cycle batteries, *Starting Batteries* have a larger number of electrode plates; however, the plates are much thinner than those of their deep cycle cousin's. This greater number of plates affords more surface area for chemical reaction to take place, hence delivering the higher current that is needed to start a motor. Since the plates are structurally weaker, they cannot handle the strain of deep cycle use. A typical starting battery cannot withstand more than a few deep discharges before it fails. The power of a marine starting battery is measured by its MCA (marine cranking amps). MCA is the number of amps a battery can deliver for 30 seconds at 32ºF without the voltage dropping below 7.2 volts. Starting batteries are engineered to supply lots of current (amps) over a short period of time (motor starting).

Dual-Purpose Batteries are part deep cycle battery and part starting battery rolled into one. Often marketed as a "universal" battery, the dual-purpose battery has its niche. If you motor frequently and your electrical demands are low, a dual-purpose battery is ideal. Also, if you have a bank of two batteries that are used for any and all loads onboard, two dual-purpose batteries will provide reliable service. However, a better dual battery system would be comprised of a dedicated starting battery and a dedicated deep cycle house battery. To gauge the relative effectiveness of various dual-purpose batteries, compare the number of deep cycles and the MCAs.

WHY BATTERIES FAIL

UNDERCHARGING

As is the case with most sailboats, the batteries of trailer sailers are repeatedly deeply discharged. However, unlike their larger relatives, trailer sailers often do not have outboard motors equipped with alternators to recharge their batteries. In fact, in lieu of an alternator, many outboards feature electric starting that exacerbates the battery's discharge condition. Even if equipped with an alternator, it is often unlikely that the boat's battery will be recharged to a capacity greater than 65–75 percent. This is mainly because sailboats rarely operate their motors for any significant length of time. Since it took a while to discharge the battery, it will take a while to recharge the battery. Recalling how a storage battery works, the uncharged 25–35 percent is in the form of lead sulfate, a relatively soft material. Over a period of time, these lead sulfate crystals (covering the battery's electrode plates) harden. This process is called sulfation. When this occurs, normal charging cannot result in the chemical reconversion to a charged state. Further undercharging and sulfation leads to further capacity loss and premature aging/battery failure.

OVERCHARGING

Because a trailer sailer lacks onboard charging capabilities, sailors frequently do their battery charging onshore. This strategy, if properly executed, has its merits. However, if left too long, some battery chargers will overcharge the boat's battery. This results in loss of electrolyte through evaporation. Also, the battery's positive electrode plates can be irreversibly damaged by excessive chemical reaction. Instead of maintaining a battery at peak charge, persistent overcharging can reduce a battery's capacity to 50 percent or even less.

EXCESSIVE DEEP DISCHARGE

During discharge, chemical energy is converted into electrical energy. This is the result of a chemical reaction, which routinely places a stress on the battery. The deeper the discharge, the greater the stress. Every time the battery is deeply discharged, some of the active material on the electrode plates is sloughed off. Over time, this shed material can build up from the bottom of the battery or even between the plates. Bridging of the plates by this sloughed-off material will short out the cell(s) and result in battery failure.

AN OUNCE OF PREVENTION

Treated properly, marine storage batteries will die of old age. Here are a few things that can help in preventing battery failure and prolonging battery life.

15. CARE AND FEEDING OF THE TRAILER SAILER'S BATTERY

MONITOR YOUR BATTERY

Periodically check the battery's state of charge with a hydrometer. Water has a specific gravity of 1.0. A fully charged battery will display a specific gravity of 1.270 or more. A specific gravity of 1.150 or less indicates a discharged battery. Be sure to measure all the cells. If you don't have a hydrometer, use a voltmeter. A fully charged battery will register 13.5 volts (if charged from a battery charger) or 14.2 volts (if charged from an alternator). A reading of 12.2 volts indicates a low battery, while a reading of 11.2 volts suggests a dead battery.

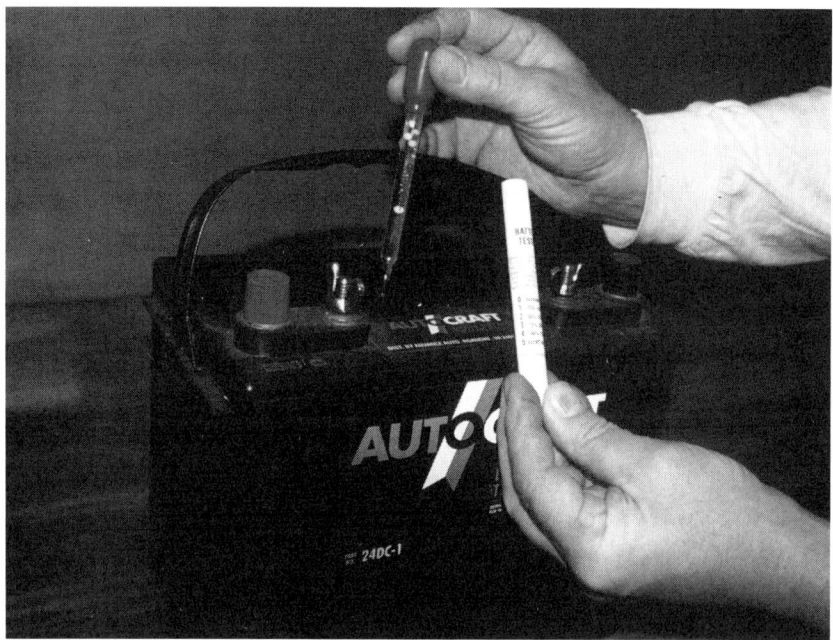

A FULLY CHARGED BATTERY WILL DISPLAY A SPECIFIC GRAVITY OF 1.270 OR MORE. IN THIS FIGURE, FOUR FLOATING BALLS EQUATES TO A FULL CHARGE.

GOOD HOUSEKEEPING

A clean, cool, and dry battery will give noticeably good performance. Clean the top and sides of the battery with water containing a small amount of detergent. Rinse the cleaned battery with water and dry it. Be sure to temporarily plug the vent holes with toothpicks during the bathing process. Remove any corrosion products with a thin paste made from baking soda and water. Again, rinse with water and dry. Burnish the battery terminals with a wire brush, coarse steel wool, or a terminal cleaner. Lightly coat them with a commercial battery corrosion inhibitor or WD-40. Impregnated felt washers that fit over the battery terminals to prevent corrosion can be found at auto parts stores. Replace them as necessary.

PERIODIC FEEDING:

If your battery is not "maintenance free," check the electrolyte level in each cell every month. If any is found to be low, add distilled water to the required level. Rainwater is an acceptable substitute for distilled water. You can avoid making a mess by using a squirt shampoo bottle for topping off your battery cells. I have found that the cells of many "no maintenance" batteries can also be accessed with a little ingenuity (gel-cells and AGM batteries not included).

15. CARE AND FEEDING OF THE TRAILER SAILER'S BATTERY

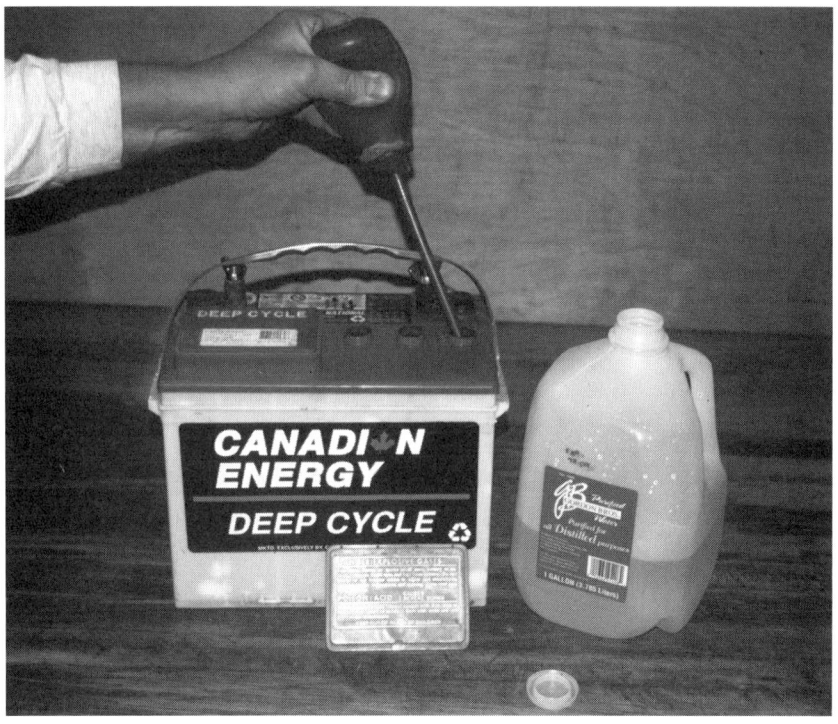

EACH MONTH, CHECK THE AMOUNT OF ELECTROLYTE IN EACH CELL.
IF ANY CELLS ARE FOUND TO BE LOW,
ADD DISTILLED WATER TO THE REQUIRED LEVEL.

PROPER HOUSING

Keep your battery in a secure and vented plastic battery case with cover. This will prevent the battery from tipping over (which would result in a short circuit) during rough conditions or excessive heel. Also, should the battery area become flooded, the cover will act as a diving bell, keeping air in and water out.

FULL CHARGE

Don't leave your marine storage battery too long with a partial charge. Over time, sulfation will reduce its capacity. Be sure to periodically bring your battery up to full charge.

FLOAT CHARGING

If you intend to leave your battery unused for a long time, be sure to first fully charge it. It will not remain in a fully charged state. All batteries will self-discharge over time. A flooded-cell battery self-discharges at 6–7 percent per month, while gel-cells and AGMs display a rate of around 3 percent per month. In cold weather, a battery can even freeze if its charge becomes too low. Therefore, during the storage period, periodically recharge or, better yet, float charge (constantly charge at a low level) your battery to keep it from sulfating. A low output trickle charger or solar panel having an output no higher than about 13.5 volts works well.

Your marine storage battery is one of the most important systems on your trailer sailer. Without it you may not be able to display your lights, call for help, pump your bilge, or maybe even start your auxiliary. However, with a little proper care and feeding your battery should provide you with years of service. But if you use it and abuse it, you may succumb to Murphy's Revised First Law: *If anything can go wrong with a system, it will, and generally at the moment that the system becomes indispensable.*

15. CARE AND FEEDING OF THE TRAILER SAILER'S BATTERY

USING A BATTERY CHARGER ONSHORE IS AN APPROPRIATE WAY TO COMPENSATE FOR A LACK OF CHARGING CAPABILITIES ON BOARD A TRAILER SAILER.

CHAPTER 16

REDUCING ELECTRICAL NOISE INTERFERENCE

A sailboat's communications gear and electronic navigation equipment can be rendered partially or even totally ineffective by electrical "noise" generated by the boat's various electric circuits.

In most instances, noise interference is usually a composite of noises from several sources and of different intensities, one layered on top of another.

An effective noise reduction program begins with the systematic removal/suppression of one noise layer after another. However, it is impossible to achieve the complete absence of noise. A successful noise reduction program is usually a compromise to an acceptable level of noise.

SOURCES OF INTERFERENCE

These are common sources of electrical noise interference, in order of severity: ignition systems; generators/alternators; voltage regulators; motors (pumps, blowers, etc.); gauges and instruments; propeller shafts and transmissions. Each of these potential sources of interference emits a distinctive sound, which can be used to identify it.

16. Reducing Electrical Noise Interference

IGNITION SYSTEMS

When a gasoline engine is used for auxiliary power, its ignition system is often the main source of interference. This is relatively easy to identify since it has that characteristic rhythmic sharp snap/pop each time a spark plug fires. This staccato sound increases in tempo with engine speed and stops instantly when the ignition is switched off.

GENERATORS/ALTERNATORS

The charging systems of both gasoline and diesel engines can produce a high-pitched musical whine. The pitch of the whine will increase with engine speed and will stop when the engine is stopped. An alternator is inherently quieter than the conventional generator.

VOLTAGE REGULATORS

Voltage regulators can generate various kinds of radio-frequency noise. Relay-type voltage regulators can produce an intermittent, ragged, rasping sound. The sound will often intensify when the charging rate is low, such as when the battery is nearly fully charged. Solid-state electronic regulators sometimes display a popping noise. Often the popping stops as the engine speed is reduced to idle.

MOTORS

Direct-current motors such as those used in bilge pumps and blowers can produce a whine or hissing sound. This noise will cease when the motor is turned off.

GAUGES AND INSTRUMENTS

Gauges and instruments can produce a variety of noises including intermittent clicking, crackling, hissing, or hash sounds. The noise interference usually worsens with rough seas because of the jarring of both the instruments and their sensors.

PROPELLER SHAFTS AND TRANSMISSIONS

Shaft noise is characterized by steady noise bursts when the prop shaft is spinning and the absence of noise when the transmission is shifted into neutral.

LOCATING THE SOURCE

The first step in noise suppression is to locate the source of the interference. Listening carefully and employing one or more of the following investigative techniques accomplishes this.

ON/OFF

The source of many noises can be identified by simply switching the suspected item on and off while listening. Since noise interference is normally layered, listen for an associated increase or decrease in the noise amount and level while turning the switch on and off.

NOISE "SNIFFER"

A pocket-type AM radio makes a great noise sniffer. Turn the volume up and tune the radio between stations. Atmospheric background hiss will be heard. Using the radio like a Geiger counter, probe around the suspected source. When the source of the interference is located, the interfering sound will be amplified through the radio's speaker.

CAPACITOR PROBE

Assemble a capacitor probe by installing clips to the hot and ground sides of a 0.5-microfarad (mfd) bypass capacitor. To use it, turn the suspected noise source on. Clip the ground of the capacitor probe to ground and briefly touch the hot terminal with the hot side of the probe. If the noise stops or lessons, the source has been confirmed. (Never connect a capacitor to the "field" terminal of a voltage regulator, alternator, or generator.)

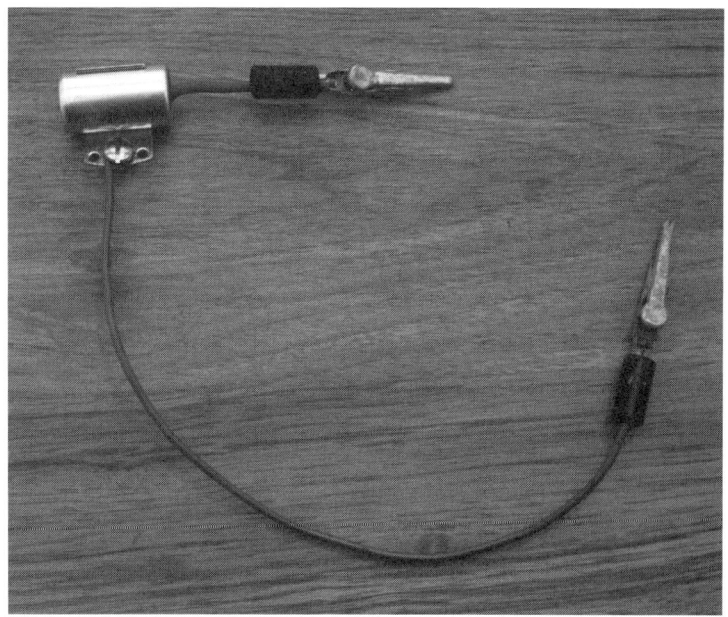

A CAPACITOR PROBE IS EASY TO MAKE FROM
A 0.5-MFD BYPASS CAPACITOR AND A COUPLE OF ALLIGATOR CLIPS.

BASIC TECHNIQUES

There are three basic techniques that are routinely employed to eliminate or reduce electrical noise interference. They are:

REPAIR OR REPLACEMENT OF FAULTY EQUIPMENT

Along with checking to see that all suppression components specified by the manufacturers are in place and in good condition, follow a diligent inspection and maintenance schedule. If your auxiliary is a gasoline engine, start with a tune-up.

For engines that are equipped with electronic ignitions, a tune-up simply entails changing spark plugs and ignition wires. When the resistance of resistor-type spark plugs exceeds 18,000 ohms, they should be replaced. Also, the resistance of resistor cables should be checked every three years and cables should be replaced when the resistance is three times that of the original value.

For engines without electronic ignitions, in addition to spark plugs and ignition wires, check and replace as necessary the breaker points, condenser, rotor, and distributor cap.

Routinely inspect all signal and power wiring. Look for and repair or replace loose connections, corroded wires, and worn or damaged insulation.

SHIELDING TO CONFINE THE INTERFERENCE TO THE SOURCE

Bonding and rerouting of wiring are also included in this technique.

Shielding can take on various forms depending upon the situation. One of the most common is the use of shielded cable. If used, make certain that you properly ground the shielding.

All low-voltage wiring should be routed away from the ignition system. Do not bundle low-voltage and ignition wires together. Avoid running wires parallel or close to wires that carry pulsating signals. Be careful that no wires are hanging in the bilge or are lying across the engine or exhaust system.

Bond together the engine, battery, and other large metal units, such as water and fuel tanks, electric motor frames, housings for electrical equipment, the mast, stanchions, and pulpits.

ADDITION OF SPECIAL COMPONENTS

These may include bypass and coaxial capacitors, filters, chokes, and so forth. These electronic components are often available at marine centers, but are more economically purchased at electronic stores, such as Radio Shack. In the following sections, a variety of specific noise suppression components are discussed. These are by no means the only ones to employ. A variety of noise suppression components are manufactured for a host of applications. They are available in various ratings of amperage, voltage, and so on. The technician at the electronics store will be able to guide you in sizing and selecting the best component for the application.

SUPPRESSING THE NOISE

IGNITION SYSTEMS

If it has been determined that the ignition system is responsible for the noise interference, the first action to take is to install a suppression resistor in the high voltage wire that runs between the coil and the center terminal of the distributor. Should the noise persist, install resistor-type spark plug cables and/or resistor spark plugs.

Make certain that the ignition coil is making good electrical contact with the engine and is securely fastened to the engine and not mounted on a bulkhead. Also, be aware that coils with metal cases emit less noise than those with plastic cases.

Check the polarity of the ignition coil. The wires may have been reversed if the coil was removed or replaced. Insert the graphite point of a wooden pencil between the spark plug wire and the spark plug. The arcing spark should flare orange on the plug side of the pencil. If not, the polarity is reversed, which can produce greater electrical noise.

Battery ignition wires that run from the ignition switch to the engine should be shielded and the shield should be grounded at the engine. Make certain that non-ignition wires are not bundled with or alongside ignition wires. All power and instrument signal wiring should be kept away from the engine.

Another way to reduce the transfer of ignition interference into the boat's wire harness is by installing a 0.1-mfd 200-volt coaxial capacitor between the ignition coil's "Batt" or positive terminal and the ignition switch. Mount the coaxial capacitor as close to the coil as possible and ground the case.

A 0.005-mfd 1,000-volt ceramic capacitor can be installed between the ignition coil's "Dist" or negative terminal and ground. Keep the capacitor's leads as short as possible.

GENERATORS

Connecting a 1.0-mfd 50-volt capacitor between the "Batt" (armature) terminal and ground (the generator's frame) will significantly quiet or eliminate the whine and snarl often associated with conventional generators. (Do not install a capacitor on the "field" terminal.)

ALTERNATORS

Alternators incorporate internal capacitors, thus making them quieter than armature and brush generators. However, they still can be a source of noise interference. As with a conventional generator, connecting a 1.0mfd capacitor between the "Batt" (output) and ground (alternator's frame) will suppress or eliminate any remaining alternator noise. Make sure that the capacitor is rated for at least 50 volts; one constructed of polypropylene or Mylar is preferred.

Another suppression technique involves the installation of a 0.5-mfd coaxial capacitor in the output line. Mount the capacitor as close to the alternator as possible and ground its case. This works well on alternators rated up to about 40 amperes. On higher rated alternators, a low-pass filter should be used instead of a coaxial capacitor. (Never connect a capacitor to an alternator's field terminal.)

To reduce unwanted radiation from the alternator's output wire, shield it from the alternator all the way to the battery. Ground the shielding at the battery. A long, unshielded wire, such as one leading to a remote current meter, is asking for radiation trouble.

VOLTAGE REGULATORS

Most modern alternators have built-in solid-state electronic voltage regulators, reducing the source of noise interference to just a single high voltage lead exiting the alternator. However, remote voltage regulators can produce severe noise interference.

Voltage regulators should be mounted as close to the alternator/generator as possible, with their field wire routed close to the engine block. If possible, shield the field wire and ground the shielding at both ends.

Placing a 1.0-mfd 200-volt capacitor between the regulator's "Batt" terminal and ground will often achieve adequate noise suppression. Keep the leads short. If this doesn't work well, install a 0.5-mfd coaxial capacitor, wiring it in series with the battery lead. Ground the case of the coaxial capacitor. (Never connect a capacitor to a regulator's field terminal.)

Consider replacing an older design electromechanical regulator with a modern solid-state electronic regulator.

ELECTRIC MOTORS

The electronic noise caused by small direct-current motors can be effectively filtered by using one or more of the following techniques:

- Insure that the motor is properly grounded.

- Connect a 0.25 to 0.5-mfd 50-volt capacitor from the motor's positive lead to ground. Install it close to the motor and keep the leads short.

- Connect a 1.0-mfd 200-volt capacitor across the power terminals of the motor. Again, keep the installation close to the motor and the leads short.

- If the noise is persistent, a small hash choke may be added in series with the positive motor lead.

GAUGES AND INSTRUMENTS

Noise caused by electrically operated gauges can be suppressed by installing a 0.1-mfd capacitor across the terminals or by connecting a 0.5-mfd 200-volt coaxial capacitor in series with the positive lead. Don't forget to ground the coaxial capacitor's case.

For persistent cases, a hash choke installed in series with the positive lead may be necessary.

Do not use capacitors to suppress noise interference from electronic tachometers. The only satisfactory suppression technique is to shield the entire length of the tachometer's pick-up cable and to ground it at both ends.

Propeller shaft and transmission: In almost all cases, shaft hash can be eliminated by installing a bronze finger or carbon brush that rides on the propeller shaft. This finger or brush is connected to the boat's bonding system by heavy gauge copper wire.

OUTBOARD MOTORS

Outboard motors, especially those with high voltage capacitive-discharge ignitions, can contribute a significant amount of noise interference. In many cases, commercial suppression kits are available from the engine's manufacturer. If not, adapt the previously outlined techniques. Additionally, household aluminum foil glued to the inside of the engine's fiberglass cover and grounded to the engine will shield much of the radiated noise.

SAILBOAT SOUNDS

While rare, an eerie electrical whine or snapping may sometimes be heard on a sailboat's radio, even though all other electrical equipment is off. The likely sources of this noise interference are the turnbuckles and shackles, and the metallic rigging rubbing together, as well as static electricity arcing from nylon line and vinyl seat cushions.

MISCELLANEOUS SOURCES

With the addition of modern creature comforts aboard ship, such as TV, DC to AC inverters, and all types of electronic navigation and entertainment equipment, new sources of interference can crop up.

Many on-board, mast-mounted TV antennas contain an amplifier that boosts weak TV signals. Because of a design flaw, strong TV signals can cause this amplifier to oscillate and radiate an unwanted signal that is strong enough to interfere with accurate GPS reception. This interference can even take place when the power to the antenna is off and the TV is not being used. Offending TV antennas are: Tandy Models 5MS740 and 5MS750, Radio Shack Model 1501624, and Shakespeare Model 2050.

Inexpensive, square wave inverters can also be a big contributor of noise interference. The more expensive, synthesized, sine wave inverters are not nearly as big a problem.

In many instances, noise suppression at the power input (usually the red wire) to the electronic device is often successful. This can be done by installing a 0.1-mfd 50-volt ceramic capacitor from the positive lead to ground.

There exists no such condition as total noise suppression, only a compromise where a tolerable level of noise exists. Even if all manmade sources are successfully suppressed, atmospheric noise is always present to some degree. And, at certain times, it can be severe (*e.g.* during periods of sunspot activity and electrical storms).

CHAPTER 17

SAIL MANAGEMENT

I purchased my first daysailer in 1979 and have been an avid "trailer sailor" ever since. My current boat is a 1984 O'Day 222 that sports its original jib and main, both still in very good condition. Many boats of this vintage have long ago bade farewell to their factory-supplied sails. Why not mine? I practice what I call sail management.

Sails are costly to replace. Therefore, it is the wise and thrifty sailor who routinely inspects, cleans, repairs, and properly stores his/her sails. While modern synthetic sailcloth can handle salt water much better than traditional natural fibers, damage caused by UV degradation, chafe, and mishandling can significantly reduce a sail's useful life.

INSPECTION

The first step of good sail management is inspection. It is with periodic inspections that early signs of damage and wear are spotted. Corrective actions can then be taken before conditions worsen. The easiest way to inspect sails is to lay them out on a clean, flat surface. With large boats having correspondingly large sails, this might be a little tricky. However, we small boat owners can easily spread out our sails on the backyard lawn or even on the family room floor. Begin the inspection process by systematically working your way around the sail's edges. Once this has been done, work your way into the center of the sail. Pay particular attention to those areas where the sail is attached to the rigging and spars. These include the tack, foot, clew, leech, batten pockets, head, and luff. In addition to chafe and UV damage, it is in these areas that stains are most likely to appear.

TACK

The sail's tack is routinely subjected to significant strain. A failure here can distort the sail and cause it to become misshapen. Examine the cringle for distortion or excessive wear. Check carefully for broken stitches and signs of chafe. On a mainsail, check where the bolt rope rubs the boom.

FOOT

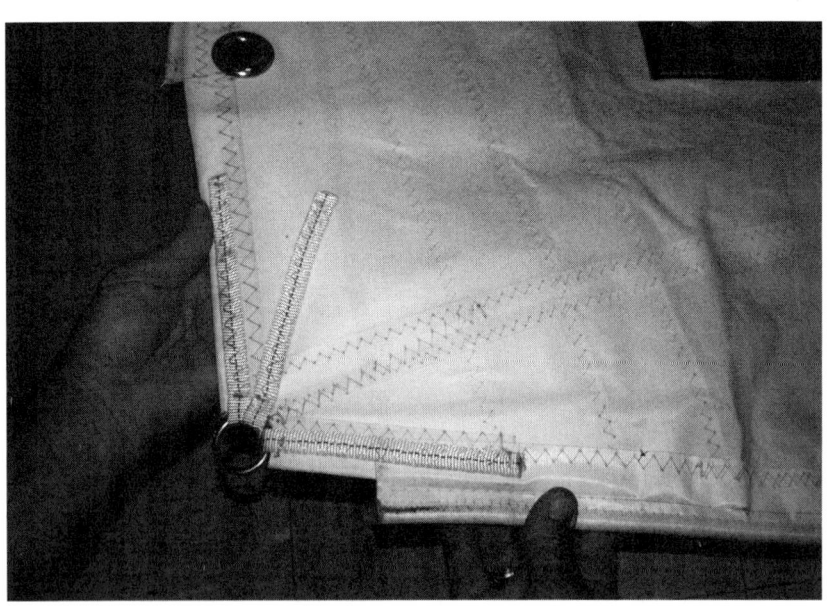

THE SAIL'S TACK IS ROUTINELY SUBJECTED TO SIGNIFICANT STRAIN.

17. SAIL MANAGEMENT

Check the integrity of the stitching along the sail's foot. Use a fingernail to scrape the thread in several places. When stitching is damaged by UV, it will slough off easily. If you can scrape away any stitching, it's time to restitch before the seams come apart. The foot on a spinnaker may show signs of wear where it rubs against the forestay.

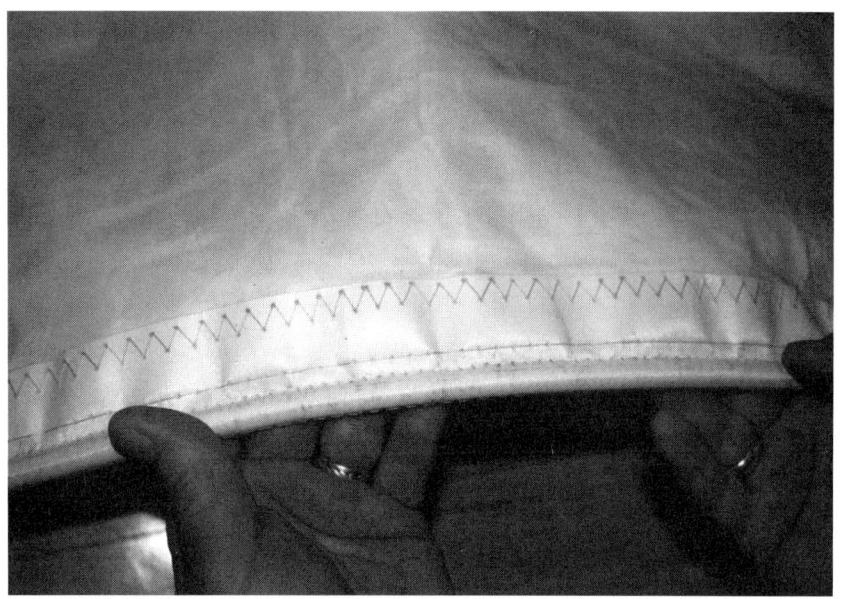

CHECK THE INTEGRITY OF THE STITCHING ALONG THE SAIL'S FOOT.

CLEW

The clew is subjected to wear similar to that of the tack. Additionally, headsail clews can exhibit chafe, due to repeated contact with standing rigging, including the shrouds and mast.

LEECH

Check the leech line hardware and make sure that it is present, in the correct position, and is operable. Topping lifts that routinely come in contact with a mainsail's leech can cause chafe. The leeches on large headsails are vulnerable to chafe from shrouds and lifelines. More and more small boat sailors are switching from hanked-on sails to roller furling. If you're one of those, the sacrificial cloth covering the foot and leech on a roller furling headsail is just that: sacrificial. Check for UV degradation by lightly scraping the surface of the fabric with a dull metal object, such as the edge of a spoon or the dull side of a knife blade. If the cloth is still in good condition, the fabric will become shiny and smoother. If not, the surface will become fuzzy or even begin to slough off. In severe cases, the fabric will rub away completely. Spinnaker fabric is susceptible to stretching. Periodically, compare the leeches to make sure one has not stretched more than the other.

BATTEN POCKETS

Examine batten pockets for damaged stitching. Make sure that the battens are the proper size and that they are not damaged. Since they must be removed prior to storing the sail, use a permanent marker to identify them and their proper placement.

HEAD

Carefully examine the headboard and determine that the rivets are all in place and are holding firm. As always, check the stitching for wear, especially in reinforced areas.

17. SAIL MANAGEMENT

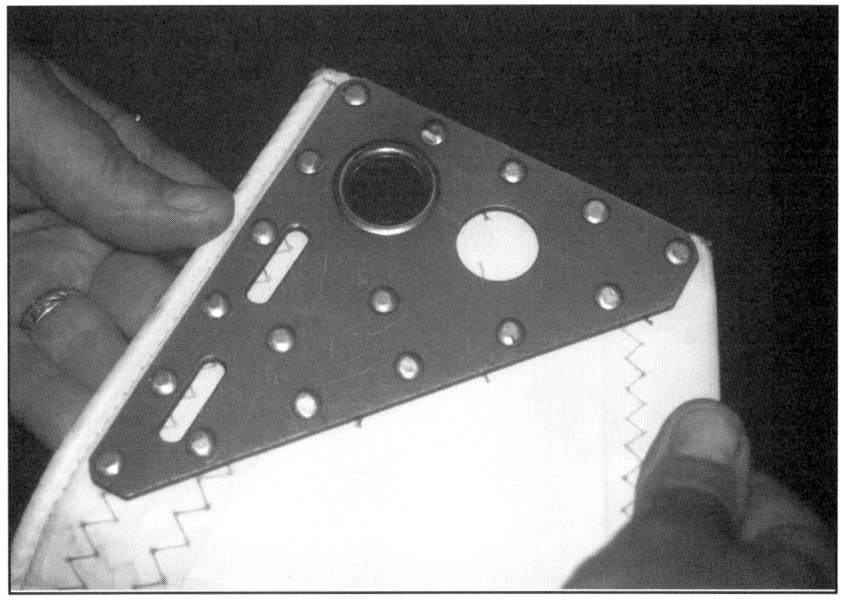

CAREFULLY EXAMINE THE HEADBOARD AND DETERMINE THAT THE RIVETS ARE ALL IN PLACE AND HOLDING FIRM.

LUFF

On a mainsail, check that all the sail slugs are properly attached, not broken or missing, and are spaced correctly. Make sure that the reefing cringle is not distorted. Look for signs of chafe along the bolt rope. The hanks on a headsail should be firmly attached and in working order. Examine the luff wire carefully to determine if there are any broken strands.

OVERALL

While examining the body of the sail pay particular attention to the reef points. Look for distorted eyelets and worn stitching. If you periodically store your sail under a sail cover while flaked on the boom, look the sail over carefully for signs of UV damage. Flaking the mainsail on the boom causes the sail to develop a memory. This leaves almost one-third of the sail (leech portion) more exposed than other areas. Even when covered, the sail is still vulnerable to UV attack. As a sail cover ages it becomes less and less effective at blocking the sun's harmful UV rays. Spinnaker cloth is particularly susceptible to UV damage.

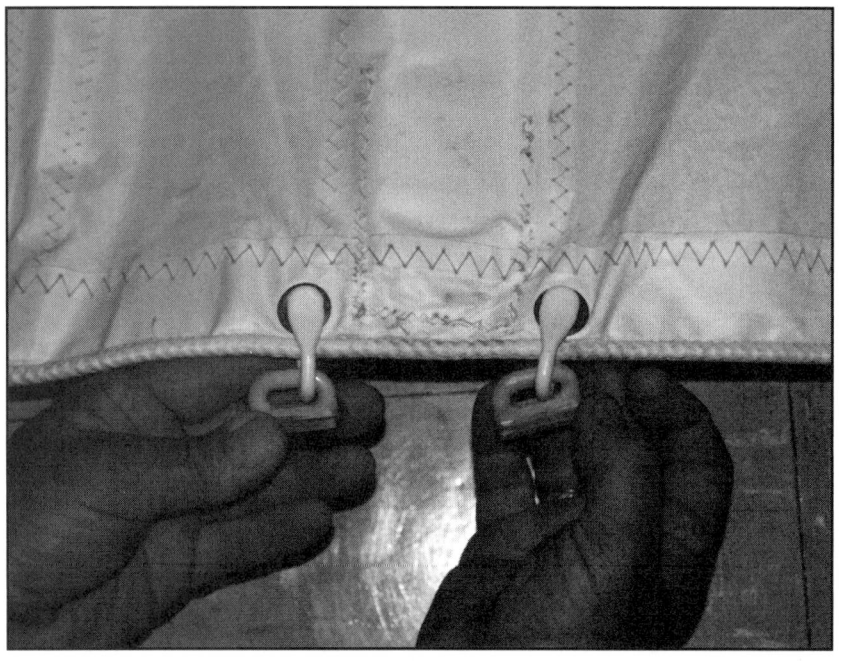

ON A MAINSAIL, CHECK THAT ALL THE SAIL SLUGS ARE PROPERLY ATTACHED, NOT BROKEN OR MISSING, AND ARE SPACED CORRECTLY.

CLEANING

17. SAIL MANAGEMENT

Dacron is the most prevalent sailcloth in use today and is highly resistant to staining. However, should staining occur, most can be removed. As with using any chemicals, common sense dictates testing the compatibility of the cleaner on a hidden area before proceeding. Spot-treat bad stains as soon as possible, preferably before washing the entire sail. Approach cautiously and employ the mildest cleaning agents first.

OIL AND GREASE

Remove the excess by blotting or scraping. Dawn dishwashing liquid is a good oil emulsifier that will often successfully remove a fresh stain. For more persistent stains try rubbing alcohol, mineral spirits, or trichloroethlyene. Dilute bleach followed by several fresh-water rinses will help lighten any remaining stain. Warning: These are all hazardous chemicals. Wear impervious gloves when handling, and do not use more than is absolutely necessary.

RUST

Treat the area with lemon juice or white vinegar followed by a detergent and a fresh-water rinse. If unsuccessful, use a weak solution of oxalic acid (1 ounce of oxalic crystals in 1 pint of hot water). Use rubber gloves and rinse thoroughly with fresh water.

MILDEW

Try lemon juice followed by a detergent and a fresh-water rinse. To lighten any remaining stain use bleach or hydrogen peroxide. Rinse thoroughly with fresh water.

BLOOD

Rinse or soak the area in cold water for up to half an hour. If the stain still persists, work in a paste made up of detergent and cold water. Bleach or hydrogen peroxide can further lighten any remaining stain. As always, rinse thoroughly with fresh water.

MUD

Washing with a mild detergent and rinsing with fresh water will remove these stains most of the time.

GENERAL WASHING

Once the stained areas have been spot-cleaned, a general washing is in order. Sails should be washed at least once a year, since salt, dirt, and stains can weaken the material. Salt is not only highly abrasive, but also hydroscopic, that is, it attracts moisture. This dampness allows mildew to form on any dirt that may be embedded in the sailcloth. Salt can easily be removed by thoroughly rinsing the sail with fresh water. To remove surface dirt, wash the sail with a mild household detergent and warm water. For embedded dirt, scrub the area with soap and a nail brush. Be careful not to damage the stitching. Because most detergents are alkaline, which can damage sailcloth, rinse the sail several times with clean water. Hang the wet sail by its luff to dry. Don't put a sail in the washing machine. Never put a wet sail in the drier or iron it. Heat can result in shrinkage and damage to the sailcloth's fibers.

REPAIR

Depending upon what deficiencies have been uncovered by the inspection, a trip to the sail loft or some quiet time with needle, thread, and a sailmaker's palm may be in order. No matter how small, repairs should be tackled promptly. If left too long they will become major problems and most probably expensive ones.

STORAGE

After the sail has been inspected, cleaned, and repaired it is now ready for storage. Starting at the foot, carefully flake the sail. Try to vary the width of the flakes to prevent permanent creases from forming. Avoid creasing any windows. After flaking, roll or loosely fold the sail and place it into a properly sized sail bag. Avoid cramming, bunching, or folding the sail too tightly. I've heard some small boat sailors say that they advocate stuffing their sails into a sail bag to eliminate repeated folds. Don't do this. Soon the sail will be severely creased and resemble a dried prune. This accelerates the breakdown of the sailcloth and stitching. The sail should be loosely flaked and folded so that air can circulate around it freely. While in storage do not allow anything heavy to rest on the sail.

SAIL CARE TIPS

Sails are expensive to replace, so it only makes sense to help prolong their life. Use the following sail care tips to help you to avoid premature sail death.

- A mini inspection can be done each time a sail is hoisted or lowered.
- While the sail is up, use binoculars to spot problem areas.
- Rinse salt off of the sail soon after a wet voyage.
- Remove dirt and stains as soon as possible.

- Always allow the sail to dry thoroughly before storage.
- Always loosely flake and fold a sail for storage.
- Avoid unnecessary stresses.
- Don't oversheet headsails.
- Don't allow sails to flog.
- Don't hoist sails in winds stronger than they were designed for.
- After use, loosen leech lines that have been tightened.
- Use a Sail Bag.
- When sails are not in use, store them below deck or, if you leave them on spars, use covers to protect them from the sun's harmful rays.

A FEW WORDS ABOUT UV RAYS

UV radiation emanating from the sun is a sail's worst enemy. Sail covers must be used when sails are stored above deck. As a general rule, when having a sail cover fabricated, bear in mind that heavier fabrics afford greater UV protection than lighter weight material. Likewise, darker colors are better then lighter colors, since they reflect UV rays better. The tropics are very hard on sails and sail covers. Two-ply acrylic covers or a single-ply cover with a foil (space blanket material) liner is the best available technology to protect against UV degradation in this harsh environment.

Effective sail management is an ongoing process, but it's worth the effort. The cost of cleaning supplies, periodic repairs, a good sail cover, and the time spent in caring for your sails will be returned many fold in increased sail longevity.

CHAPTER 18

THE TRAILER SAILOR'S GALLEY

Eating well is an integral part of boat safety. A hungry crew is more prone to seasickness, lethargy, and lower morale. Any one of these conditions can adversely affect the cruise. However, many trailer sailors seem to overlook this aspect, concentrating instead on the mechanics of sailing. I suspect that the spartan galleys of most typical trailerable sailboats make food preparation a daunting task. Believe me, this does not have to be the case. As with any other aspect of sailing, a little forethought, preparation, and the proper equipment can add to the safety and enjoyment of the outing.

TYPES OF GALLEYS

A trailer sailor's galley can take on many forms depending upon the type of trailersailing you do. For example, if your trailersailing is predominantly day sailing, your galley may be nothing more than a picnic basket, cooler, and insulated thermos. While this is the simplest galley, it can be extremely versatile, allowing for maximum creativity ranging from cold-cut sandwiches to wine, caviar, and pâté; from paper plates to leaded crystal and linen napkins. You are only limited by your imagination. You may choose to dine on board or, depending upon your sailing area, in a secluded cove, on a picturesque beach, or at a picnic area. Its versatility is what gives this galley its appeal.

Trailerable pocket cruisers used for weekend adventures or longer usually have a dedicated galley of sorts, and your planning and creativity needs to center around it for the most part. For a couple of days on the water, you can rely more on perishable, previously home prepared, and otherwise bulky food stocks. Normally, weekenders have the added versatility of enjoying a lot of activities on shore. Grilling and picnicking on shore allows you to use your standard backyard barbecue techniques for meals and also provides you with unlimited space, a commodity not available on your boat.

For those trailer sailors who spend most of their cruise on the water, the galley takes on a new dimension. Just because your galley may be small does not necessarily mean that your meal options need to be limited. However, as the amount of time you spend on board increases, you will want to decrease the amount of perishable, previously home prepared, and otherwise bulky food stocks on board. Your types of onboard galley equipment will also change with increased time on the water. Don't be envious of the daysailer with his wine and caviar. With careful planning and equipping of the galley ahead of time, you can also be enjoying those finer things. Think "out of the box," or in this case, "out of the boat" while functioning "in the boat."

Cruising on a 22-foot trailerable pocket cruiser, Joyce and I have developed a galley that allows us maximum versatility and variety in a minimal amount of space. Here's how we do it...

GALLEY EQUIPMENT

Our approach to the galley on board *Splash* is not that much different from our approach to backpacking. Having close to 30 years of Scouting experience, we have slightly modified our proven woodland techniques to account for our change in venue. Before we go any further, let's make one thing perfectly clear. When we're talking about backpack provisioning, we're not talking about trail mix, beef jerky, and freeze-dried foods. Rather, we enjoy meals such as rice scampi, calzones, and beef pot pie.

Our technique for selecting galley equipment—or for that matter, sailing gear and even provisioning—is based on our tried and true "three pile" method. Everything (and we mean everything) that goes on board, goes through the same selection process. Pile one consists of those items that we absolutely, positively have to have on board. In pile two are those things that would be nice to have on board, making life easier or more comfortable. Lastly, pile three contains those items that can be broadly classified as "luxuries." Once we have our three piles established, we stow everything from pile one, skip pile two altogether, and select one or two things from pile three. How else could we reasonably include our wineglasses and corkscrew? Once things are stowed, we check for space. This is our opportunity to stow a few things from pile two.

Instead of relying on disposables, we use real/unbreakable dishes, cups, glasses, and flatware. They have nonskid bottoms, or have been modified by the addition of silicone beads to their bottoms. Another way to make these items nonskid is by using rubberized nonskid drawer liners as placemats. Using real eating utensils makes us feel more at home and decreases the amount of trash that we need to store on board. Going back to one of our backpacking corollaries, what you bring in, you need to bring back out: If we bring in a minimum amount of disposables, we'll have a minimum amount of trash to bring out. This is especially important aboard a boat. It is possible to generate a lot of trash if you do not plan carefully. Once the trash is generated, it becomes unwanted cargo until you reach a port where it can be disposed of.

Refrigeration on a trailer sailer means ice chest. Depending on your space, ideally two ice chests would be best: one for frozen items, which is opened up maybe once a day, and a second one that you go into more frequently. But most trailer sailers will only allow space for a single ice chest. In any case, consider keeping a separate smaller soft-sided cooler containing cold drinks and snacks readily available in the cockpit. The fewer times you open your galley ice chest, the colder the food will stay.

EXCEPT FOR A SINGLE-BURNER BUTANE STOVE,
THIS IS ALL OUR GALLEY GEAR.

Food preparation usually requires some degree of slicing or dicing. An assortment of knives and a cutting surface are essential in the galley. Our knife assortment consists of a small paring knife, a mid-size serrated edge knife, and a large chopping-type knife. With these three knives we can prepare fruits, vegetables, meats, and even fish. Some pocket cruisers are equipped with a cutting board that covers the galley sink when not in use, but ours is not. We have had good luck using an inexpensive plastic cutting mat purchased from a marine retailer.

For traditional cooking, our collection of pots and pans has been scaled down to a stainless steel nesting backpack kit. The kit consists of a frying pan and three pots. Because of their nesting characteristic, they take up a minimal amount of space. For serving/cooking pieces, we have found that the oversized fork and spoon from a stainless steel government surplus mess kit are sized just right. Our Scouting adventures gave us a lot of experience cooking in heavy cast iron Dutch ovens. While we don't consider a Dutch oven to be a good choice in your trailer sailer's galley, we find that Dutch oven pliers come in very handy. These are versatile pliers that are meant for grasping hot cooking vessels, either with the pliers portion itself or by using the hook on the opposite end to loop the bail on a pot or kettle.

Having to clean our nondisposable galley equipment is a price we are willing to pay to avoid having any extra space filled with used disposables. Our galley gear is washed with the salt or lake water and dish soap, then rinsed using a spray bottle of potable water to which a few drops of chlorine bleach has been added as a sanitizer. The rinsed gear is placed in a mesh bag and hung outside to air dry. For those times when the gear needs to be quickly stowed below, we dry it with a chamois. We have found that a synthetic chamois works just as well as the more expensive natural chamois.

Even though one can minimize clean-up by not using real dishes, cups, and flatware, the cooking utensils still need to be cleaned. However, we have discovered a cooking technique that enables us to never scrub our cook pot.

THE BAKEPACKER®

The most novel galley item that we discovered from backpacking and have found to be very useful aboard our trailer sailer is the BakePacker®. The BakePacker® is a cook pot accessory in the shape of a 7⅜-inch diameter vertical aluminum grid.* It was developed

---

*FOR MORE INFORMATION ON THE BAKEPACKER® AND ITS ACCOMPANYING RECIPE BOOK, CONTACT: STRIKE 2 INDUSTRIES, INC. E. 508 AUGUSTA AVE., SPOKANE, WA 99207, (509) 484-3701, WWW.BAKEPACKER.COM.

and originally promoted as a way to help American soldiers reheat prepared foods in winter conditions. Further development allowed the BakePacker to become popular among outdoorsmen as a better way to prepare their food.

THE BAKEPACKER®, AN ALUMINUM GRID
THAT FITS IN A 7½- TO 8-INCH POT..

This cook pot accessory is designed to cook solid foods, although it is not a steamer or pressure cooker. It is an aluminum grid, which fits into your 7½- to 8-inch cook pot, and functions as multiple mini-heat exchangers. Water is poured into the cook pot to the top level of the grid. The food to be cooked is placed in a one-gallon freezer/storage plastic bag and then set inside the pot on top of the grid. The cook pot is then covered with its lid, and the water is boiled. The rate of heat transfer from the water via the BakePacker grid to the food in the plastic bag is higher than that of traditional cooking techniques. This is all accomplished at a relatively low temperature (212°F). Cooking is done by means of the grid, not from the boiling water per se. Since the food is cooked in a plastic bag, it does not get scorched or dried out. Because of the high heat transfer rate, foods cook faster, and you can actually bake in the cook pot! The BakePacker Standard version cooks enough food to serve 3–4 people.

Now, just picture this: Your meal is done and everyone is feeling good, until you remember that you need to clean up. Well, with the BakePacker, clean-up of the cooking vessel is nonexistent. What you are left with is a cook pot containing about an inch of hot water, which you can use to wash your eating utensils, unless you decide to use it for making coffee or tea!

As the length of time on the water increases, it is important to us to have cooking versatility. We wouldn't want a steady diet of one-pot meals from the BakePacker. By combining traditional type cooking methods (with our stainless steel nesting backpack kit) along with the BakePacker cooking method, we can vary our diet and meal types.

MEAL PLANNING

With both of us having scientific backgrounds, we tend to take a rather analytical approach to life in general. When it comes to meal planning for our trailersailing, an analytical approach helps to decrease the amount of unwanted surprises and disasters in the galley. Another one of our corollaries is, no experimenting with a new recipe on board. All recipes are tried and true on shore, even using the same pots, pans, stove, and utensils that will be used on-board. This not only determines the viability of the recipe, but also its complexity, timing, and whether or not we even like it.

When planning a sail, we also plan the meals. Once the menu is down on paper, we figure out the ingredients that are needed. Keeping in mind that space is at a premium, we usually don't have a full size container of anything aboard, unless we know that the whole container's worth is necessary for the planned recipes. Typically, we take just enough onion powder, garlic, flour, paprika, or whatever, that is called for in the recipes. We use little vials and pouches specifically designed for small amounts of spices (available at outdoors stores), 35mm film canisters that are labeled, and even labeled zipper-type bags to hold what we'll need. Fast food restaurant packets of condiments are great, unless a recipe calls for a larger amount. Many food products that you buy will be exorbitantly packaged. Eliminate any unnecessary and bulky packaging before you stow it in the galley.

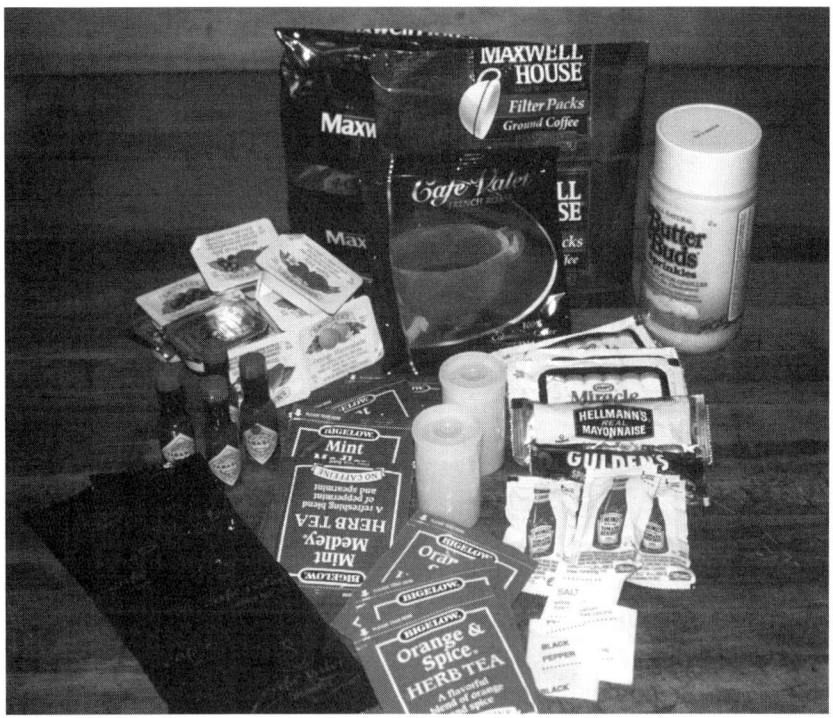

WE USUALLY DON'T HAVE A FULL-SIZED CONTAINER OF ANYTHING ABOARD. FOR CONDIMENTS, FAST FOOD RESTAURANT PACKETS ARE GREAT.

18. The Trailer Sailor's Galley

The galley aboard a trailer sailer is what you make it, and can range from a brown bag to a gourmet meal. All it requires is a little forethought, imagination, and the right equipment (knowing a little bit about how to cook is also helpful).

Bon appétit!

SECTION V

SNAKE OILS AND ELIXIRS TO KEEP YOUR BOAT HEALTHY AND HAPPY

The other day Joyce informed me that we needed milk and that I should pick some up on my way through town. As is sometimes the case, I didn't catch all the particulars, but how hard could it be? Surprise! Once at the supermarket, I was presented with a variety of choices. Did I want whole milk, 2% milk, 1% milk, or skim? Am I interested in organic milk or milk fortified with synthetic vitamins? How about milk from cows treated with BST or not? What about quantity—gallons, half gallon, quarts, or pints?

Where is this all leading? Check out your local chandlery and you'll see what I mean. The chapters in this section demystify those magic, mouse milk, marine potions that can help you keep your trailer sailer in tiptop condition.

CHAPTER 19

SEALANTS AND ADHESIVES

During a visit to the local home improvement center, I experienced a chance meeting with a fellow sailing club member. Barnacle Bob, as he's sometimes called, had a shopping basket containing about half a dozen 10-ounce tubes of sealants/adhesives. Among them were an automotive windshield urethane adhesive, a rubber-based gutter sealant, and a siliconized latex caulk. After a cursory examination of his purchases, I suggested that some, if not most, of the items might not be well suited for the marine environment that he was planning to use them in. I continued by saying something such as, "It's not that marine products are simply superior to similar products found in hardware and home improvement stores, but also the fact that adhesive/sealant manufacturers formulate their products for specific applications and environments. The reactives, additives and solvents, as well as the grades of ingredients in a product, are selected for specific applications. For example, marine-grade urethanes are considered structurally permanent, yet automotive windshield urethanes repeatedly flex with temperature changes and vehicle motion and are routinely removed for windshield replacement. A rubber-based gutter sealant is not constantly exposed to water and after curing shrinks excessively and becomes brittle. Latex caulks not only shrink and become brittle, but also have limited adhesive strength and are more cosmetic than structural."

He wouldn't hear of it, but rushed off after delivering the retort, "It all comes from the same factory, just the packaging and price are different."

It was this chance meeting, combined with my 17 years in the specialty chemical industry, that precipitated the discussion that follows.

Selecting the proper sealant or adhesive is definitely the most important part of the job, for if the wrong product is used, or for that matter the right product is used incorrectly, failure is inevitable. Don't rely totally on the manufacturer's labels. Many companies do include helpful job-specific information; however, many provide little help or even overstate performance claims. Despite the dizzying selection, sealants and adhesives are all made from one of five base or backbone polymers: rubber, latex, silicone, polysulfide, or polyurethane. For the most part, the base polymer determines what general characteristics the product will exhibit, such as what substrate materials it will adhere to, how easily the joints can be smoothed, its paintability, and its durability.

Sealants, often referred to as caulk, are lower performing materials than adhesives. That is, they are not expected to do as much work. Caulks are generally designed to "weatherproof," while adhesives are designed both to weatherproof and bond. Some of this bonding or adhesion of an adhesive is mechanical; however, most of it is chemical. Chemical bonding is achieved in the following three steps:

- The adhesive is wet out and spread to obtain intimate molecular contact with the substrate.
- During the setting, the solvents (water, organics, etc.) evaporate.
- A chemical reaction occurs during the curing, and a cross-linking, or in situ polymerization, takes place.

The quality of the sealant or adhesive joint depends very strongly upon the nature of the substrate (composition, structure, morphology, cleanliness). As stated earlier, even the right product when used incorrectly will fail.

To help you better understand and differentiate among the various products/chemistries, let's first take a broad look at what's available. Hopefully, through this process of education and subsequent elimination, you'll be able to separate the wheat from the chaff, so to speak, and pick the right product for the job at hand.

RUBBER (ELASTOMERICS)

Manufacturers often use the terms elastomer and rubber interchangeably. In actuality, any material that exhibits elastomeric properties (stretches and bounces back) is an elastomer. For this discussion, we'll use the terminology rubber-based.

Materials in this group are stretchy and non-structural. Contact cement falls into this category. These products are generally made with any of the following synthetic rubber compounds:

- Isoprene (synthetic natural rubber)
- Butadiene (SBR or styrene butadiene rubber)
- Nitrile (acrylonitrile butadiene)
- Polychloroprene (Neoprene, the first widely used synthetic rubber)

Rubber-based caulks will adhere to almost everything, even damp and oily materials. Their solvents are highly flammable, are dangerous to breathe, and will melt styrofoam, which is sometimes used for flotation or insulation. Once the solvent evaporates, rubber-based caulks can shrink as much as 35 percent. They are resistant to hydrocarbons (oil & gasoline), water, and many solvents. If (and a

19. SEALANTS AND ADHESIVES

big if, at that) used aboard ship, they are limited to special purpose applications, such as creating seals and gaskets for fuel tanks/ systems.

LATEX

Latex originally referred to the milk-white substance occurring in certain trees and plants. This natural rubber latex occurs in the *Hevea brasiliensis* tree and the guayule plant. Prior to the advent of the synthetic latices, the foregoing definition may have been adequate; it is no longer today. A more suitable definition is: Latex is a stable dispersion of a polymeric substance in an essentially aqueous medium (a dispersion in water, the final product of emulsion polymerization).

Some latex-based sealants are also labeled acrylic caulk or vinyl caulk. In the first instance, the product contains an acrylic polymer (polymethyl methacrylate) and in the second a vinyl polymer (ethylene-vinylacetate). In either case, the chemistry is a C=C polymer dispersed in water; it is through the addition of these polymers that the products' performance characteristics are enhanced.

About five to seven years ago new technology produced siliconized latex. Siliconized latex caulks are acrylic, and contain a small amount of silane (a silicon-based material). This combination promotes better adhesion. Do not confuse siliconized latex with 100 percent silicone.

Unlike the vast majority of sealants and adhesives, latex caulks do not contain volatile solvents. This allows them to be smoothed out with a wet finger and the excess cleaned up with soap and water. They are inexpensive, fast drying, and paintable (some are even pretinted); however, they can mildew, have limited adhesive strength and flexibility, and often shrink after curing. They should be relegated to household use only, not marine applications.

SILICONE

Silicone is derived from silicon, the non-metallic element commonly found in sand. This sealant is available in two types. Each type is based on the specific curing agent employed. One type is acetoxy-cure silicone, whose technology was developed in France in the 1950s. It is also called acid-cure or moisture-cure silicone. Acetic acid is the catalyst in the formula, thus the characteristic vinegar smell. Even though many marine silicone sealants are of this variety, be aware that this "acid" version can be corrosive to metal, particularly aluminum. The neutral-cure or natural-cure variety of silicone sealant, which is ammonia-based, uses newer technology. It gives off little or no odor and is not corrosive.

Silicone sealants are fast cure (they skin over in ½–1 hour and completely cure in 24 hours), virtually nonshrinking, soft, elastic, and resistant to solvent and fuels. They can withstand temperatures (recommended for form-in-place engine gaskets), and have a long service life (20 years is often given by manufacturers). They afford excellent insulating properties, making them ideal for bedding dissimilar metals and potting electrical junctions (insulation and corrosion prevention). Silicone sealants are also compatible with plastics. They exhibit very tight cohesive qualities; that is, once they are cured, they form a tough, resilient gasket that is difficult to tear apart. This quality makes silicone sealants most suitable for use as a form-in-place gasket under compression, such as the bedding of a stanchion base, which is then held in place by mechanical fasteners.

However, silicone sealants are not perfect. For starters, they are difficult to smooth and will not hold paint. In fact, silicone in any of its forms (sealant, wax, lubricant) is a scourge to painters. Should silicone be used on or even near a surface that may be painted or varnished (in some cases even years later) contamination can occur; all attempts to paint or varnish will be repelled. In addition to a product called Release from Boatlife, there are cleaners one can borrow from the auto painting business that will help to remove silicone residue (DuPont's Prep Sol and Martin Senour's Kleanz Easy), but the silicone residue can continue to leach out of the substrate for years. The use of silicone is one reason why an epoxy barrier coat or an epoxy primer is almost universally recommended under polyurethane paints on fiberglass hulls and decks (both were exposed to silicone mold release agents during manufacturing). When silicones are involved, it is always recommended to paint the substrate before applying them. By the way, silicones come in clear and a variety of colors.

Paint and varnish are not the only materials that do not adhere to silicone. Silicone itself does not adhere well to silicone. A damaged seam or seal made of silicone must be completely removed and the surface cleaned and fresh material applied. With silicone sealants, applying a little dab of new material over the damaged old material will be a short-lived solution.

Silicone sealants lack significant adhesive strength and rely on mechanical compression to maintain a seal when used as a bedding compound. This makes them suspect when applied in bead form to working seams or in applications where it is necessary to fill a large void.

A naturally occurring bacterium (*Bacillus niger*) attacks silicone. This microorganism can cause discoloration (mildew) and deterioration. Silicone sealants sold in hardware stores and home centers contain mildewcides; however, they yellow when exposed to sunlight (ultraviolet rays). To help prevent yellowing, marine silicone sealants also contain a UV inhibitor in addition to a mildewcide.

Silicone sealants are universally not recommended for use below the waterline as seam sealers. This is because their low adhesion coefficient makes them extremely poor seam sealers, especially underwater. With prolonged continuous exposure to water, their performance worsens. However, poor adhesion is not an issue and therefore not a problem when silicone is used in conjunction with compression. Furthermore, unlike polysulfide and polyurethane (two major marine adhesives/sealants), silicone is compatible with plastics. By default, silicone becomes the sealant of choice for use under mechanically fastened plastic through-hulls.

Before it sets, silicone can be worked by smoothing it with a wet finger. Clean up with soap and water before it has cured; after curing, mineral spirits will help soften the sealant prior to mechanical removal.

Consumer products commonly available at marine centers that fall into this category include: Boatlife Marine Silicone Sealant, GE 8200 Bedding & Trim Sealant, 3M Marine Grade Silicone Sealant, and West Marine Marine Silicone Sealant.

POLYSULFIDE

Its technology dates back to the 1940s when, under the name Thiokol, it was used to patch bullet holes in airplanes, as well as to make aircraft fuel tanks leak- and explosion-proof. Polysulfide is perhaps the most versatile marine adhesive sealant combination available.

Polysulfide adhesive sealants exhibit strong adhesion, high elasticity, and a resistance to fuels and solvents; in addition, they are toolable, sandable, and paintable, and are generally unaffected by movement associated with stress and temperature change. Because of their high bonding strength, high elasticity, and resistance to fuel and solvents, including harsh teak cleaners, polysulfide adhesive sealants are the choice for bedding oily woods, such as teak, to a variety of substrata—including fiberglass, wood, and steel—regardless of whether or not mechanical fasteners are used. The black caulking between planks of a teak deck is invariably polysulfide.

Polysulfide adhesive sealants are available in both one- and two-part formulations. They are also available in a variety of consistencies, from pourable (thickness of honey), to gun-grade (applied through a caulking cartridge), to a knife-grade (applied with a putty knife). Depending upon the formulation, polysulfides can contain a variety of solvents (xylene, toluene, acetates, alcohols, ketones, petroleum distillates, chlorinated solvents or a combination of these). The average boat owner seldom runs across the two-part types, which are more commonly marketed to boat manufacturers and commercial boatyards. Typically available at marine centers are the one-part, gun-grade versions; however, depending upon the manufacturer, the solvent package may vary.

The one significant weakness associated with polysulfide adhesive sealants can be directly attributed to its solvent package. Polysulfide adhesive sealants are incompatible with most plastics, mainly rigid thermoplastics such as acrylic (Plexiglass), polycarbonate (Lexan), ABS, and PVC. The solvent(s) can leach the plasticizer from this class of plastics and cause them to harden and crack. Higher quality fittings made from epoxy, glass-filled epoxy, nylon, Delrin, or Marelon (glass reinforced nylon), are unaffected and can be safely bedded with polysulfide adhesive sealants.

When compared to silicones and polyurethanes, polysulfide adhesive sealants cure the slowest (tack-free from 30 minutes to 72 hours, with a full cure time ranging from 2 to 10 days, depending upon formulation/manufacturer). Exposure to moisture in the air is what cures polysulfides; consequently, higher humidity levels will cause them to set more quickly. Polysulfides will continue to cure underwater and, in an emergency, can even be applied underwater as a temporary repair. Ambient temperature also affects the rate of cure (the warmer the temperature, the more rapid the cure).

Polysulfide adhesive sealants are readily paintable with no special priming required. The "primers" for polysulfide that are often seen on chandlery shelves are not for priming the adhesive sealant prior to painting, but for priming oily woods (be it teak or woods exposed to oily bilge water) prior to applying the polysulfide, when no mechanical fasteners will be used. In this instance, the polysulfide will be the sole bonding agent. If mechanical fasteners will be used, no priming is required. In this instance, the sealant will be functioning as a gasket.

Although the adhesion of polysulfide is less than that of polyurethane, this is an advantage, especially when polysulfide is used on fittings that might have to be removed some time in the future. When it comes to removal or cleanup, uncured polysulfide can be cleaned up with mineral spirits, lacquer thinner, or naptha (lighter fluid). However, once it begins to set, methyl ethyl ketone, toluene, or xylene must be employed. Mechanical removal (cutting, scraping, sanding) is required on fully cured material.

Polysulfide-based products that are commonly available at marine centers include: Boatlife Life Caulk Sealant, Boatlife Life Caulk Deck Sealant (this is a two-part product), 3M Marine Sealant 101, and West Marine Multi-Caulk Sealant.

POLYURETHANE

What is this stuff that we call polyurethane? In general chemical terms, it is any polymer that has been extended by the reaction with di- or poly-isocyanate. And since isocyanates can react with any compound containing at least one active hydrogen, the door's open for the creation of materials possessing a wide range of properties. For the average boat owner, polyurethanes are state-of-the-art adhesive sealants, with the accent strongly placed on the word adhesive. They are tough, waterproof, flexible (ranging from less flexible than silicones to about the same as or close to polysulfide), permanent adhesives much like epoxy.

Polyurethanes are excellent for hull-to-hull, hull-to-keel, chainplate, and centerboard trunk installations. Since they are considered permanent, polyurethanes should not be used in any applications where future disassembly may be required. Polyurethanes are not just difficult to remove: it is nearly *impossible* to remove them without the part or substrate or both sustaining damage.

With a few exceptions and subtleties, polyurethanes exhibit a lot in common with polysulfides. For example, like polysulfides, polyurethanes can be tooled, sanded, and painted. Wet sanding of cured material is often recommended, which suggests that polyurethanes don't easily sand. Also, since polyurethanes are not generally UV stable, it is best to paint or otherwise protect any exposed material.

Polyurethanes bond to a variety of substrata, much like polysulfides, including wood (oily or not), fiberglass, and metal. However, unlike polysulfides, polyurethanes are not as tolerant of fuel and solvents, including some teak cleaners (most notably the two-part teak cleaners). Repeated or continuous exposure to any of these will permanently soften polyurethanes.

The warning against using polyurethanes with thermoplastics is the same as for polysulfides. However, instead of the polyurethanes' solvent leaching the plasticizer from the plastic, the problem is the exact opposite: Solvents leaching from the plastic can react with the polyurethanes and weaken the bond.

Polyurethanes are also available in both one- and two-part formulations. One-part formulas are commonly available at retail marine outlets, while two-part polyurethanes are relegated solely to boat manufacturers. While polyurethanes cure faster than polysulfides, like polysulfides their cure times are a function of ambient temperature and humidity, also the volume of surface area of the adhesive. Tack-free ranges from 30 minutes to 48 hours, while 3–7 days is the range expressed for a full cure, depending upon formulation/manufacturer. Even though polyurethanes can be used above and below the waterline, their use as an underwater temporary fix is not recommended.

Lastly, uncured polyurethane can be cleaned up with acetone. However, once the material begins to set, the same industrial solvents recommended for polysulfide cleanup, including 1,1,1-trichloroethane, are needed to remove it. Once cured, these solvents may help soften polyurethane prior to mechanical removal. Also, a couple of relatively new products, Anti-Bond 2015 and DeBond 2000, are said to assist in removing fully cured polyurethane.

Products whose chemistry is based on polyurethane and are routinely available at marine centers are: Boatlife Life Seal, 3M 4200 Fast Cure, 3M 5200, 3M 5200 Fast Cure, Sikaflex 291 LOT, Sikaflex 291, Sikaflex 292, and West Marine Quick Cure Polyurethane Adhesive/Sealant.

OF SPECIAL NOTE

As indicated earlier in this discussion, sealants and adhesives are polymers. And it is this polymer base or "backbone" that determines the product's general characteristics. The specific characteristics—such as UV stability and compatibility with various substrata, to name two—are dependent upon two things:

1. The compound or compounds the base polymer has been combined (chemically reacted) with. For example, an aliphatic polyurethane (one which does not contain benzene rings) is UV resistant; however, an aromatic polyurethane (one which *does* contain benzene rings) is not UV stable.

2. The additives that may have been incorporated into the product's formulation. Typical additives include:

    - Fillers—increase modulus, provide reinforcement
    - Catalyst package—speed up or retard reaction rate

- Rheology modifiers—control viscosity for dispensability, also sag characteristics (non-sag/self-leveling)
- Moisture scavengers
- Pigments
- Flame retardants
- UV stabilizers

Simply stated, the reactives and the additives are the two reasons why there are different types of silicones, different types of polysulfides, and different types of polyurethanes, each exhibiting different characteristics. This then leads to a few marine sealants/adhesives worthy of special note:

GE 8100 Hatch & Window Silicone Sealant, the only silicone sealant recommended by GE for sealing polycarbonate (Lexan).

Boat Life Teak Deck Sealant (formerly called Boat Life Sandable Silicone), a blend of silicone rubber and a proprietary ingredient.

Boat Life Life Seal, a combination of polyurethane and silicone.

3M 4000 UV, a polyether-based cosmetic sealant for applications where aesthetic appeal is a priority. It is UV stable and can be used with plastics, including ABS and Lexan.

Sikaflex 295 UV-a polyurethane adhesive sealant for bedding and sealing acrylic (plexiglass) and polycarbonate (Lexan)

SUMMING IT UP

So, what should you use the next time that you need to "glue" something together and keep the water out? For bedding applications, choose between silicone and polysulfide. Keep in mind that silicone is a good gasket material and electric insulator, while polysulfide is great for bedding everything except plastic. As for seam sealing, select either polysulfide or polyurethane. If you want to take it apart in the future, use polysulfide. Polyurethane is permanent.

SELECTION GUIDELINES

Stanchions	Polysulfide	Silicone
Bow/stern pulpits	Polysulfide	Silicone
Winches	Polysulfide	
Windlass	Polysulfide	
Clutches	Polysulfide	
Deck organizers/turning blocks	Polysulfide	
Cleats and chocks	Polysulfide	
Chainplates	Polyurethane	Polysulfide
Wood trim	Polysulfide	Polyurethane
Toe rails	Polysulfide	Polyurethane
Deck seams (teak/oily woods)	Polysulfide	Polyurethane*
Glass to metal	Silicone	
Glass to vinyl	Silicone	
Glass to fiberglass	Polysulfide	Silicone
Hull to deck	Polyurethane	
Hull to hull	Polyurethane	
Centerboard trunk	Polyurethane	
ABS/Lexan/PVC/Plexiglass	Silicone	
Fittings made of epoxy, glass-filled epoxy, nylon, Delrin, or Marelon	Polysulfide	Polyurethane
Electric insulator	Silicone	
Bedding dissimilar metals	Silicone	
Fuel line/fuel tank repairs	Polysulfide	
Engine gaskets	Silicone	
Bronze thru-hulls	Polysulfide	
Fittings/thru-hulls of unknown plastic composition	Silicone	

*Can be permanently softened by some teak cleaners.

For further information, contact:
BoatLife Industries   www.boatlife.com
3M Marine   www.3m.com
Sika Corporation   www.sikasolutions.com
West Marine   www.westmarine.com

CHAPTER 20

ENGINE LUBRICANTS

Most trailer sailers rely on outboard motors as their means of auxiliary propulsion. Many of these are of the 2-cycle variety; however, 4-cycle outboard engines are becoming increasingly more prevalent. Also, there are those trailerable cruisers that are fitted with inboard engines. It is these 4-cycle power plants, both inboard and outboard, that this chapter targets.

The motor oil in any sailboat's auxiliary engine is second in importance *only* to the supply of fuel and air. If neglected, certain—and often—sudden engine failure will occur. This being the case, let's take a look at the complex role motor oil plays.

THE PURPOSE OF MOTOR OIL

Motor oil has four primary functions: to lubricate, to seal, to cool, and to clean.

In order for motor oil to be a good lubricant, it must maintain a slippery surface between moving parts. The oil film must tenaciously adhere to the engine's metal surfaces and resist being pushed off regardless of temperature or pressure.

As a result of combustion, gases are formed under high pressure. This pressure acts against the piston head, producing working horsepower. Therefore it is necessary to keep these gases from leaking past the pistons and valves. Oil acts as the sealant.

The cooling system (water) removes the bulk of unwanted heat from the engine. However, oil assists the cooling system by removing heat from some critical areas, such as the bearings. In doing so, it frequently becomes much hotter than the cooling water.

A variety of waste materials are formed as byproducts of combustion. The type of fuel—gasoline or diesel—influences the nature and quantity of these waste materials. A few of the most common and troublesome waste materials include water, soot, carbon, and acids. It is a job of the motor oil to maintain these contaminants in a state of dispersion, so that they may be removed with routine oil changes and not form harmful deposits.

INFLUENCING FACTORS

Some of the major chemical and physical factors that make the job of engine lubrication challenging include: temperature extremes, oxidation, corrosion, contaminants, and foaming.

Motor oils encounter both high and low temperatures. When cool, motor oil becomes viscous and resists flowing. In cold weather, oil may become so thick that it will not circulate freely throughout the engine. This can result in excessive engine wear. In extreme cases, the oil can become so thick that the engine cannot be started. On the other hand, when it is hot, oil thins out. If it becomes too thin, high oil consumption and engine wear will occur.

When oxygen in the air comes in contact with the oil, a chemical reaction called oxidation begins to take place. Oxidation occurs very slowly when the oil is cold. However, heat rapidly speeds up the reaction. Products of oxidation include deposits and acids. Also, motor oil becomes more viscous as it oxidizes.

Two types of corrosion commonly take place in a sailboat's auxiliary engine. They are atmospheric corrosion and acid corrosion. While atmospheric corrosion is caused by water or moisture in the air, acids are a byproduct of the combustion process. Both water and acids are routinely formed in quantities significant enough to cause engine damage in a short time.

Most sailors are under the false impression that their motor oil requires to be changed because it has broken down or worn out. Not so. The oil needs to be removed because it has accumulated contaminants in the course of performing its job. These contaminants include water, soot, carbon, acids, metallic particles, and dirt. If allowed to remain in the engine, they can combine and form sludge.

Foaming can take place when oil and air are beaten together in the crankcase, producing small air bubbles trapped in an oil film. Foaming reduces lubrication effectiveness and can result in the malfunctioning of such engine components as the oil pump and hydraulic valve lifters.

VISCOSITY

Viscosity is that physical property which determines the oil's ability to flow. Oils that are thick offer great resistance to flow and possess a high viscosity. Those that flow easily possess a low viscosity and are often termed nonviscous.

Oil viscosity controls the ease of engine starting in cold weather; or, to put it another way, it determines the temperature below which an engine cannot be started.

It is viscosity that determines the thickness of an oil film in an engine. A viscous oil leaves a thicker film under any one set of conditions than does a nonviscous oil. This fact influences engine wear.

Oil viscosity also explains the reason for most oil consumption, since consumption increases as oil viscosity decreases. Oil can be too heavy; in this case it can fail to uniformly lubricate or remove excess heat.

ADDITIVES

For many years the naturally occurring chemical and physical characteristics of motor oil were adequate. Since World War II major changes began to take place. Varying compression ratios, higher temperatures, greater power-to-weight output, and emission controls have made it necessary to incorporate a number of additional agents into the oil.

These additives are designed to enhance the oil's performance level. They include detergents, antioxidants, corrosion inhibitors, and antifoaming agents.

For the most part, these additives are expendable. They can be depleted if the oil is used for too long. Routine oil changes not only insure that these additives are replenished, but also insure that destructive contaminants are removed.

SYNTHETICS

Synthetic motor oils have been commercially available since the early 1930s, when they were used primarily for military applications. During World War II, they were used to prevent the oil from freezing in army tanks during the winter months. Synthetic oils are often made from a mineral oil base stock, which may be partially disassembled and reconstructed to meet a set of specific performance requirements. Synthetic motor oils are generally more expensive than conventional motor oils.

SPECIFICATIONS

That combination of letters and numbers one sees on a container of oil was created by the combined efforts of the American Petroleum Institute (API) in conjunction with the American Society for Testing and Materials (ASTM) and the Society of Automotive Engineers (SAE).

It is the motor oil's service classification and identifies in which type of engine and under what conditions the oil can be used.

The API Engine Service Category S indicates that the oil is designed to provide service in a gasoline (Spark) engine. The letter immediately following the S suggests the type of additive package the oil contains. For example, SD indicates use in gasoline engines 1968 through 1970, while SG is for gasoline engines beginning with the 1989 model year.

The API Engine Service Category C indicates that the oil is designed for use in diesel (Compression) engines. As is the case with category S oils, the letter immediately following the C also defines the oil's use. CA oils were widely used in diesel engines in the late 1940s and early 1950s. Diesel engines manufactured since 1983 require oils with an API Engine Service Category of CE.

The second letter in the API Engine Service Category is issued in alphabetical order. The oldest and least complex oils are SA and CA. The most current are SL and CF. In most instances, higher API Engine Service Category oils are "backwards compatible"—that is, they may be used in place of earlier recommendations.

The SAE viscosity numbers constitute a classification of crankcase lubricating oils in terms of viscosity. These SAE grade recommendations are linked directly to temperature. The lower the number (*e.g.* SAE 5), the thinner or less viscous the oil, while the higher the number (*e.g.* SAE 40), the more viscous the oil. Thin oils meet SAE low temperature requirements, while more viscous oils meet high temperature requirements. A multi-SAE or viscosity graded oil (*e.g.* SAE 10W-30) is one which, at low temperature, meets the SAE requirements of a lower grade number and also meets the high temperature requirements of the higher or heavier grade oil.

20. ENGINE LUBRICANTS

FROM LEFT TO RIGHT:
A MULTI-WEIGHT, SYNTHETIC OIL FOR GASOLINE AND DIESEL APPLICATIONS;
A STRAIGHT WEIGHT MOTOR OIL FOR DIESEL SERVICE;
AND A TYPICAL MULTI-WEIGHT MOTOR OIL FOR GASOLINE SERVICE.

ROUTINE MAINTENANCE

While today's modern motor oils are amazingly effective, they are not magical. They have an operating life and need to be replaced periodically. Follow the engine manufacturer's recommendations regarding the proper API Engine Service Category, SAE viscosity, and change frequency.

Before changing the oil, bring your engine up to operating temperature. This ensures that any damaging contaminants are in suspension and can be pumped out with the old oil. In addition to periodic oil changes based on hours and conditions of usage, always change the oil before seasonal lay-up. And be sure to change the filter with every oil change.

CHAPTER 21

ENGINE COOLANTS

While most trailerable cruisers, especially older ones, rely on outboard motors for auxiliary propulsion, there are those trailer sailers that are outfitted with inboard engines. This chapter addresses those sailboats having inboards.

In order for your inboard auxiliary engine to age gracefully while performing well, two things must be constantly controlled: friction and heat. In Chapter 20, we discussed the role of proper lubrication in minimizing friction and dissipating heat. But while motor oil does a great job, it can't do it all. It needs the help of another key player: the engine coolant.

An estimated 50 percent of gasoline engines found on boats are raw water cooled. In these systems, raw water is taken from the sea and pumped through the engine block and then discharged. The remaining percentage of gasoline engines and all modern diesels, which must be fresh water cooled, utilize a closed cooling water loop. This fresh water closed loop is, in turn, cooled by raw water circulated through a heat exchanger. While it is impossible to treat the raw water system, the closed fresh water cooling loop *can* be treated. This is done by adding an engine coolant, commonly (and erroneously) referred to as antifreeze.

21. ENGINE COOLANTS

COMMON TYPES

The most common types of engine coolants are based on ethylene glycol or propylene glycol. Ethylene glycol, introduced in 1937 as "permanent antifreeze," is still the most widely used form of engine coolant. It is usually green in color and always highly toxic.

A relative newcomer, propylene glycol, usually red or blue in color, is considerably less toxic than ethylene glycol. While it can be used in place of ethylene glycol, it is more commonly used in systems where ethylene glycol would be inappropriate, such as in a boat's potable water system. Since it is "Generally Recognized as Safe" by the Food and Drug Administration (FDA), propylene glycol is often labeled as being nontoxic. Nevertheless, it should not be thought of as safe for consumption.

COMMON ETHYLENE GLYCOL-BASED COOLANT ON THE LEFT AND A PROPYLENE GLYCOL-BASED COOLANT ON THE RIGHT.

HOW THEY WORK

Both ethylene glycol and propylene glycol engine coolants are alcohol-based compounds that are added to the cooling water in order to do the following:

- Lower the water's freezing point
- Increase the water's boiling point
- Inhibit corrosion of the engine's water-side internals
- Provide lubrication to the water pump

In climates where the temperature can drop below freezing, water expands as it freezes and can crack an engine block as if it were an eggshell. A 1:1 ratio of coolant to water protects against freezing down to about −40 degrees Fahrenheit.

This same 1:1 solution can increase the cooling water's boiling point to about +276 degrees Fahrenheit. This is especially important in warmer climates. Thus, in addition to being an antifreeze, the engine coolant is also an "antiboil."

Engine cooling systems often contain a range of electrochemically incompatible metals (aluminum, cast iron, copper, lead solder, et cetera). This presents a potential for galvanic corrosion. Over time, both glycol-based coolants degrade to oxalic acid, which is highly corrosive. To protect this mixed-metal environment and inhibit the gradual conversion of alcohol to acid, coolant manufacturers add corrosion inhibitors.

In addition to corrosion inhibitors, lubricants such as silicone are often included in the engine coolant's additive package. These lubricate the water pump and various seals located throughout the cooling system.

APPLICATION

While separate standards have been published for gasoline and diesel engine use by the American Society for Testing Materials, a 1:1 ratio of engine coolant to water is the accepted industry norm. Fifty percent of this mixture is a known commodity, while the other 50 percent, the water, is not. Therefore, it is strongly recommended that only distilled water be used to dilute the engine coolant. The reason is that tap water generally contains dissolved minerals that, when heated, drop out of solution and form scale in the narrow cooling passages. This mineral scale can restrict water flow and inhibit heat transfer. Ultimately, engine overheating can result.

One way to eliminate the need for mixing coolant with water is to purchase a coolant that is already diluted with distilled water to form a 50/50 blend. This is also a convenient way to carry a spare supply of properly diluted coolant aboard ship. Should one have to occasionally top-off the cooling system, no mixing will be required.

To insure that the proper concentration of coolant is present at all times, you must test the cooling water periodically. Bear in mind that while too much coolant

A 50/50 BLEND OF ETHYLENE GLYCOL AND DISTILLED WATER

can actually contribute to overheating, too little doesn't afford adequate corrosion protection.

For systems containing ethylene glycol, you can use an inexpensive hydrometer. Hydrometers measure the specific gravity of the liquid. The specific gravity of ethylene glycol varies directly with its concentration. As the one increases, so does the other.

The concentration of propylene glycol cannot be determined by using a hydrometer. Instead, a coolant refractometer must be used. The refractometer will determine the refractive index of the coolant and relate it directly to a freezing point.

As stated earlier, both ethylene glycol and propylene glycol degrade over time into corrosive acids. To inhibit this degradation, coolant manufacturers have added corrosion inhibitors to their products. These inhibitors include such inorganic materials as silicates, borates, and phosphates. The life expectancy of these additives is about two years, hence the recommendation that the typical engine coolant be changed at two-year intervals.

New organic acid technology (OAT) coolants or extended life coolants (ELC) contain additive packages based on organic carboxylates rather than the traditional inorganics mentioned previously. Consequently, they offer an extended service life of five years. Typically, ELC engine coolants contain a red, pink, or yellow dye to differentiate them from conventional inorganic coolants, which are typically green or blue. ELC engine coolants are also considerably more expensive. Although these newer formulations still contain glycol, they may not be compatible with conventional engine coolants. Don't mix the two. If changing from one to the other, a thorough flush, preferably professionally done with acid, is recommended.

While the coolant manufacturers are quick to point out their claims and recommended change intervals, the final word is best left to the engine manufacturer. They warrant the engine and have a compelling self-interest in its performance.

CHAPTER 22

SIMPLY CLEAN

We live on a small farm in rural northeastern Ohio, where we are nestled in amongst the fourth largest Amish community in the world. All of our neighbors live, work, and play as though it were still the eighteenth century. Having a "Yankee" (that's what non-Amish are called) living in their midst is not only a constant reminder to them of the "outside" world, but also affords them with a degree of entertainment.

Initially, one would think that farming and sailing would be conflicting interests, since their activities occur at the same time of the year. However, the flexibility afforded by trailersailing continues to work well for us.

Each spring as I prepare for plowing, I also use the tractor to pull our trailer sailer from its winter storage place next to the barn. I then place it in the center of the rear yard, where I can get it ready for the upcoming sailing season. At this time my spring commissioning ritual becomes entertainment for my neighbors, especially Noah Hostetler. This elderly gentleman, a retired dairy farmer, possesses the uncanny knack of appearing out of nowhere, especially when I'm messing about the boat.

This past spring's commissioning was no different. As I was cleaning the cockpit, I heard a noise behind me. It was Noah, rummaging around in my crate of cleaning supplies, all the while shaking his head.

"What is it, Noah?" I asked.

"Got a lot of fancy chemicals here," responded Noah.

Knowing from experience that this cat-and-mouse discussion could take quite some time, I cut to the quick. "What's your point?"

It turned out that Noah did me a favor and provided me with the recipes for several proven, homemade cleaning supplies that can be made from ingredients commonly found aboard. Needless to say, this transfer of knowledge took several months of Noah's visits to complete!

No, I haven't entirely given up (nor would I advocate giving up) commercially prepared cleaning products. But there are those times when you run out of your favorite product and need something right now to get that stain out. You just may find that one of the following homemade substitutes is a lifesaver. Common sense dictates that before you use any cleaner, commercial or homemade, you first test it on a hidden area to determine compatibility.

ALL PURPOSE CLEANER

> Mix and dissolve in a pail of soft, warm water (Noah uses rainwater) the following ingredients: 1 cup of ammonia, ½ cup of vinegar, and ¼ cup of baking soda.

ALL PURPOSE CLEANER & DISINFECTANT

> Dissolve ½ cup of borax in one gallon of soft, warm water.

MILDEW REMOVERS

> Try one of the following:

- Mix ½ cup white vinegar and ½ cup liquid bleach in 2 quarts of water. Rinse well with clean water to which ½ cup of white vinegar has been added.
- Mix ½ cup of white vinegar and ½ cup of borax in 2 quarts of warm water. Rinse with fresh water. (The borax is said to inhibit mold growth.)
- Scrub with equal parts of white vinegar and table salt.
- Clean mildewed area with equal parts of lemon juice and table salt.

WINDOW CLEANERS

Noah's family each had a favorite. We use formula #2 with great success.

1. Mix ⅓ cup of vinegar (cider or white) with 2 pints of water. Use a soft rag to wash and crumpled newspaper to dry and polish the window.
2. Mix ⅓ cup of alcohol with 2 pints of rainwater.
3. Use formula 1 followed by 2. (According to Ada, Noah's wife, #1 is the grease cutter and #2 is the polisher.)
4. Blend 1 quart of hot water with ½ cup of kerosene. Dampen a soft cloth with the solution and wring it out well before using. The residual kerosene film will keep the glass cleaner longer.
5. For clear plastic windows, including Lexan, use 1 part vinegar to 2 parts water.

BRASS & COPPER CLEANER/POLISH

To remove tarnish from these metals, use a mixture of 2 parts table salt to 1 part lemon juice and 1 part vinegar. Apply the liquid to the metal with a sponge and let it dry. Rinse it off with hot water. Worcestershire sauce by itself works well on brass.

CHROME CLEANER/POLISH

Clean with cider vinegar and polish with baby oil.

ALUMINUM CLEANER

Dissolve 2 tablespoons cream of tartar in 1 quart of hot water.

STAINLESS STEEL CLEANER

Use window cleaner or ammonia and a soft cloth.

CLEANING LINES

Soiled lines can be cleaned in a tub filled with water and Woolite. Avoid using bleach; it will not only discolor the lines but also weaken them. Rinse the lines several times with clean water. Add a small amount of fabric softener to the final rinse. Allow the lines to air dry. The lines will be both clean and less abrasive to your touch. Noah uses this technique on his synthetic harnesses with good results.

TO REMOVE WATERMARKS FROM CABIN INTERIOR WOOD FINISHES

Try one of the following:

- Rub the area with the meat of a nut.
- Apply either mayonnaise or cooking oil with a small amount of baking soda.

- Rub the area with toothpaste on a damp cloth. (Always rub with the grain of the wood when using mild abrasives.) Wipe up any residue and buff with a soft cloth.

WAXED WOOD POLISH

Mix one part vegetable oil and one part lemon juice or vinegar into a solution. Apply a thin coat and rub in well.

UNWAXED WOOD POLISH

Use vegetable oil or lemon oil to replenish the shine.

VARNISHED WOOD CLEANER

Use equal parts vinegar and water.

VARNISHED WOOD CLEANER/POLISH

Use 3 parts olive oil and 1 part white vinegar to clean. Polish with straight olive oil.

VARNISH REMOVER

Mix 1 cup turpentine and 2 cups ammonia together. Brush this mixture on the old finish. This may take a few applications. Once all of the old finish is removed, wipe with a solution of 1 cup vinegar to 1 quart of water.

SCREEN CLEANER

Clean with kerosene and rinse with water with a few drops of dishwashing detergent added.

SCOURING POWDER

To remove stains from pots and pans, make a paste of 3 parts baking soda, one part table salt, and a little water. Rub the paste onto the metal and let dry. Rinse with hot water and wipe with a soft cloth. For stubborn stains, repeat the process.

BURNT POT RESIDUE

Mix baking soda with water in the pot. Allow the mixture to boil for a few minutes. The burned material will lift right off.

QUICK, MILD ABRASIVES

Sprinkle borax, baking powder, or dry table salt onto a damp sponge, scour, and rinse.

GREASE CUTTER

To remove that dull, greasy film from the galley, use ½ cup white vinegar mixed into ½ gallon of warm water. *Or* use lemon juice straight.

DRAIN CLEANER

To keep drains clog-free, pour in 1 cup of baking soda followed by 1 cup of hot, white vinegar. Allow the mixture to stand overnight. Rinse with hot water.

HEAD CLEANER

Sprinkle baking soda into the bowl and drizzle some vinegar on top. Scour with a toilet bowl brush. This both cleans and deodorizes. Every couple of days, add two tablespoons of vegetable oil to an almost empty toilet bowl and pump it through. This will make pumping easier and extend the life of the seal, piston ring, and joker valve.

DEODORIZER

To deodorize upholstery and carpet, sprinkle baking soda over the affected area and let rest overnight. Vacuum. If no vacuum is available, use a whiskbroom or beat it out.

LAUNDRY BLEACH ALTERNATIVE

Use ¼ cup of lemon juice.

LAUNDRY SPOT REMOVER (GENERAL)

Hydrogen peroxide straight from the first aid kit. Let it sit overnight and then wash as normal. Or use lemon juice in place of hydrogen peroxide.

LAUNDRY SPOT REMOVER (RUST)

Cover the spot with a paste made of lemon juice and salt. Allow the garment to dry in the sun. Wash as normal.

LAUNDRY SPOT REMOVER (INK)

Apply a paste made from lemon juice and cream of tartar. Allow the garment to dry. Wash as normal.

INSECT REPELLANT

Blend six cloves of crushed garlic, one minced onion, and one tablespoon of soap in one gallon of hot water. Let the mixture age one or two days. Strain. Apply with a spray bottle.

FISHY ODOR REMOVER

After preparing fish, rub your hands and the counter with lemon juice.

ANT KILLER

Sprinkle cream of tartar, red chili powder, dried peppermint, or boric acid where the ants are.

COCKROACH KILLER

Use equal parts baking soda and powdered sugar. The sugar attracts them and the baking soda kills them.

BIRD DOO-DOO REMOVER

To lift from your boat's deck the calcified droppings birds leave behind, mix baking soda and a little detergent with water. Allow the mixture to sit for a little while and then scrub off with a deck brush.

While not necessarily as alluring as a "magic bullet" product that promises to clean everything in mere seconds, most of these homemade formulas are just as effective, cost less, and are nonpolluting. These are classic cleaning recipes that Noah's grandmother (and her grandmother) used and Noah still uses today.

CHAPTER 23

CHOOSING THE RIGHT ANTIFOULING PAINT

In 1625 William Beale registered the first patent for a toxic underwater paint. It was a mixture of iron powder, cement, and copper. How effective it was is anyone's guess. But one thing is for sure: Bill's paint was the opening shot in the war against marine fouling, a war that still rages today.

Antifouling paints have come a long way since 1625. Not only are they more advanced, but they are also becoming more ecologically friendly. They come in a variety of formulations, types, and even colors, thus making the selection process a bit involved. Therefore, before heading off to the chandlery with checkbook in hand, you need to consider a few preliminaries.

PRESELECTION GUIDELINES

Many variables directly influence the selection of an antifouling paint. Such variables include fresh or saltwater use, water temperature, nutrient content, how the boat is used, the length of the sailing season, the material the hull is made of, and if the bottom is currently painted.

Consider the following: Boats that sail in fresh water generally experience different kinds of biological growth than their saltwater cousins. For example, fresh water sailors don't even think twice about barnacles or Toredo worms. They are, however, extremely aware of slime formation, and Great Lakes sailors are concerned with zebra mussels. Water temperature also has a direct bearing on fouling. A boat kept in the cool waters of Lake Superior or off the coast of Maine will not foul as quickly or extensively as one kept in the warm and sunny waters of Florida. Waters with a high nutrient content, such as the lower Great Lakes (which experience significant agricultural runoff) and coastal waters in proximity to highly urbanized/industrialized areas, provide an almost unlimited food source for marine organisms. While a variety of bottom paints that contain a high biocide content will generally perform well under most of these cases, strength isn't always the answer.

For example, boats that are regularly used can benefit quite nicely from a polishing or "soft" antifouling paint. This is a type of antifouling paint that continuously exposes fresh biocide as the boat moves through the water. Boats that spend considerable time at their moorings may possibly be better protected by a "hard" antifouling paint that slowly releases biocide at a controlled rate. Trailer sailors who routinely launch and retrieve their boats need to consider a paint that doesn't lose its effectiveness when exposed to air and can also withstand the routine abrasion of sliding off and on a trailer. A single-season paint may work well for boats with short sailing seasons, while multi-season paints are more economical for boats that sail year around.

If your boat is fiberglass or even wood, most types of antifouling paints will work equally well. In these instances it's often economics that plays the dominant role. However, if the hull is metal, especially aluminum, the field of choice is narrowed considerably. Since copper is the active biocide in most antifouling paints, think galvanic corrosion. Metal boats require barrier coatings and/or special antifouling paints.

The last consideration when selecting an antifouling paint has to do with compatibility. On a bare hull, your pallet of paints is endless.

However, if the boat's bottom is currently painted, your selection is automatically narrowed. This is especially true if you either don't know what the current paint is or don't want to remove it.

BASIC INGREDIENTS

While formulas may differ among companies and products, modern antifouling paints consist primarily of four basic ingredients: resin, solvent, pigment, and biocide.

The resin gives the product its mechanical properties. It holds the product together, forms the coating film, and controls the release of the biocide. Many different resins are used, including tree rosins (with an o), alkyds, one-part epoxy esters, vinyl, and Teflon.

The solvent impacts the product's application characteristics, especially its flow and drying speed. It keeps all the product's solids in suspension until it evaporates as the paint dries. Some of the more common solvents include petroleum distillates, alcohol, and water.

Pigments not only add color to antifouling paint, but also affect the product's thickness. Some pigments can act as a passive biocide by inhibiting normal metabolic growth. Zinc oxide and, to a greater extent, zinc pyrithione (the active ingredient in many anti-dandruff shampoos) act as sunscreens inhibiting algal growth.

Biocides are the active ingredients that repel, are toxic to, or inhibit marine biological growth. The most common biocide in use today is copper and its oxides; that's because they're not very toxic to marine life. They function more as repellents than as biocidal agents. Less used materials include zinc compounds and hydrogen peroxide. Recent technology based on cybutryne (a triazine compound) inhibits photosynthesis. When blended with conventional copper-based antifouling paints this material increases anti-slime protection. Cybutryne is marketed by Interlux under the trademark of Biolux and by Pettit and West Marine as Irgarol.

THE RIGHT PAINT FOR THE RIGHT JOB

Antifouling paint takes two different forms: polishing (soft) or hard. For the most part, their selection can be dovetailed with the type of water and sailboat use.

Polishing types of antifouling paints are of a soft composition and include the traditional sloughing paints, ablatives, and copolymers. Except for the multi-season copolymers, the soft rosin sloughing paints and the more durable ablatives are single-season products. All are formulated to gently wear away like a bar of soap as the boat moves through the water. This erosion exposes fresh biocide, reduces the thickness of the paint, and sloughs off any biological growth. Through normal action, the paint will eventually disappear altogether, exposing the bare hull. During the paint's active life, the paint should not be scrubbed. Scrubbing will remove not only the paint but also the biocide, reducing the product's lifespan. Polishing paints are depleted by mileage, not by time in the water. They are generally regarded as being maintenance-free. With minor surface preparation, polishing paints will overcoat most existing antifouling paints.

Hard antifouling paints include epoxy esters, dry lubricants (Teflon), and vinyl paints. Antifouling paints in this group function by what is termed contact leaching. Upon contact with water, the binder in the paint begins releasing its biocide at a steady, controlled rate. Unlike polishing paints, the active biocides in hard antifouling paints will be depleted with time, not mileage. Once the biocide has been exhausted, the hard paint binder still remains. The typical lifespan of a hard antifouling paint is approximately 12 months (when in contact with water). All of the hard antifouling paints produce a very thin film and can be over-coated several times before stripping is required.

Unlike polishing antifouling paints, which are all quite similar, the three types of hard antifouling paints possess distinct differences. Epoxy ester-based hard antifouling paints include some of the best selling products on the market. They are suitable for both fresh and saltwater applications, are reasonably priced, and can over-coat most other products. Dry lubricant (Teflon) paints produce a coating with the lowest drag coefficient available. It's no surprise that this class of hard antifouling paint is favored by racing sailors. Its ultra-thin film is tough and unaffected by air, making it a good choice for trailerable boats. Its antifouling properties aren't the best in saltwater and it can't be over-coated with other paints. Lastly, vinyl-based antifouling paints produce an extremely durable film. It too is liked by racing sailors, especially since it can be wet sanded and burnished to a slick racing finish. Unlike Teflon-based paints, vinyl-based products can be over-coated by most anything else; however, they will not over-coat anything but themselves.

WHAT'S ON THE MARKET

Below is a partial listing of antifouling paints available from the major paint manufacturers. This list is by no means exhaustive.

Polishing-Sloughing
   Interlux Bottomkote
   Interlux Bottomkote XXX
Polishing-Ablative
   Interlux Fiberglass Bottomkote ACT
   Interlux Trilux 33
   West Marine CPP Plus
Polishing-Copolymer
   Interlux Micron Extra
   Interlux Micron CSC
   Pettit Ultima SR
   West Marine PCA Gold
Hard-Epoxy Ester
   Interlux Fiberglass Bottomkote

Interlux Ultrakote
  Interlux Ultra
  Pettit Vivid
  Pettit Trinidad
  Pettit Trinidad SR
  West Marine Bottom Shield
  West Marine Bottom Pro Gold
Hard-Dry Lubricant (Teflon)
  Interlux VC17m
  Pettit SR-21
  West Marine FW-21
Hard-Vinyl
  VC Offshore

COMPATIBILITY

While selecting the right paint for the right job is important, knowing if the new paint is compatible with old paint is critical. Carefully review the compatibility chart on the facing page.

FINAL WORDS

Detailed instructions covering the preparation or removal of antifouling paints, including the preparation of new hulls, plus step-by-step application instructions, can be found at one or more of the following websites: www.yachtpaint.com, www.pettitpaint.com, and www.westmarine.com.

23. CHOOSING THE RIGHT ANTIFOULING PAINT

COMPATIBILITY CHART

OLD PAINT (across top) / NEW PAINT (down side)	Polishing-Sloughing	Polishing-Ablative	Polishing-Copolymer	Hard-Epoxy Ester	Hard-Dry Lube (Teflon)	Hard-Vinyl
Polishing-Sloughing	Lightly Sand & Apply	Sand Well & Apply	Sand Well & Apply	Sand Well & Apply	Remove Completely	Sand & Apply
Polishing-Ablative	Remove Completely	Lightly Sand & Apply	Sand Well & Apply	Lightly Sand & Apply	Remove Completely	Sand & Apply
Polishing-Copolymer	Remove Completely	Lightly Sand & Apply	Lightly Sand & Apply	Lightly Sand & Apply	Remove Completely	Sand & Apply
Hard-Epoxy Ester	Heavily Sand & Apply	Sand & Apply	Sand & Apply	Sand & Apply	Remove Completely	Sand Well & Apply
Hard-Dry Lube (Teflon)	Remove Completely	Remove Completely	Remove Completely	Remove Completely	Clean & Apply	Remove Completely
Hard-Vinyl	Remove Completely	Remove Completely	Remove Completely	Remove Completely	Remove Completely	Sand Well & Apply

CHAPTER 24

APPLYING BOTTOM PAINTS

Before you apply any bottom paint to your sailboat, some basic preparation is in order. This includes not only having the proper application equipment and the correct amount of paint on hand, but also having the necessary safety and cleanup equipment assembled.

By its very nature, bottom paint is toxic. And since the majority of the work will be conducted overhead, bodily contact with the paint is seemingly unavoidable. Proper personal protective equipment (gloves, clothing, eye goggles, and a respirator) will help prevent an overexposure to any sanding residue or to the paint. It's also a good idea to place a tarp beneath the boat to protect the ground. The tarp will not only collect any sanding/scraping debris or paint splatter, but will also prevent dust from rising onto the freshly painted surface.

SURFACE PREPARATION

Adhesion of the new paint is directly related to the quality of what's beneath it. If the old bottom paint is in good condition, all you need to do is sand it with 80-grit paper, wash off the dust, and roll on a fresh coat or two of new bottom paint. With an uneven or thick build-up of paint, it may be necessary to resort to a more aggressive approach such as scraping or chemical stripping. Once the loose or flaking old paint has been removed, the surface should then be sanded. If this is

24. APPLYING BOTTOM PAINTS

the first time that boat's bottom is to be painted, or if, after sanding/stripping, a significant amount of raw fiberglass is showing, it would be wise to either apply a primer or sand the boat's hull with 80-grit paper prior to applying the first coat of bottom paint. Fiberglass by itself is not the best material for holding paint. The application of a primer or sanding the bottom will create a surface porous enough for the bottom paint to adhere to. Additionally, a new boat that has not been previously painted has mold release wax on its fiberglass. This wax must be removed before any kind of paint will stick. Clean the hull thoroughly with a dewaxing solvent, changing rags often throughout the process. Once cleaned, the hull is ready for sanding or priming, prior to the application of bottom paint.

APPLICATION

At last, it's time to roll on the bottom paint. Assemble your application and cleanup equipment: short-nap roller, sponge brushes (for use in tight areas where the roller can't reach), paint tray, mixing stick, solvent, and rags. Once you've marked off the waterline with masking tape it's time to don your disposable clothing, such as a Tyvek suit, and put on your gloves and goggles.

Mix the paint thoroughly with your mixing stick, making sure to stir up all the sediment from the bottom of the can. In most instances, it's the cuprous oxide biocide that's on the bottom of the can. Once the paint is well mixed, decant some into the paint tray. To make cleanup easier, use a disposable tray liner. Place the lid securely back on the can to minimize evaporation and to save losing $$-worth of paint, should you accidentally kick it over. This is the voice of experience speaking.

Start your painting at the bow. Try to work at a comfortable height. Kneepads can help, and a roller handle extension saves a lot of stretching and will make painting the keel easier. Dip your roller into the paint tray, unload the excess paint on the tray's slope, and begin by rolling up and down on the hull from waterline to keel. To insure proper coverage, go over the area from side to side. Using this technique, work your way aft. The cuprous oxide is a high-density material that settles fairly rapidly. Therefore, each time you refill the tray, be sure to stir the paint. If the cuprous oxide is not evenly distributed within the paint, some areas of your hull won't be adequately protected. Apply an extra coat of paint along the waterline and on the leading and trailing edges of the keel and the rudder. Bottom paint doesn't last as long in areas where there is constant water turbulence.

KEEP IN MIND

Generally speaking, the performance of bottom paint is directly proportional to its thickness. Don't try to economize by either thinning the paint or by applying it too thin. Follow the manufacturer's recommendations. For the first coat (the flag coat), use a bottom paint of a different color. When applying additional coats or when sanding, the flag coat will signal when complete coverage is obtained or you've sanded enough.

There's no need to paint the prop or the shaft. Also, be sure to leave all zinc anodes unpainted. And if you're planning on installing fresh zincs, make certain that their mounting locations are paint-free. To protect any underwater transducers, use specially formulated transducer antifouling paint.

Lastly, keep your receipts and make note of the paint's batch number, just in case there's a problem later on.

CHAPTER 25

RESTORING LUSTER TO YOUR DECK

Over the years, I've owned several "experienced" fiberglass sailboats. These were boats that have had at least one or two owners prior to me. One thing I noticed was that by the time I got my hands on a boat, the cosmetic condition of the fiberglass laminate was usually fair to poor. I'm not speaking of scratches, scrapes, and collision damage, or even age-related gelcoat crazing, but rather the fading and chalking due to the boat's routine exposure to the elements, especially the harsh rays of the sun. Without exception, I've found it necessary to buff out, polish, glaze, and finally wax the topsides. This technique restores the majority, if not all of the boat's original gloss. While this four-step procedure has served me well with regards to the boat's hull, it doesn't lend itself to the horizontal deck surfaces, especially the molded-in nonskid areas.

Having worked for many years in the specialty chemical business, I fortunately have contacts in various industries, including coatings, adhesives, and paint. Periodically, I glean a gem of an idea from my sources and successfully apply it to the upkeep and maintenance of my boat. It was with my dull deck dilemma (say that three times fast) that I queried my friends. What I finally came up with has not only worked wonders on my decks, but is also simple and easy.

- Before I do anything, I wash the deck thoroughly using a mild abrasive cleaner and a brush. The combination of

Soft Scrub with bleach and a nail brush works well. This somewhat mildly aggressive cleaning approach insures the removal of dirt, most stains, and loose oxidization. It also affords a deep cleaning of the molded-in nonskid.

- After the entire deck has been washed, I go over it again with clear water and, using the nailbrush, brush out the nonskid. This step removes any abrasive residue.

- I usually do the cleaning at midday, when the sun is high and the deck surface is warm. I then kick back with a beverage and allow the deck to thoroughly air dry.

- Late afternoon or early morning the next day, I begin the final step. (Don't do this in direct sunlight.) Using a 3-inch-wide paint roller with a very short nap (maybe ¼ inch), I apply a *thin* coating of Penetrol to the entire deck. Penetrol works best if it is applied in *very thin* multiple (2-3) coats. To do so, I roll out most of the moisture so that I don't clog the nonskid. *Thin* coats dry very fast...in minutes. It has been my experience that if applied too heavily, Penetrol can flake off and leave the surface blotchy. Two *thin* coats are better than one thick coat. Excess Penetrol should be cleaned up quickly with mineral spirits and a lint-free cloth. Tee shirt material works great. If dried, Penetrol can be removed with any paint remover formulated specifically for use on fiberglass.

What is Penetrol? Penetrol is a petroleum-based additive that was originally developed to increase the penetration and adhesion of oil/alkyl paints and varnishes. When used alone, it was discovered that this deep penetrating oil reaches down into the fiberglass and restores the original color. And upon drying, Penetrol cures to a tough, flexible, and shiny finish. One can find Penetrol in many hardware stores, most paint stores, and the local chandlery.

All fiberglass laminates are permeable to some extent and will allow moisture to penetrate them. As an added benefit and as its name implies, Penetrol penetrates the porous fiberglass and impedes moisture penetration. It also eliminates the need for other surface coatings, such as polishes, that dry out quickly.

The Penetrol coating isn't slippery, but one should always be careful on wet fiberglass, especially on older boats whose nonskid may be severely worn.

As far as reapplication goes, I've learned to apply Penetrol based on need rather than schedule. And reapplication should always follow the same four steps: clean, rinse, dry, and apply.

SECTION VI

MARLINESPIKE SEAMANSHIP

In the book *Piloting, Seamanship and Small Boat Handling*, Charles F. Chapman categorizes marlinespike seamanship as the selection and care of rope; knots, bends, and hitches; splices; and blocks and tackle. For the landlubber, the mention of the word knots evokes a mental picture of a young Boy Scout sitting around a campfire intently concentrating on a jumble of line, in hopes of passing his Tenderfoot requirement. To the sailor, however, marlinespike seamanship is about shipboard organization on a real world level. This is where docking lines droop, reef points loosen and spill sails, and sheets mysteriously untie. This section is the ammunition you'll need to win the everyday battle against these small-scale forces of chaos.

CHAPTER 26

CORDAGE

A few years ago, after carefully inspecting all of my running rigging, I decided that it was time for me to replace much of it. On a sheet of paper I identified each line and recorded its diameter, length, and color (long ago, I found it a lot easier to tell an eager-to-help nonsailor to release the yellow line instead of the boom vang). With my list in one hand and checkbook in the other, I arrived at the local marine store. Soon I found myself standing speechless in front of a wall of spools of rope. Just about every color of the rainbow was represented, as well as a variety of diameters and materials of construction. I was amazed at the selection of cordage available. While I was comfortable with the basics—nylon, Dacron, three-strand twist, and double-braid—I was at a loss when it came to the newer high modulus fibers. I decided that before I opened my checkbook, a bit of research was in order.

> Is it line or is it rope? Most sailors (as do I) define rope as the raw material, which becomes line when it is cut for a specific use (*e.g.* anchor line).

CONSTRUCTION TECHNIQUES AND TYPES

All rope begins as individual fibers. In the process of rope manufacturing, these fibers are first twisted into yarn. Following the formation of yarn, a number of yarns are then twisted into strands or plaits (braids). Finally, the strands or plaits are combined—either twisted or braided—to form rope.

The most common of ropes is the three-strand twist. Three-strand twist rope maintains its form because it is always under self-tension. This self-tension results from the alternate twisting of the individual fibers, yarns, and strands. This creates internal friction among these various components, and working in concert with each other, forms the rope. Three-strand twist is inexpensive and is quick and easy to splice. It can become difficult to knot and coil properly, especially when it progressively stiffens with age. Its twisted form of construction makes it the ideal candidate for docking and mooring lines as well as anchor rodes. In these applications, stretch and shock absorption are valued attributes.

Like three-strand twisted rope, braided rope is also made up of fibers, yarns, and strands; however, they are laid out differently and are not under self-tension. Single-braid rope is braided with 12 strands. Half of the strands revolve to the right and half to the left. In the case of double-braid rope, the cover can be comprised of 16, 20, 24, or 32 strands, again half revolving to the right and the other half to the left. A rope constructed from eight strands is called plaited line. While braided line is round, plaited rope is flat. Polypropylene ropes are often plaited.

Single-braid line exhibits less stretch than three-strand twisted, is easier to coil and store, works better in self-tailing winches, and is kinder on the hands. However, it can be difficult to splice, is more expensive to produce, and has limited popularity.

Double-braided rope, which is a hollow-braided cover over a hollow-braided core, makes up the bulk of all running rigging used aboard contemporary sailboats. This rope is held together by the geometry of its interlocking cover and core. This interlocking method produces a softer and more flexible rope that exhibits greater strength and less stretch. The core and cover share the load equally, assuming that the materials of construction are the same. The core can be comprised of a host of different materials to take advantage of differing properties. For example, a high strength core material can carry 90 percent of the load. The core can also be woven at low angles or even laid-up as parallel fibers to reduce stretch even further and increase strength. There are ropes with low-twist three-strand cores claimed to be 40 percent stronger than double-braided and that stretch only half as much.

Double-braids are the easiest on the hands, afford excellent grip, and can be woven in a multitude of colors for quick identification. Also, the cover of double-braided rope can be finished either smooth or hairy. Hairy finished ropes won't be as strong as smooth ones, though they are easier to handle and work better in rope clutches and jam cleats. Double-braided rope is a bit more expensive to manufacture and splicing takes some practice.

MATERIALS OF CONSTRUCTION

Historically, rope was always made of natural fibers. These included such materials as cotton, flax, sisal, hemp, and manila. However, these days, synthetics rule the high seas.

The evolution from natural fibers to synthetics started in the late 1950s with the application of three-strand twisted nylon as halyards and sheets. The rest is history. Nylon was soon replaced by polyester; nearly half a century later, advancements in synthetic fiber technology continue to put new cordage aboard sailboats. While none can equal the durability of polyester, when it comes to UV and saltwater exposure each of these new breeds of synthetics has found a niche in this complex arena we call sailboat rigging.

NYLON

Nylon can be chemically described as a polyamide (a polymer of amines). Its basic ingredients are coal and water. Nylon, developed by E. I. DuPont de Nemours and Co. Inc. in the 1930s, has the honor of being the very first synthetic fiber. The Nylon name became instantly generic and Du Pont declined to register it as a trademark. Nylon is strong, affordable, and offers excellent resistance to abrasion, rot, and flexural fatigue. While nylon is prone to stretching (as much as 15 percent), this stretchiness can be useful when it comes to absorbing shock loads imposed on mooring lines and anchor rodes. Nylon is susceptible to UV degradation and readily absorbs water. This tendency to absorb water can reduce the rope's strength by as much as 10 to 15 percent. Also, when soaked, the individual nylon fibers swell and the rope temporarily shrinks a little in length. Another downside to nylon's absorbent nature is that impurities are drawn into the rope over time. This results in discoloration and a progressive stiffening of the rope. Nylon has a specific gravity of 1.14 (meaning it weighs 1.14 times the weight of fresh water) and, when dry, is lighter than polyester. Nylon is not recommended for running rigging applications. It makes for great dock lines and anchor rodes. When protected from UV by means of a polyester cover (Polyon), it makes the ideal mooring pendant.

POLYESTER

Polyester is often referred to as Dacron, which is another synthetic fiber that was created in the DuPont laboratories. While nylon has become a generic term, Dacron has not, but is, in fact, a registered trademark. While it is not as strong as nylon, polyester performs very well in high stress applications, such as running rigging. It is resistant to rot, abrasion, and flexural fatigue. Unlike nylon, polyester is UV stable, does not absorb water, and exhibits very low stretch. Even greater stretch resistance can be achieved by prestretching the rope to its elastic limit and heat-setting it. However, this leaves the rope markedly stiffer and more difficult to splice. Polyester takes to coloring very well and is ideal for color-code lines, making them instantly identifiable. While polyester has a specific gravity of 1.38, making it a heavy material, it is usually the first and most economical choice for virtually all running rigging applications. Prestretched polyester ropes are ideal for halyards and offer a cheaper, albeit inferior, alternative to HMPE (high modulus polyethylene).

POLYPROPYLENE

Polypropylene is an inexpensive, hard-wearing fiber that is weaker than both nylon and polyester. It is stiff, slippery, brittle, and hard to knot. Polypropylene is heat sensitive and melts if run rapidly over a winch. It exhibits poor UV stability and is very susceptible to fading. Its low resistance to weathering further prevents it from being widely used. However, polypropylene has stretch characteristics approaching those of polyester. It doesn't absorb water, and it has a specific gravity of less than 1.0. Polypropylene's claim to fame is that it's extremely light...it floats! This makes it an excellent candidate for MOB rescue lines and towing dinghies.

HMPE

High modulus (high strength) polyethylene is more commonly known by the trade names Dyneema and Spectra. It is a high strength, low stretch synthetic fiber that affords resistance to both weather and abrasion superior to that afforded by polyester. When coated during its manufacturing, HMPE exhibits reasonable resistance to UV degradation. However, for the long term, a polyester cover works best. It is expensive and second only in strength to PBO (polybenzoxazole). In addition to its cost, HMPE tends to creep (elongate) under sustained loads. With a specific gravity of 0.97, it is a much lighter fiber, one reason why it's often found aboard racing yachts. For example, a 7/16 inch (10mm) halyard comprised of a HMPE core with polyester cover is not only stronger than a ½ inch (12mm) double-braid polyester line of identical length, but because of its inherent lightness and smaller diameter, it is also 40 percent lighter. Likewise, in light air HMPE spinnaker sheets would allow the sail to fly, when heavier polyester ones might possibly lead to the sail's collapse.

PARA-ARAMIDS

This family of high modulus synthetic fibers consists of Kevlar and its sister fibers Twaron and Technora. Para-aramids are said to be stronger than steel by weight. While these fibers are quite vulnerable to UV and abrasion, they are exceptionally stretch resistant. Para-aramids are brittle, do not bend well, and are difficult to splice. They tend to break down when flexed over small radius blocks. Technora is the exception; this material can handle turns better than Kevlar and Twaron. Also, as a core material, para-aramids tend to cut through polyester covers. On high-tech racing boats, these fibers are usually sheathed in shrink-on black plastic. Even though these synthetics display outstanding strength-to-weight properties, their many drawbacks and high cost make them less functional aboard cruising boats.

POLYESTER-POLYARYLATE

Vectran is the only brand of polyester-polyarylate high modulus fiber used in the construction of marine rope. Its characteristics of high strength, extremely low stretch, and little or no creep make it similar to those of the para-aramids. Like the para-aramids, Vectran is degraded by UV and has a limited flex life. However, it displays much better abrasion resistance, and therefore will last longer when turning around sheaves. Like all the newer high modulus fibers, Vectran is expensive. But unlike most, when covered with polyester it can perform most running rigging tasks aboard high-tech racing boats.

PBO

Poly-para-phenylene-2 6-benzobisoxazole (or PBO for short) is the strongest of the synthetic high modulus fibers. In fact, it is 20 percent stronger than its nearest competitor, HMPE. It displays exceptional stretch resistance and very low creep. However, it is susceptible to UV degradation, needs chafe protection, and has a limited flex life. On high performance ocean racers, PBO, covered in shrink-on black plastic, is used as standing rigging, where it is substantially lighter than stainless steel rod rigging. However, considering its cost and maintenance, PBO is best relegated to where the pockets are as deep as the water sailed.

26. CORDAGE

SO, WHAT'S THE BOTTOM LINE? (PUN INTENDED)

While there may be some high-tech racers rigged entirely with HMPE or polyester-polyarylate, the majority of cruisers coming off of the assembly line are rigged mainly with double-braid polyester. However, a few manufacturers are beginning to offer HMPE halyards.

Experienced (previously owned) boats, I suspect, sport a mixture of fibers: halyards and sheets of double-braid polyester, docking and anchor lines of three-strand twist nylon, and MOB heaving lines and dinghy towing bridles of plaited polypropylene.

While high modulus fiber ropes are slowly making their way on board cruising boats, they're still pricey. However, once the economics of scale kicks in, prices will come down.

The majority of sailors are content with good performance double-braid polyester, while banking the difference between it and those high performance, cutting edge fibers. So educate yourself and shop around before you buy.

CORDAGE SELECTION GUIDE

Genoa sheets
Jib sheets
Boom vang
Reefing lines
Main sheet
Spinnaker sheet
Traveller control lines
Cunningham/downhaul
Outhaul
Barber hauler
Spinnaker pole uphaul & downhaul
Backstay adjuster
	Standard Performance (SP):
	    Double-braid polyester
	High Performance (HP):
	    HMPE, Polyester-polyarylate
	    (covered with polyester)

Spinnaker guy	SP: Double-braid polyester HP: HMPE, Polyester-polyarylate, Para-aramid (covered with polyester)
Main and Jib halyards	SP: Double-braid polyester HP: HMPE, Poylester-polyarylate, Para-aramid, PBO (covered with polyester)
Spinnaker halyard	SP: Double-braid polyester HP: HMPE (covered with polyester)
Preventer Lazy Jacks Flag halyards	Nylon or Double-braid polyester

CORDAGE SELECTION GUIDE

Headsail furling line Fender lines Topping lift Headsail downhaul	Double-braid polyester
Dock lines	Nylon (three-strand twist or braided)
Anchor line	Nylon (three-strand twist)
Mooring pendant	Nylon (braided) or nylon covered with polyester (Polyon)
Life sling line Heaving lines MOB lines Dinghy towline	Polypropylene (plaited)

CHAPTER 27

KNOTS

During my two-plus decades of Boy Scouting (as a Scout during my youth and later as a Scoutmaster), knots and knot-tying played an integral role in the program. Without them how could the lashings of a signal tower be begun or ended, or the lines of a tent be properly secured and made taut?

As a sailor, I took knot-tying for granted along with sail trimming, bottom painting, using proper nautical terminology, and so forth. However, it wasn't until my most recent experience as skipper for a Sea Scout ship that I realized that knots, on a real-world level, are very important tools.

There are approximately 4,000 different knots in existence. Many of them are highly specialized, used for one-of-a-kind applications, and a few are even patented. In Scouting, I used about 25 knots to get what I needed done, done. In sailing, I have found that the following dozen knots can get the tasks aboard ship completed in good seamanship fashion.

KNOWING THE PROPER TERMS

What is a knot? A knot can be a generic term for any loop or entanglement of line, created intentionally or accidentally. More precisely, as distinct from a bend or hitch, a knot secures the two ends of the same line.

27. KNOTS

What's a bend? A bend joins two separate lengths of cordage together. A hitch, on the other hand, is generally used to attach a line to a post, rail, or ring.

A few other terms that will help simplify what appears to be a universal knot-tying dilemma deal with the line itself. They include the *bitter end, standing part, bight,* and *loop.* The bitter end of a line is its very end, while the standing part is the main section of the line. A bight is formed by bending the standing part of a line into a U-shape, while a loop is a small circle formed in the standing part.

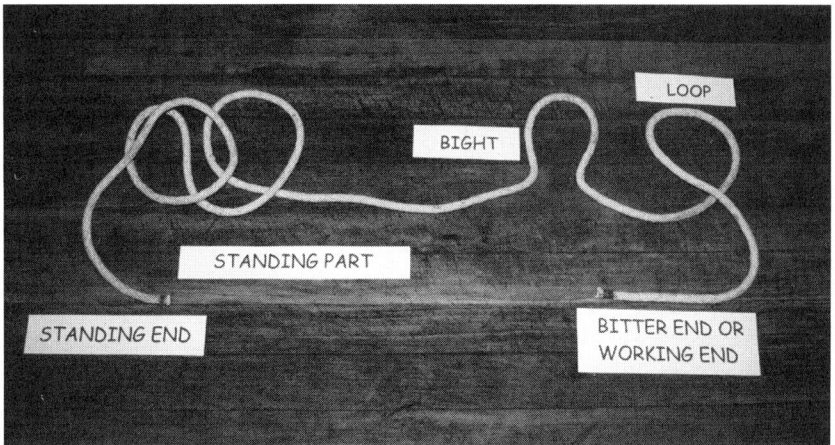

KNOT-TYING TERMS

By their design, some knots are easily untied, while others require some degree of coaxing. Although a knot is used to secure, there may be instances where a "quick release" modification may be desired. This is called making a knot "slippery" and is usually accomplished by incorporating a bend in the last step of the tying process. One of the most common slippery knots is the bow knot used to tie your shoes. In actuality it is a double slipped square knot. Some other knots that can be made slippery are the figure eight, sheet bend, clove hitch, two half hitches, and cleat hitch.

Lastly, a few words concerning relative knot strength or efficiency. Based on a rope strength of 100 percent, the efficiency of a knot is that percentage of breaking strength left after that knot has been tied in it. Do not confuse breaking strength with safe working load. The breaking strength is commonly 5 times that of the safe working load.

THE FIGURE EIGHT KNOT

A PROPERLY TIED FIGURE 8 "STOPPER" KNOT

The figure eight, the sailor's number one stopper knot, is believed to have gotten its name from Darcy Lever in his book *Sheet Anchor* (1908). It is used to prevent jib and main sheet ends, halyards, and other control lines from coming unreeved from blocks and fairleads. It is not only easy to tie, but more importantly easy to untie, even when wet. To make the most of the knot, tie it at least four inches from the bitter end. As is always the case, the breaking strength of a line is reduced when there is a knot present; a figure eight is no exception. It reduces the line's strength to 45 to 50 percent of unknotted line.

REEF KNOT (SQUARE KNOT)

"REEFING A SAIL OR TYING A PARCEL, A REEF KNOT THE ROLE WILL FULFILL."
MASTER MARINER S. GRAINGER

The reef or square knot is said to be one of the most useful knots known. The Ancient Greeks, Romans, and Egyptians all used this knot. The Romans called it the Hercules knot. This knot is used to tie together two ends of the same piece of line, such as conventional sail ties, tying in battens, tying lashings, and so on. It is easy to tie and untie, except when wet and under heavy load. If used on "small stuff," which can pull very tight, it becomes very difficult to undo. In this instance, use a sheet bend. It affords superior performance and is simpler to tie. A reef knot is not a bend and is quite weak, reducing the breaking strength of the tied line to 45 percent.

SHEET BEND

"WHEN TYING TWO ENDS ALWAYS USE BENDS."
MASTER MARINER S. GRAINGER

The sheet bend is simple, honest, and easy to tie. Stone Age fishing nets have been found with mesh knots resembling sheet bends. However, it was first called by this name in David Steel's book *Elements and Practice of Rigging and Seamanship* (1794). The sheet bend is principally designed to attach two lines of different diameters. It is ideal when using a lightweight throwing line as the messenger to haul a heavier working rope into position. The sheet bend is neither a strong nor a secure knot. It is easily untied and it is almost 50 percent the strength of that of the smaller line.

FISHERMAN'S KNOT

PULLING TWO OVERHAND KNOTS TOGETHER FORMS A FISHERMAN'S KNOT.

The fisherman's knot is actually a bend. In Isaak Walton's *The Complete Angler* (1653), it was also called the water knot. Throughout the centuries that followed, the fisherman's knot has been referred to by several names, including angler's knot, ring knot, gut knot, true lover's knot—and the list goes on. The fisherman's knot is a strong and secure bend used for joining two similar lines together. It can also be used to form endless loops or slings. In addition to tying together line, it works well with webbing tape, such as tape sail ties. The efficiency of the fisherman's knot is about 70 percent.

BOWLINE

IN THE DAYS OF SQUARE RIGGERS, IT WAS SAID
"...THE DEVIL HIMSELF WOULD MAKE A GOOD SAILOR,
IF HE COULD ONLY TIE A BOWLINE AND LOOK ALOFT."

The bowline is the most common knot seen aboard sailboats. In early nautical history it was referred to as the seafarer's knot. However, it wasn't until 1794 that David Steel illustrated the "bow line knot" in his book *The Elements and Practice of Rigging and Seamanship*. Not only is the bowline the most common knot aboard a sailboat, but it is also possibly the most useful knot aboard. Use it wherever a loop is needed. It is ideal for securing jib sheets to the clew. It is easy to untie, even after having been dunked in the water and put under heavy load. The bowline is 40 percent weaker than the line and 30 percent weaker than an eye splice, giving it an efficiency of 60 percent.

ANCHOR BEND

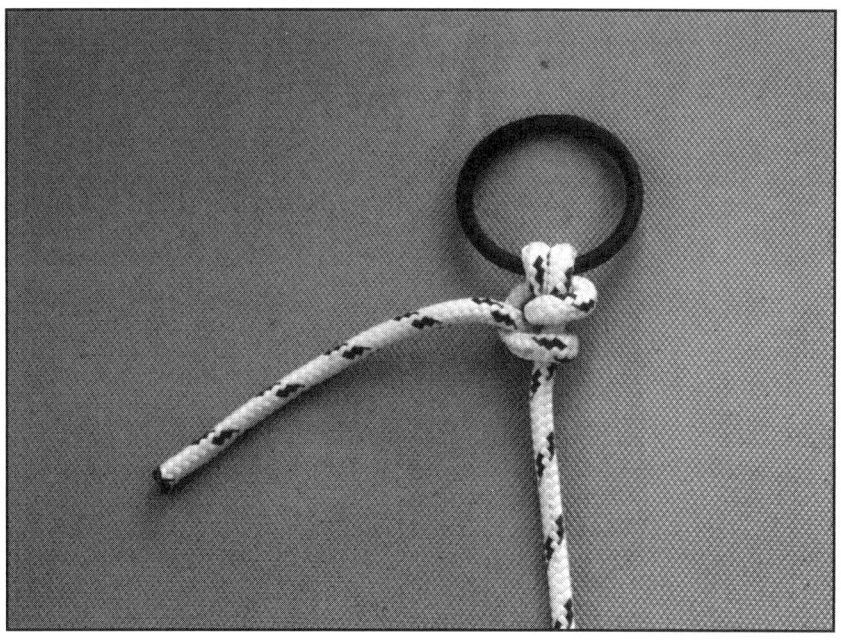

AN ANCHOR BEND TIED TO A RING.

Sometimes called the fisherman's bend (not to be confused with the fisherman's knot), the anchor bend's name is misleading. It is actually a hitch. David Steel recommended this knot in his 1794 book. The anchor bend makes a more secure loop than a bowline and is handy for making fast to a buoy, spar, or ring. It is an especially secure hitch for wet and slimy conditions, such as are often found on an anchor. Because it is only 25 percent weaker than the line (75 percent efficient), the anchor bend is often preferred to a bowline, but it is difficult to untie.

CLOVE HITCH

CLOVE HITCH USED TO SECURE A LIFELINE
TO A STANCHION ON A GANGPLANK.

The clove hitch is a simple yet versatile knot that is held in place by friction. Though it was once called a builder's knot, William Falconer in his *Universal Dictionary of the Marine* (1769) gave it its current name. It is a good knot for tying fenders to lifelines and for securing a line around a post or piling. The clove hitch is not designed for heavy pulling. It is easy to tie, but will hold well only when the load on the knot is steady and at right angles. If pulled around, the clove hitch will work itself loose. When wet it can jam and be difficult to untie. Its breaking strength is about 60 percent.

TWO HALF HITCHES

On shapes and in places where the clove hitch won't go, two half hitches is probably the best choice, both for simplicity and security. In 1794, David Steel referred to this hitch by name, in *Elements and Practice of Rigging and Seamanship.* Two half hitches is commonly used for making a line fast to a bollard, pile, or spar. It is easy to tie, adjust, and untie. Two half hitches has a breaking strength of approximately 70 percent. Taking a round turn before tying the two half hitches increases that percentage.

A ROUND TURN AND TWO HALF HITCHES

TAUTLINE HITCH

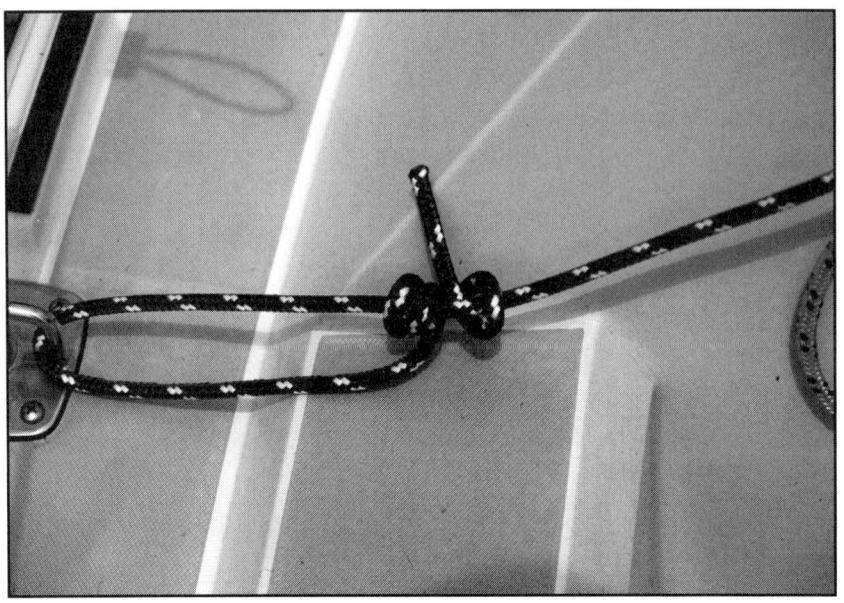

TAUTLINE HITCH — WORK THE ENTIRE KNOT BEFORE USING IT.

Although more commonly found around the campsite securing the guy lines of a tent, the tautline hitch is equally at home aboard ship. Two common variations of this "slide and grip" knot are the classic midshipman's hitch and the newer Tarbuck knot, which was devised by climber Ken Tarbuck in 1952. The tautline hitch is primarily used to tension a line that tends to sag over time, such as a clothesline or the guys of a tarp or cockpit tent. The tautline hitch holds in one direction, but can be slid along itself in the other direction for easy adjustment. The efficiency of this one-way "ratchet" knot is about 65 percent.

ROLLING HITCH

A ROLLING HITCH WILL SLIDE ONE WAY ALONG THE LARGER LINE
BUT NOT THE OTHER.

A close cousin to the venerable clove hitch, the rolling hitch exhibits the "slide and grip" functionality of the tautline hitch. In earlier times, it was often refered to as Magner's hitch or a Magnus hitch. This knot allows a small line to be secured to the standing part of a larger line. It is useful for applying tension to a sheet, constructing a towing bridle, or to assist in extracting a fouled anchor. Like its cousin the clove hitch, the rolling hitch's breaking strength is about 60 percent.

KNUTE HITCH

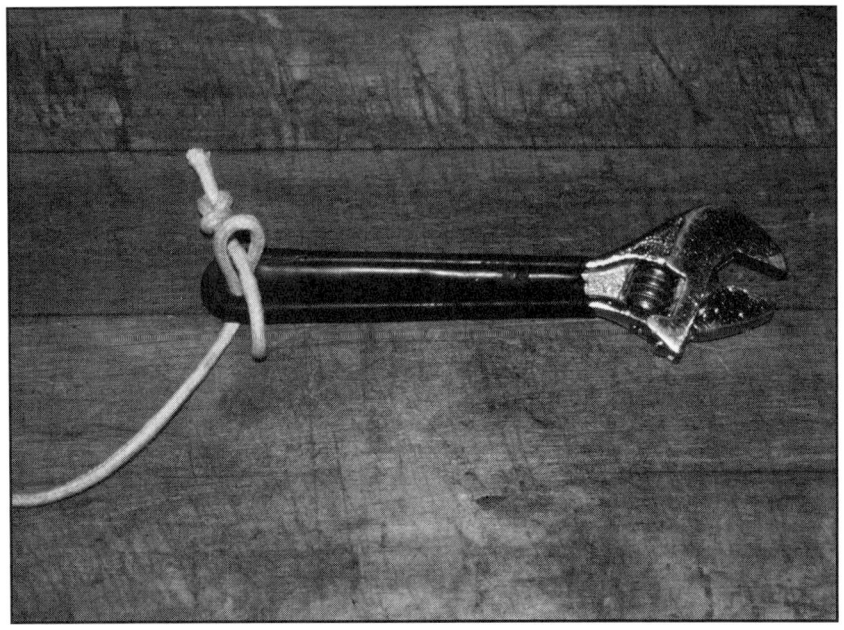

KNUTE HITCH

This is a simple yet effective hitch to attach a line to anything with a hole in it, not much larger than twice the diameter of that line. It is probably centuries old, but master rigger Brion Toss gave it its name in 1990. The knute hitch is used for fixing lanyards to knives and tools, thus keeping them out of Davey Jones' locker. It can also be employed to attach halyards to flags and even sails. The efficiency of this knot is somewhere in the neighborhood of 55 percent.

CLEATING

PROPERLY CLEATED LINE

One can tie a knot through a cleat or pass a loop over both ends. However, the proper way is to use a figure eight pattern around the cleat and finish this off with a twisting loop, making sure that the free end of the line is underneath the final wrap. Cleating a line is not a hitch, bend, or even a knot, but rather an age-old method of making fast. It is universally used to secure halyards, outhauls, downhauls, docking lines—the list is almost endless. It is never used for fastening sheets, as sheets often have to be released in a hurry. The efficiency of a properly cleated line is nearly 80 percent.

Learning how to tie knots can be confusing at first. However, with a little practice and some hands-on application, sailing will be both easier and safer. Bear in mind that there may be more than one way to tie a knot. It doesn't matter how it's tied, as long as the end product is correct.

CHAPTER 28

WHIPPING AND SPLICING

Periodically I conduct a cursory examination of my running rigging. I make mental notes of those lines that need to be monitored, as well as those that are potential candidates for repair or replacement, and if necessary I make corrections on the spot. By doing this often enough, I hopefully can avoid any potential failures—I don't like surprises.

On an annual basis I carefully inspect all of my cordage. This usually is accomplished in the fall, prior to putting the boat away for its annual winter's sleep. I check not only the running rigging, but also the docking lines, mooring pendant, heaving lines, and anchor rode. If anything significant is discovered, I have all winter to correct the situation.

During a recent inspection, although I didn't uncover any major problems, it struck me that not all of the bitter ends of my lines were finished off in a proper seamanship-like fashion. That is to say, all of the ends were not whipped, but rather most had been heated and fused together—which is functional, but not nautically acceptable. I vowed to correct this deplorable situation. Also, I planned to use the winter months to make a few changes and upgrades in my cordage.

28. WHIPPING AND SPLICING

WHIPPING

Whipping makes for a nicer appearance, but its primary functions are to prevent the line's ends from unlaying and to make them easier to reeve through blocks and eyes.

The simplest type of whipping and the one most often seen is "common whipping." Whipping (twine, waxed cord, etc.) is laid along the line to form a loop. The whipping is then tightly wound around both the line and the loop for a distance equal to the line's diameter. To finish, the working end of the whipping is passed through the loop and is pulled out of sight under the turns, by pulling the loop end. Finally, both ends of the whipping are trimmed off. Consider this type of whipping temporary. To make it permanent, add a drop or two of super-glue to the whipping. Common whipping can be used on both three-strand and braided lines.

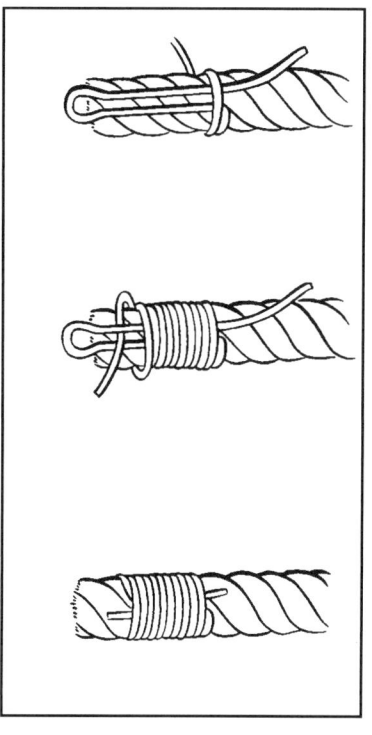

COMMON WHIPPING

The finest whipping is "needle whipping." It takes a bit longer to accomplish, but its superiority justifies the extra time. It is performed most easily on three-strand line, but can be used on braided line. A doubled length of whipping is passed under one strand of line—or in the case of braided line, a few braids. The ends of the whipping are tucked under the turns, which are put on doubled rather than single, as with common whipping. Once the desired length of whipping has been achieved, the working end of the whipping is brought under a strand (few braids) of line and follows the lay of the line back to the whipping's start, where it is drawn under another of the line's strands (few braids). After having followed the three lays back and forth over the turns of whipping (three or four times for braided line), the whipping is finished by bringing the working end up through the center of a strand and trimming it short. In the case of braided line, the whipping is finished by bringing the working end up through approximately one-third of the line's body and then trimming it short.

Here are some things to remember when whipping a line. All whipping should be started "inboard" and the turns wound towards the end of the line. Whipping should not be put on close to the line's end, but rather several inches from the end. Once the whipping has been completed, the excess line is cut off not less than ⅜ inch from the whipping. The width of the whipping should generally equal the diameter of the line to be whipped.

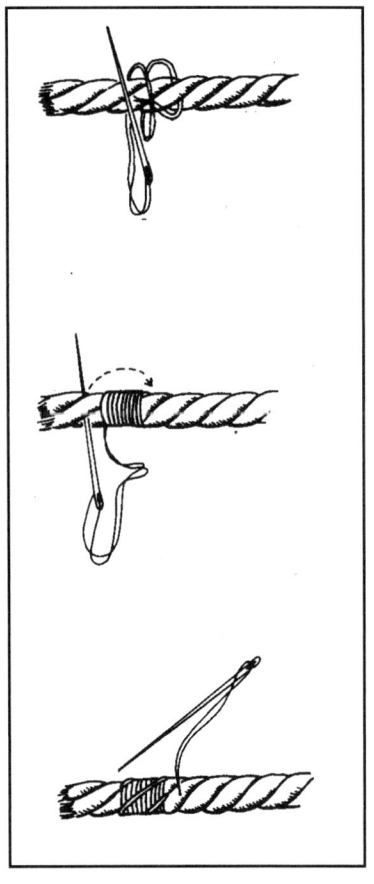

NEEDLE WHIPPING

BACK SPLICING

Another way to prevent three-strand line from unlaying is by back splicing. This technique works well and looks great on docking lines and even some heavier lines. Since back splicing almost doubles the end of the line's diameter, the line may not pass through blocks and eyes. This may be good or not so good, depending upon how the line is used.

28. WHIPPING AND SPLICING

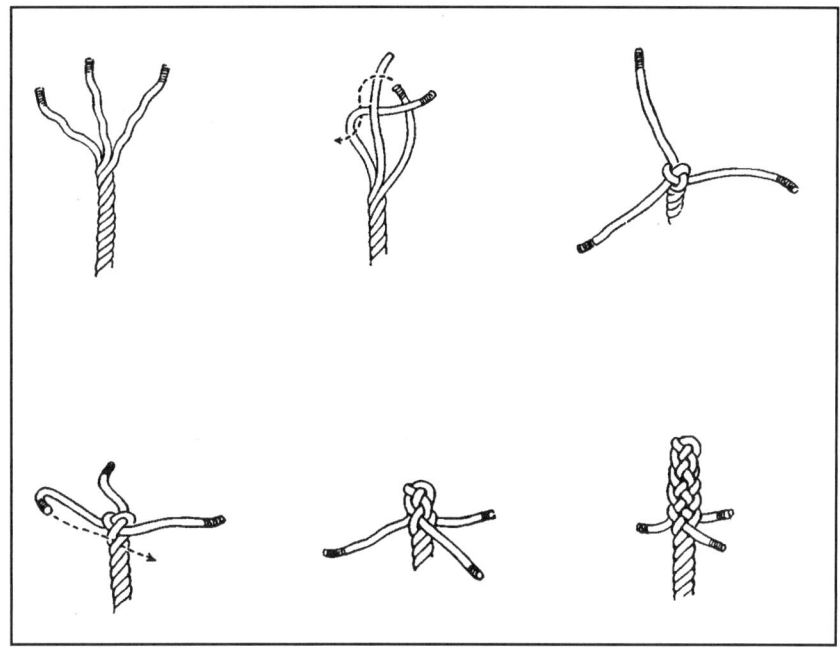

BACK-SPLICING

Back splicing starts with a crown knot, which is very simple and is most easily described by illustration. Moving counterclockwise, each strand of unlaid line is crossed over its neighbor on the left, with the final strand enclosed in a bight. The strands are drawn tight and emerge from the bottom of the knot, ready for back splicing.

To back splice, working from left to right, you bring one of the crown knot's strands over a laid strand of the standing line and under the next. This process is repeated with the other two remaining strands, completing a series of three over and unders. The working strands are pulled snug and the series of three over and unders, with a snugging in between, is repeated until the strands are too short to work.

ROPE TO CHAIN SPLICING

In addition to finishing off three-strand line in a unique nautical fashion, a crown knot and back splice is an excellent method for attaching rope to chain without the use of a thimble. A perfect application is a combination rope and chain anchor rode. If you have a windlass with a rope-chain gypsy, hands-free operation demands a proper rope-to-chain splice. Thimbles and shackles won't go through without jamming. They even can hang up in bow rollers.

In this application, the crown knot is tied through the first link of the chain and the strands are then back spliced into the line. Properly done, the line is spliced tight enough to the chain so as not to allow any movement, thus eliminating chafe potential. Any movement that does take place is between the other links of the chain.

EYE SPLICE

If a crown knot and back splice combination is not employed, a properly executed and snug eye splice is required around the thimble in a rope-and-chain anchor rode to insure that it doesn't pop out. Also, eye splices are what make the loops at the ends of docking lines. It is the strongest rope loop and one that can easily be mastered with a little practice.

Unlay the line for a distance of approximately 12 times the line's diameter. To keep the line from further unraveling, it's a good idea to put a temporary clove hitch or whipping at the point where the strands begin to unlay. This hitch or whipping should be removed after the splice is formed.

Bring the unlayed working end of the line up to form a loop. Untwist the standing part of the line at the point where the splice is to start. All tucks are made from right to left and against the lay of the line.

Pass the middle unlaid strand under one of the strands in the line. Pass the left unlaid strand over the strand that the middle unlaid

28. WHIPPING AND SPLICING

strand went under, and under the next strand in the line to the left. With the loop turned over, pass the remaining unlaid strand from right to left under the last laid strand. With the loop turned back over to its starting position, pull all working strands tight.

From this point on, working from right to left, in a series of three over and unders with a snugging pull in between, the unlaid strands are braided into the line until they are too short to work. The ends can then be trimmed off and the splice made fair by rolling it under foot or pounding it gently with a wooden or rubber mallet.

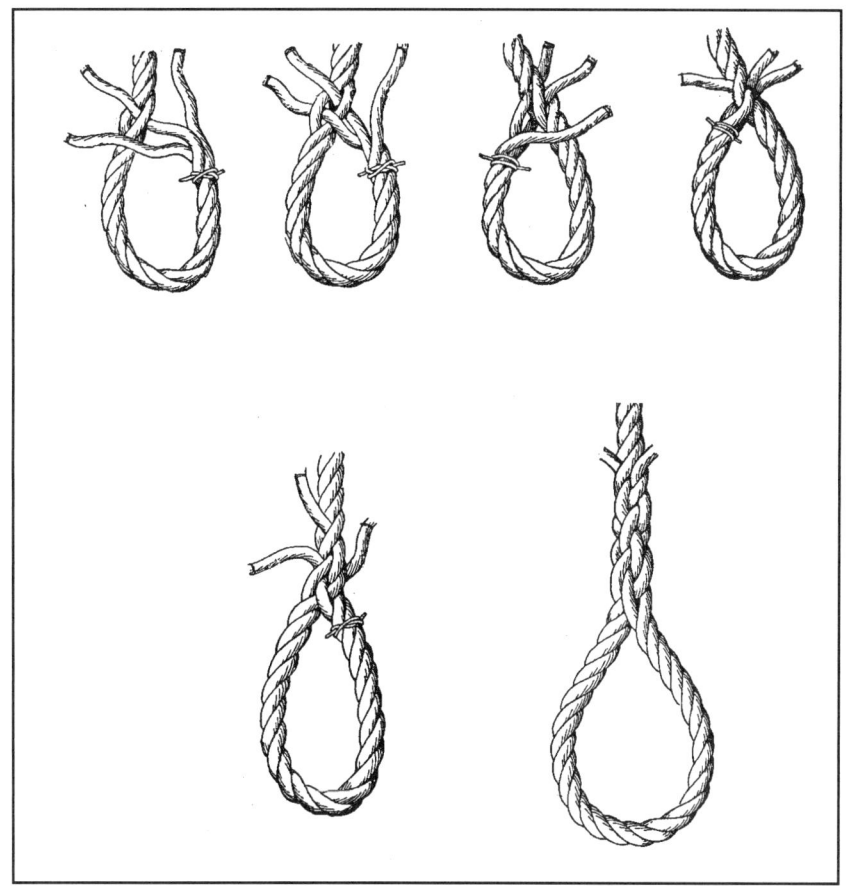

EYE SPLICE

ARTS OF THE SAILOR

Whipping and splicing are just two of the many skills born of necessity and nurtured through the centuries by riggers, sailmakers, and able-bodied seamen. While old as the romantic Age of Sail, these traditional skills still find application on today's modern boats.

CHAPTER 29

TACKLE

On a sailboat, rigging is the collective term used to describe all the lines, wires, and gear used to support the mast and to control the spars and sails. Rigging is divided into two categories: standing rigging, which supports; and running rigging, which controls. Common to both is an old-fashioned mechanical appliance called tackle.

BLOCKS AND TACKLES

A block is simply a nautical pulley. It consists of a sheave or roller, which turns on either a pin or bearings, between two wooden, metal, or plastic cheeks. Depending upon the number of sheaves, the block can be a single, double, triple, and so on. In addition to simply redirecting lines, blocks combine with rope to form tackle. It is tackle that performs the work by increasing the pulling power (mechanical advantage).

The following terms are commonly used in conjunction with tackle:

- Fall: the rope that is passed through the blocks
- Fall End: the end of the rope to which power is applied
- Standing Part/End: the end of the rope that is fixed
- Standing Block: a block that is fixed to a permanent structure

- Running Part: the portion of the rope that is not fixed and moves when power is applied
- Running Block: a block that is attached to the object to be moved
- Overhaul: to separate the two blocks
- Round In: to bring the two blocks together
- Two Blocks: both blocks are tight together
- Reeve: to pass a rope through a block and over a sheave
- Becket: a block with a stationary eye to which a rope (the standing end) is made fast

THE ADVANTAGE

Tackle affords excellent power for pulls of a short distance, such as the boom vang, main sheet, and Cunningham. Because of the multiple falls, tackle also lessens the line load, thus allowing the use of smaller diameter rope.

The power gained by using tackle is referred to as its mechanical advantage. This increase in power is commonly expressed as a ratio of force to weight necessary for lifting. This ratio can be easily calculated by counting the number of falls leading to and from the moveable block of the tackle. The number obtained is the theoretical number of times that the power is increased—theoretical, because power lost through friction is not accounted for. The loss of power attributable to friction will vary depending upon the type of pins and bearings, lubrication, sheave diameter, and line used.

The power gained through the use of tackle is achieved at the expense of distance. There is a direct correlation between mechanical advantage and the amount of rope that must be pulled. For example, using a 4 to 1 tackle, one must pull 4 feet of rope to move an object 1 foot. This imposes a practical limit on the use of multiple purchase tackles.

29. TACKLE

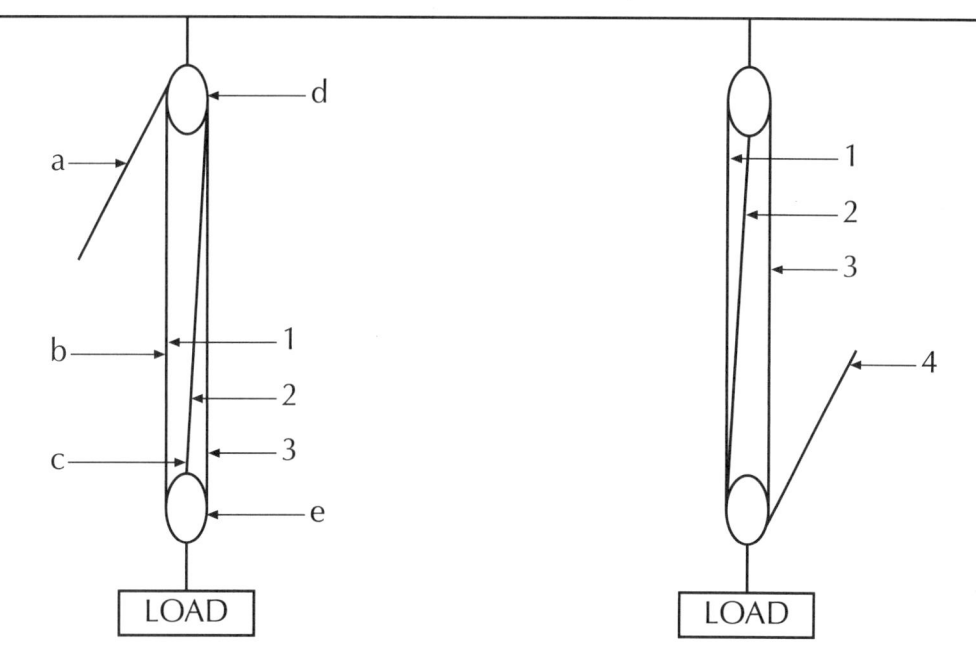

1:3 Mechanical Advantage   1:4 Mechanical Advantage

a — fall end
b — running part (of the fall)
c — standing part (attached to the becket)
d — standing block
e — running block

THE NUMBER OF FALLS LEADING TO AND FROM THE MOVEABLE BLOCK
DETERMINES THE THEORETICAL MECHANICAL ADVANTAGE (IGNORING FRICTION).

TYPES OF TACKLE

Tackles are commonly named according to the number of sheaves in the blocks that comprise the tackle (single, two-fold, three-fold, and so forth). Sometimes their names are synonymous with the work they perform (main sheet tackle, vang tackle, etc.) or from names that have been handed down from the past (gun tackle, luff tackle, and the like). Tackles that are routinely found aboard cruising sailboats are:

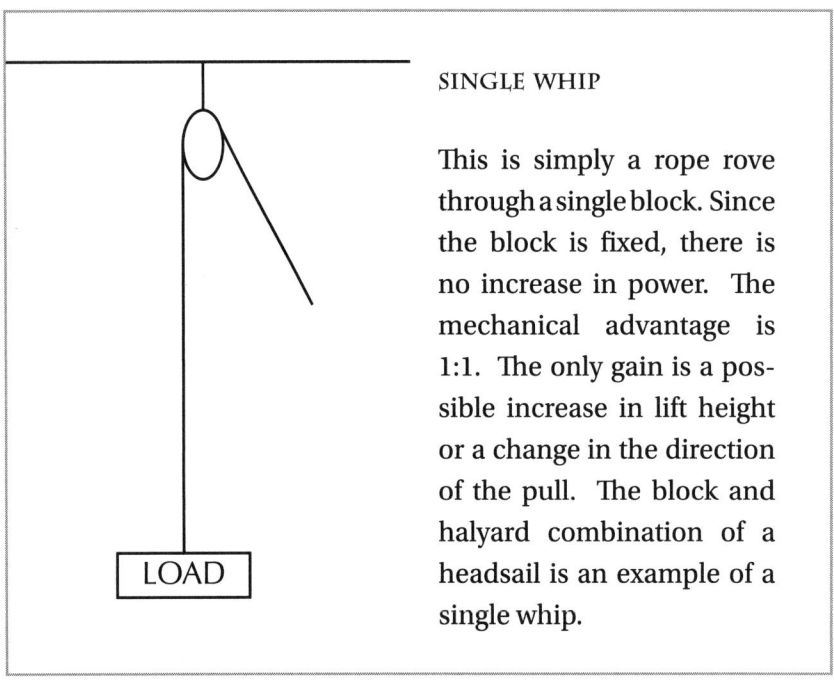

SINGLE WHIP

This is simply a rope rove through a single block. Since the block is fixed, there is no increase in power. The mechanical advantage is 1:1. The only gain is a possible increase in lift height or a change in the direction of the pull. The block and halyard combination of a headsail is an example of a single whip.

29. TACKLE

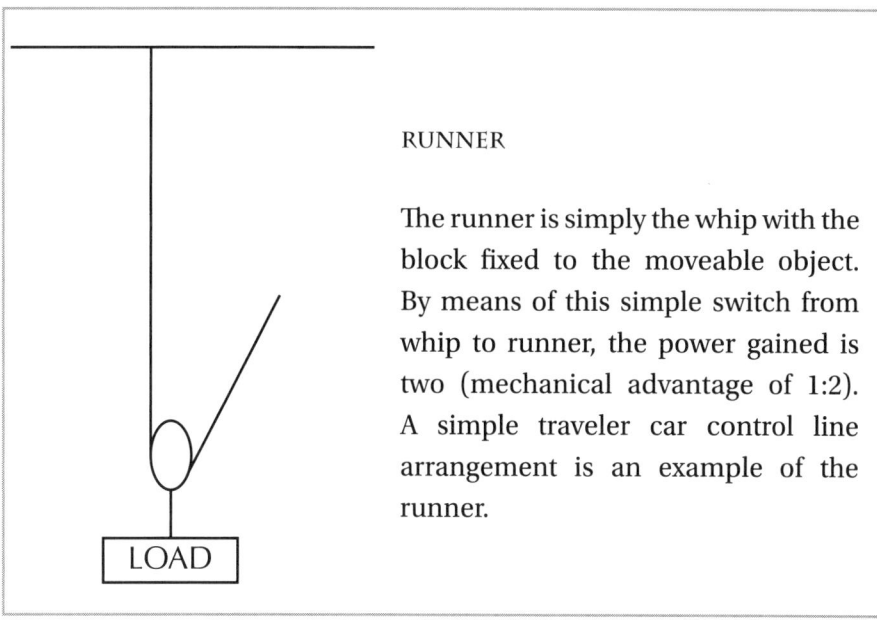

RUNNER

The runner is simply the whip with the block fixed to the moveable object. By means of this simple switch from whip to runner, the power gained is two (mechanical advantage of 1:2). A simple traveler car control line arrangement is an example of the runner.

GUN TACKLE

This tackle consists of two single blocks, one with a becket. If the lower block is moveable, the mechanical advantage is 1:2. The mechanical advantage is increased to 1:3, should the upper block be moveable. In the Age of Sail, this form of tackle was attached to gun carriages and used to train the smooth bore cannons on enemy ships. This type of tackle finds many uses, including Cunninghams and outhauls.

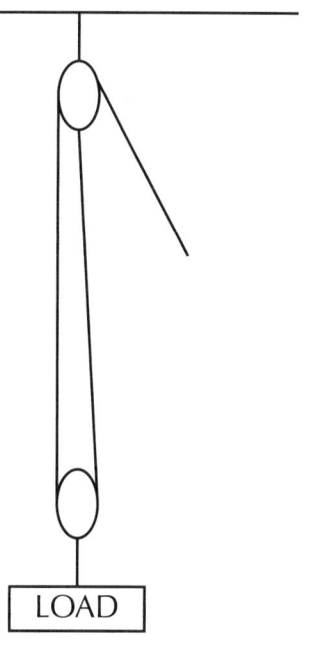

LUFF TACKLE

This consists of a single block and a double block. The standing part of the fall is made fast to the becket on the single block. The fall is then alternately rove through the sheaves of the two blocks. When the single block is moveable, the mechanical advantage is 1:3. When it's the double block that moves, the power gained is four. Backstay adjusters and vangs are two examples where luff tackle can be used.

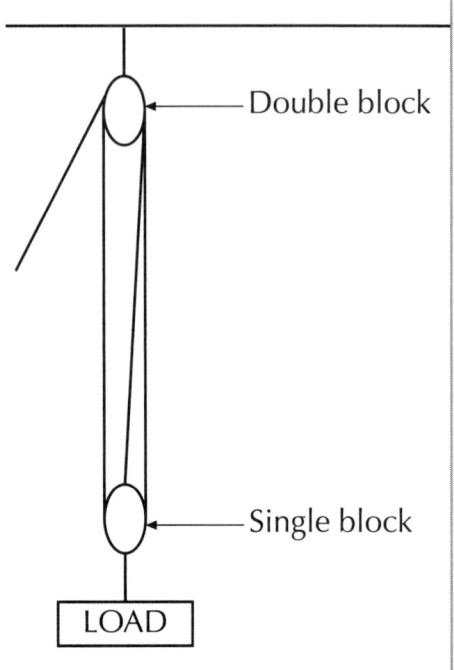

TWO-FOLD OR DOUBLE PURCHASE

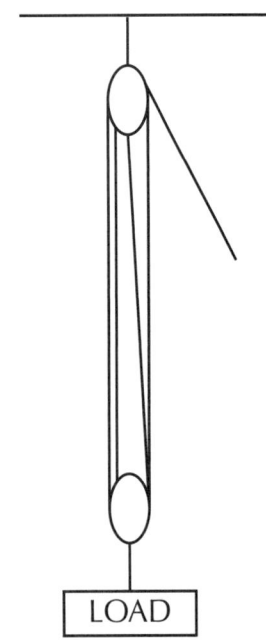

Two double blocks rove together make up the two-fold tackle. The power that is gained using a double purchase is either four or five, depending on which of the blocks is moveable. Mainsheets are excellent candidates for two-fold tackle.

Tackles in excess of the two-fold purchase are becoming more and more common aboard modern sailboats. One of the most common is the three-fold purchase, which consists of two triple blocks. This tackle is often used on mainsheets and backstay adjusters.

OPTIMIZING EFFICIENCY

In order to obtain the greatest mechanical efficiency, the following four points should be kept in mind when installing and using tackle:

1. The fall end should lead from the block with the most sheaves.
2. If both blocks have the same number of sheaves, lead the fall end from the moveable block.
3. The block with the greatest number of sheaves should be the moveable block.
4. When using a triple block, reeve the fall end through the center sheave, thus avoiding potential binding.

Just as electronics and satellite technology have become more dominant players in the field of navigation, modern winches and even hydraulics have taken on a portion of the line-handling load. However, good old-fashioned tackle still remains a simple, foolproof way to pull an object a short distance.

CHAPTER 30

A HANDY HEAVING LINE

Being a skipper of a small trailerable sailboat, I spend considerable sailing time on various inland lakes, reservoirs, and other smaller bodies of water. One common thread they all share is the lack of on-the-water assistance, especially towing. It boggles the mind how often fellow sailors/boaters are in need of a tow. I once belonged to a small sailing club of 50 members that routinely experienced at least four "loose" boats a year. Add to this the fishermen whose motors run out of gas or won't start, and a Good Samaritan can keep pretty busy.

So at least once a year I find myself volunteering to go aboard someone else's boat to assist in a tow. And without fail, a multitude of well intentioned but ineffective techniques are routinely employed in trying to pass the towline from one boat to the other. The last time, I was prepared. You should have seen the mouths open in awe when contact was made with the first toss. *Not really awe, but you get the picture.* I used a heaving line.

A proper heaving line is about 50 feet in length, made of 3/16-inch to 5/16-inch diameter line, and has a monkey's fist knot tied on one end. While the knot's bulk and round shape make it ideal for this application, the addition of a little weight increases the heaving line's accuracy and distance. This is achieved by inserting a rubber or wooden ball into the knot as it is being tied. Rubber or wood also aids in flotation, which is very important if the line is used in a MOB

30. A HANDY HEAVING LINE

situation. A 1¼-inch diameter ball works well with 3/16-inch line and a 1½-inch diameter ball fits nicely into a knot made with 5/16-inch line.

HEAVING LINE WITH MONKEY FIST KNOT
AND THE WORKING END OF THE LINE
WHIPPED AND SEIZED TO THE STANDING PART.

To fashion a monkey's fist knot, take a bight of the rope about 5 feet from one end and wrap 4 turns around the four fingers of your left hand. Be sure not to cross the wraps over on another, but rather allow them to lie next to each other. Once this is complete, pass the working end of the line between your fingers and take 4 turns around the first set of turns. At this point, remove the knot from your hand and insert the weight. Once the weight is in place and surrounded by the two sets of turns, pass the working end of the line inside of the knot and wrap the second set of turns and the weight with 4 turns. With the completion of this last set of turns, you now have a loose monkey's fist knot that needs to be dressed. Start with the second set of turns. Working in both directions, begin taking out the slack. While dressing the knot, align the turns next to one another to maintain the knot's symmetry and uniformity. Once the knot is snug, finish off the working end. The working end should be no longer than 2 feet. It can be spliced into the standing part of the line or its end whipped and seized to the standing part. Lastly, place a seizing around the two lines close to the monkey's fist knot.

With the heaving line completed, go outside and practice, making accuracy and distance your goal. Secure the bitter end to something stationary. Coil the line in fairly large loops. Hold these loops loosely in one hand and grasp the weighted knot end, at the splice or seizing, in the other hand. Swing the weighted knot end in a vertical circle and throw underhanded. Allow the coils to reel off your hand unobstructed. If the line tends to kink, correct this by tying it between two trees and pulling repeatedly on the center portion or by affixing a weight in the center and allowing the line to stretch for 24 hours. Once all the kinks have been removed, allowing the line to uncoil smoothly, try heaving the line again. Practice makes perfect.

CHAPTER 31

ROPE MATS

The old-school sailor had a complete repertoire of knots, both plain and fancy. The fact that some knots were beautiful or decorative was secondary to their usefulness. The one infallible sign announcing to all who trod that they were on a sailing ship, or for that matter in the home of a sailor, was the presence of a rope mat. For hundreds of years, rope mats were found on every sailing vessel and well-kept yacht. They were primarily used as chafing gear, to provide skidproof footing for the helmsman, at the companionway threshold, and on the gangway. Many of these mats were quite decorative and all were fashioned by able-bodied seamen. However, in recent times, this art has been neglected by yachtsmen and is rarely seen.

Fear not. With a little effort, the modern sailor can again benefit from the functionality and beauty of the rope mat. Here are three mats that can be easily fashioned and that will add functionality and a bit of nautical flare to both your boat and home.

FLEMISH COIL

The simplest and most basic rope mat is called the Flemish coil. It can be fashioned in either a round or oval configuration. This mat is nothing more than a rope that has been coiled carefully, with the turns lying close, flat, and smoothly next to one another. Once the

Flemish coil has been laid to the desired size, the turns of the coil are stitched together. A simple overhand stitch, using a single length of heavy polyester or nylon thread and a large sail needle, works well. If the stitches are placed beneath the surface between the coils, the mat is reversible and can be used either side up. While it is possible to sew the turns together as the rope is being coiled, this is not advisable, for the end result is usually a distorted, lumpy mat that does not lie flat. Therefore, it is best to first coil and then stitch.

Not only is the Flemish coil the easiest mat to fashion, but it is also the plainest of mats. One way to dress it up is by using colored line. Another way is to start with a decorative flat knot in the center and finish up with the Flemish coil.

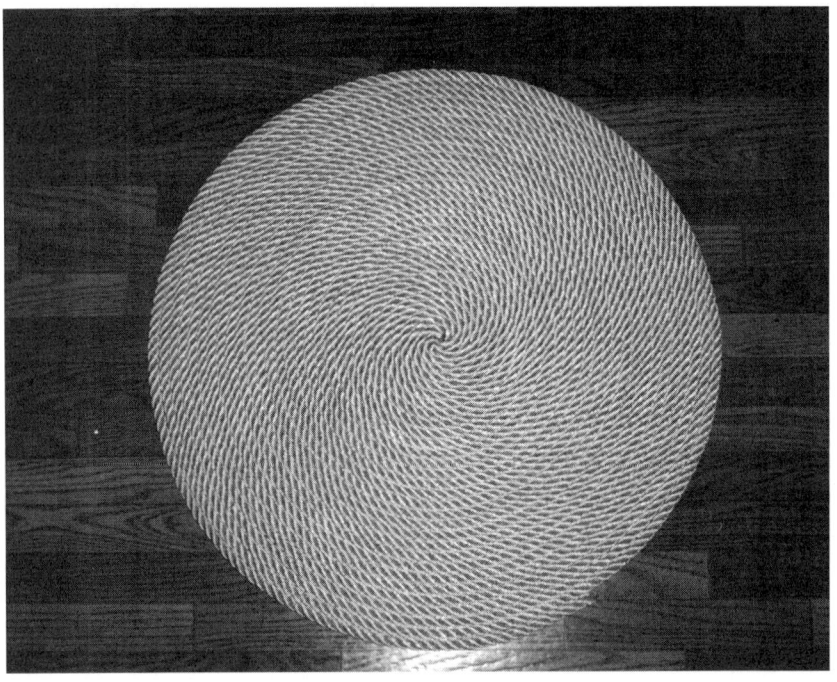

FLEMISH COIL (IN THE ROUND)

31. ROPE MATS

OCEAN PLAT

While it may look involved, the ocean plat decorative knot can easily be fabricated in about a half hour's time.

Since the weave of the ocean plat crosses over and under itself, the knot thickness is doubled. Therefore, when incorporating the ocean plat within the Flemish coil, it is best to use rope that is one diameter size smaller than that used for the Flemish coil. Approximately 35 feet of ⅜-inch rope makes for a striking triple-passed ocean plat decorative knot. Around this, coils of ½-inch rope are laid to achieve the desired mat size. The knot will hold together without sewing; however, it must be stitched to the coil where it touches the coil. Also, the coil itself needs to be stitched together as described previously.

To begin the ocean plat, start with a bight at approximately 12 feet from one end of the rope. Arrange the rope loosely as shown in the accompanying picture series. This leaves one long end and one short end. Weave the long end to the location from where the short end emerges. Continue to weave the long end through the knot, making two complete circuits. This will result in a triple-pass ocean plat decorative knot. At this point it should look like the finished knot, albeit loose and maybe a bit lopsided. Finish the knot by starting with a bight anywhere in the knot and begin to take out the slack. Work in both directions until it lies close together and the knot is symmetrical. Once this is achieved, the ends should be whipped and stitched to the knot's underside. To complete the mat, add the Flemish coil as previously described. The completed knot will flatten out with use. Pounding it with a wooden mallet will accelerate the flattening process.

THE OCEAN PLAT IS A BIT TRICKY TO START.
HOWEVER, ONCE YOU'RE SURE OF WHICH PART OF THE LINE
GOES OVER AND WHICH PART GOES UNDER,
YOU SIMPLY FOLLOW THE PATTERN AROUND,
WEAVING OVER AND UNDER FOR TWO MORE FULL ROUNDS.

31. ROPE MATS

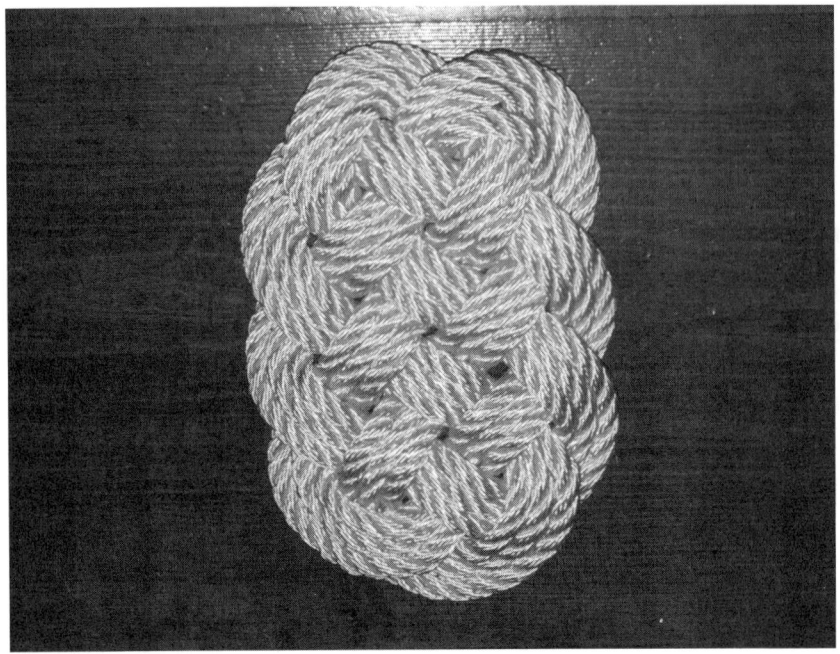

LADDER-STEP MAT

The last of the rope mats is the ladder-step mat. It is sometimes referred to as the sailor's true lover mat weave. It is fashioned in much the same way as the ocean plat.

Approximately 25 feet of 5/16-inch rope can easily be transformed into a four-pass ladder-step mat. If you want to improve the mat's water absorbing capabilities, use cotton rope such as good quality clothesline. Begin by laying the rope up as illustrated in the accompanying picture series. Pass one end of the rope in a complete over-and-under circuit around the knot. Throughout this process, remember to keep the knot loose. Repeat the weaving for a total of three more passes, four in all. Whatever end of the rope you're using, always lay the next pass against the same side of the previous

31. ROPE MATS

rope. Avoid crossing over. Snug up the knot by removing the slack as was done with the ocean plat. Keep the knot symmetrical during this process. The ends should be whipped and stitched to the knot's underside, where they are hidden.

With a little patience and practice, a complete set of these mats should take about two hours, from start to finish. Once done, place one of the mats in the cockpit beneath the helmsman's feet, another at the companionway threshold, and the third at the foot of the companionway ladder to absorb water from dripping foul weather gear. On second thought, maybe three's not enough. What about the main saloon, just outside of the head, and at the foot of the v-berth, to name a few others.

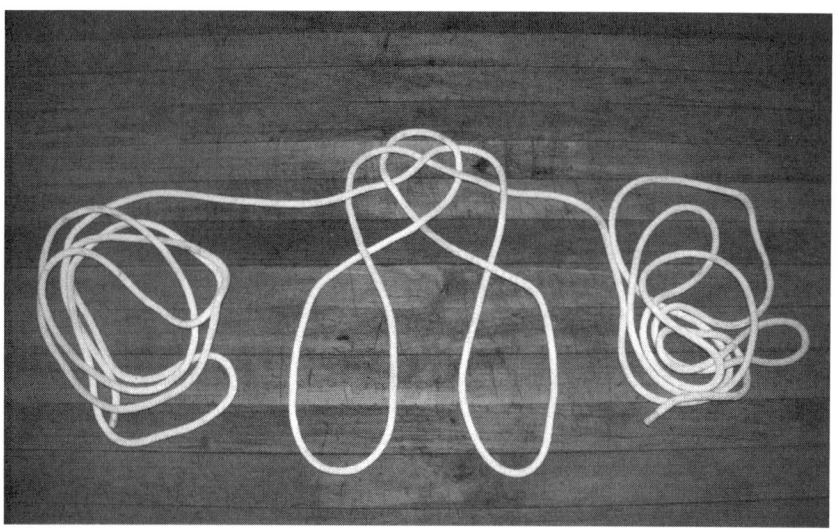

THE LADDER-STEP IS SIMILAR IN CONCEPT TO THE OCEAN PLAT.
THE KEY TO SUCCESS IS THE INTRICATE SETUP.

VI: MARLINSPIKE SEAMANSHIP

31. ROPE MATS

SECTION VII

YOUR TRAILER SAILER AT REST

No book, pamphlet, seminar, lecture, or discussion with an expert, either genuine or of the dockside variety, can teach a novice skipper the technique and art of anchoring. It must be learned (taught) on the water and it must take into consideration a host of variables. These include the boat, the subsurface, the weather and sea conditions, the type of ground tackle, and the abilities of the skipper and crew. This section is provided to give the reader both a glimpse and a few novel hints into this ancient, yet modern technique.

CHAPTER 32

ANCHORS

Just like anything else, proper anchoring begins with the right equipment. Although new anchor designs seem to crop up on a continual basis, a few have successfully withstood the test of time. It is with these chosen few that we will spend the bulk of this chapter.

The very first step in selecting the proper ground tackle (ground tackle is the collective term for anchor, chain, line, swivels, and shackles) is to carefully mate it to the size of your boat and your anticipated sailing grounds. As a general rule, anchor size (weight) is determined by the size of the boat: The bigger the boat, the bigger the anchor. If you expect to encounter different bottom types, you should carry or have available more than one type of anchor. Aboard *Splash* we carry three anchors, each of a different type. One is a lunch hook and the other two are slightly oversized.

Generally speaking, there are two basic anchor types: the lightweight or fluke-type and the heavy burying-type.

FLUKE-TYPE ANCHORS

The most popular style of anchor is the fluke-type, with the most common being the Danforth and Fortress. Two long, sharp pivoting flukes and a long shank easily identify this style of anchor. Most fluke-type anchors are either constructed of steel, high tensile steel,

32. ANCHORS

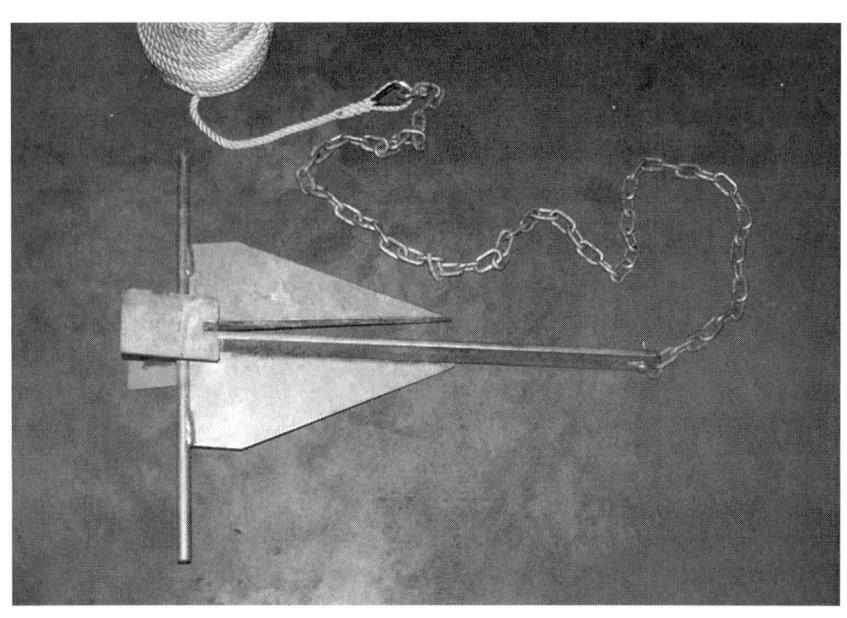

THE MOST POPULAR STYLE OF ANCHOR IS THE FLUKE-TYPE,
WITH THE MOST COMMON BEING THE DANFORTH (PICTURED ABOVE)
AND FORTRESS (PICTURED BELOW)

or, in the case of the Fortress, alloyed aluminum. The high tensile Danforth is said to be more effective because its points will remain sharper and penetrate better than its steel cousin. Being fabricated out of an aluminum alloy, the Fortress is both strong and very light. This allows the use of a much larger anchor. This is a good thing.

Most fluke-type anchors perform best in sandy or muddy bottoms. A round rod situated across the anchor's crown prevents the anchor from rotating on the bottom as the flukes bury themselves. The fluke-type anchor releases easily when pulled from a different direction. This is because its flukes pivot so that the shank can be pulled at a more vertical angle. Anchors in this category offer excellent holding-to-weight ratio and a significant amount of straight-line holding power. To perform properly, they require maximum scope. Fluke-type anchors are unsuitable for rock or coral bottoms and can foul on branches and underwater debris and on their own rode as the rode swings about in a changing current.

Fluke-type anchors do not store well in bow rollers; however, their light weight, especially the aluminum version, makes them easy to hang them from the pulpit or lift aboard, where they'll stow flat on deck. Speaking of on deck, vinyl-coated models are available to protect your deck from the anchor's points. The vinyl coating also inhibits the anchor from penetrating a bottom harder than soft mud. Leave the vinyl-coated version at home or, better yet, on the store's shelf.

BURYING-TYPE ANCHORS

The most common heavy burying-type anchors are the CQR, the Delta, and the Bruce. These anchors are often classified as plow-type anchors, especially the CQR and the Delta.

The CQR is manufactured in Scotland of drop forged steel with a plow-shaped fluke and a hinged shank. It is so named because, when spoken, the letters sound like the word secure.

32. ANCHORS

The CQR works well on a variety of bottoms, including sand and mud. The combination of its plow design and weight makes it more effective in weedy bottoms than the lighter weight fluke-type anchors. Like most other burying-type anchors, the greater the pull, the deeper the CQR buries. Its shank pivots side to side, while remaining parallel to its fluke (opposite to what a fluke-type anchor does). This enables the CQR to remain buried during moderate changes in wind or current direction. The manufacturer claims that the CQR will reset itself if a change in pull trips it. Its design also allows for a relatively easy release, when pulled vertically. The CQR is not foolproof. It can resist digging when pulled through thick weeds and it slips through soft mud.

Because it is more three-dimensional than many lightweight anchors, the CQR is more difficult to stow and is best carried on a bow roller. For years, the CQR has been the choice of the cruising community.

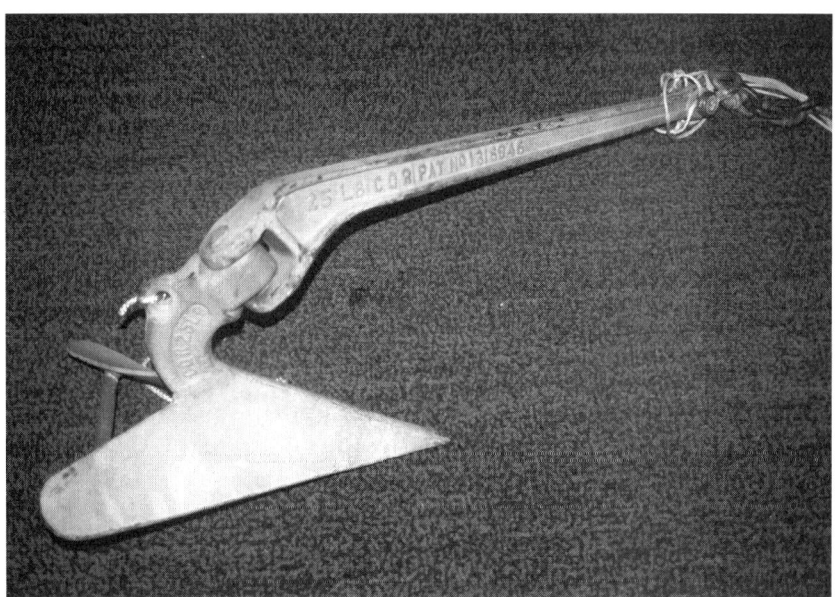

FOR YEARS, THE CQR HAS BEEN THE CHOICE OF THE CRUISING COMMUNITY.

The Delta, also of Scottish origin, is the modified cousin of the CQR. It is of robust construction with more fluke area per weight than the CQR and lacks the hinged shank. Even without the moving joint, the Delta has good veering capability. It possesses a sharp, fixed point and a low center of gravity. This allows the Delta to better penetrate weeds and grass. In some instances the anchor can foul on underwater debris. In doing so, it will collect debris beneath its shank. The Delta is much handier to stow on a bow roller than on deck, where its design allows for self-launching. While it is a relatively new addition to the group, the Delta is gaining wide acceptance.

WHILE IT IS RELATIVELY NEW, THE DELTA IS GAINING WIDE ACCEPTANCE

The Bruce anchor was originally developed to moor gas and oil-drilling rigs in the North Sea. The scaled-down version is becoming popular with sailors. Its super-strong, one-piece construction features a scooping plow with three rounded flukes. This design allows the anchor to hold fast, even with a 360-degree directional change in pull. Reportedly, the Bruce is designed to reset itself within two shank lengths. Like the other burying-type anchors, when pulled vertically the Bruce loosens easily. Since its flukes are not sharp enough to effectively penetrate, this anchor is not ideal for grass or hard sand. Its one flaw is the anchor's ability to foul on a rock that fits neatly into its three-fluked grasp. While the Bruce fits nicely in a bow roller, its flukes take up lots of space in all three dimensions. Even so, the Bruce is widely used by charter fleets and is becoming popular with cruisers.

THE BRUCE IS WIDELY USED BY CHARTER FLEETS AND BECOMING POPULAR WITH CRUISERS.

OTHER TYPES

The five anchors previously discussed probably account for better than 80 percent of the anchor types in active use today. Most of the remaining 20 percent are variations or permutations of these five favorites and include, but are not limited to, the following:

The Bulwagga anchor has three large flukes that, no matter how the anchor is oriented, will always be properly aligned to dig into the bottom. Its center-located shank pivots to help keep the load on the two working flukes. It's an awkward piece of ground tackle that might be useful as a kedge anchor, provided the boat has a large stowage space.

The Claw anchor is nothing more than a Bruce look-alike produced by Lewmar. Simpson-Lawrence of Scotland manufactures the Bruce.

The Fisherman, closely related to the Kedge, Yachtsman, and Herreshoff anchors, was the traditional anchor-type used during the days of sail. It's strongly made and good at hooking onto things. It must be much heavier than burying-type anchors to achieve equivalent holding power. Unless it can be disassembled, and most can't, it's difficult to stow.

The Flook resembles a flying wing. According to the manufacturer, launch this pantograph hook from your boat's bow and it will glide gracefully down to the bottom at a 5:1 scope angle. The makers claim that the Flook anchor will hold boats up to 25 feet in normal-to-strong conditions.

The Hydrobubble incorporates the concept of the plow anchor but adds a broader fluke and an air-filled bubble to the shank. Upon deployment, the bubble forces the anchor to meet the bottom at the correct angle. A new variation of the anchor has a release latch on the fluke. If the Hydrobubble gets fouled, the release is activated and the anchor is retrieved.

The Manson Supreme is a product of Plastimo USA. It has a scoop-like, sharply pointed fluke, a rigid shank, and a roll bar that supposedly ensures that the anchor is always properly oriented to the bottom.

The Northill is a lightweight cousin of the Fisherman. It's made of aluminum and offers a high strength-to-weight ratio. The Northill exhibits the same handling vices as the Fisherman anchor.

The old Navy anchor is a heavy stockless device. If it's heavy enough to hold, it is too heavy to handle; and if its weight is kept within reason, it cannot be trusted to hold.

West Marine's Oceane is similar to the Manson Supreme; however, it has a C-shaped shank that's attached at the front of the scoop and does away with the roll bar. The Oceane's unique shape makes it difficult to stow on a bow roller.

The Prasolux is a German-made version of the Bruce fabricated out of stainless steel.

The Rocna is almost identical to the Manson Marine and one would suspect that it affords similar performance.

The Sarca anchor consists of a large triangular blade with a sharp point, a roll bar, and a fixed shank with a slot cut into its entire length. This slot allows the shackle to slide forward during retrieval.

The French-designed Spade closely resembles the Oceane, but with a longer, less pronounced C-shaped shank; this anchor's fluke is heavily weighted close to its point.

The Super Max is designed for use with an all-nylon rode, as opposed to chain. It is a variation of the Bruce with two notable exceptions. Its three flukes are much less pronounced, thus resulting in one large scoop-like fluke. Also, the shank of the Super Max is adjustable. This adjustable shank provides three different angles for different bottom conditions.

The stainless steel Wasi has a roll bar, a flat, heavy triangular blade, and a shank angled at about 30 degrees.

The XYZ anchor exhibits a bat-wing design and features a short shank with a knob that helps the anchor flip over if it lands upside down on the bottom. The shank and blade can be disassembled for stowage.

Selecting the anchor(s) for your trailer sailer depends to a large degree on where you will be sailing and under what conditions. With so many anchors to choose from, the process may seem daunting.

Don't despair; select your primary and your secondary from the proven five. If you plan to have a third anchor, anything's game.

It's a good idea to formulate a plan on what anchor(s) to use where; how to quickly, easily, and safely make changes; and how to deploy a second anchor in the event that your primary anchor fails.

There's more to anchoring than just stopping the boat and tossing the hook overboard.

CHAPTER 33

ANCHOR RODE BAG

One of the most convenient features found on many newer boats is a dedicated anchor locker located on the foredeck. My boat, an O'Day 222, unfortunately lacks this amenity, as do many older trailer sailers. When I purchased the boat, I found the anchor along with its rode "stored" in the lazarette, beneath a tangle of PFDs, fenders, and enough docking lines to tie off the QEII. Recalling that someone once said, "good seamanship is nine-tenths preparation and one-tenth application," I set about developing a better storage system for my ground tackle.

My goal was to create an arrangement that would afford easy access, provide protection, and be out of the way when not in use. After considering several ideas, I decided to suspend the anchor from the bow pulpit using stainless steel brackets designed for that exact purpose. With half of my ground tackle stored, I directed my attention to the other half, the 150-foot nylon and chain rode, which I had temporarily stored in a paper bag. Epiphany!

Using that same #20 paper bag as the basis for a pattern of what was to become my anchor rode bag, I added a zippered lid and extended the "back" side of the bag, both up and down. The "up" portion was extended 6" and when rolled in half and zippered to itself, formed a sleeve, which would be used to wrap around the top rail of the bow pulpit. The 4" "down" portion was rounded and a large grommet placed near the center's edge. By adding a short length of line to the grommet, the bag could be secured to the base of the pulpit. To finish it off, two grommets were equally spaced in the bag's bottom, one for drainage and one for the rode's bitter end to protrude from.

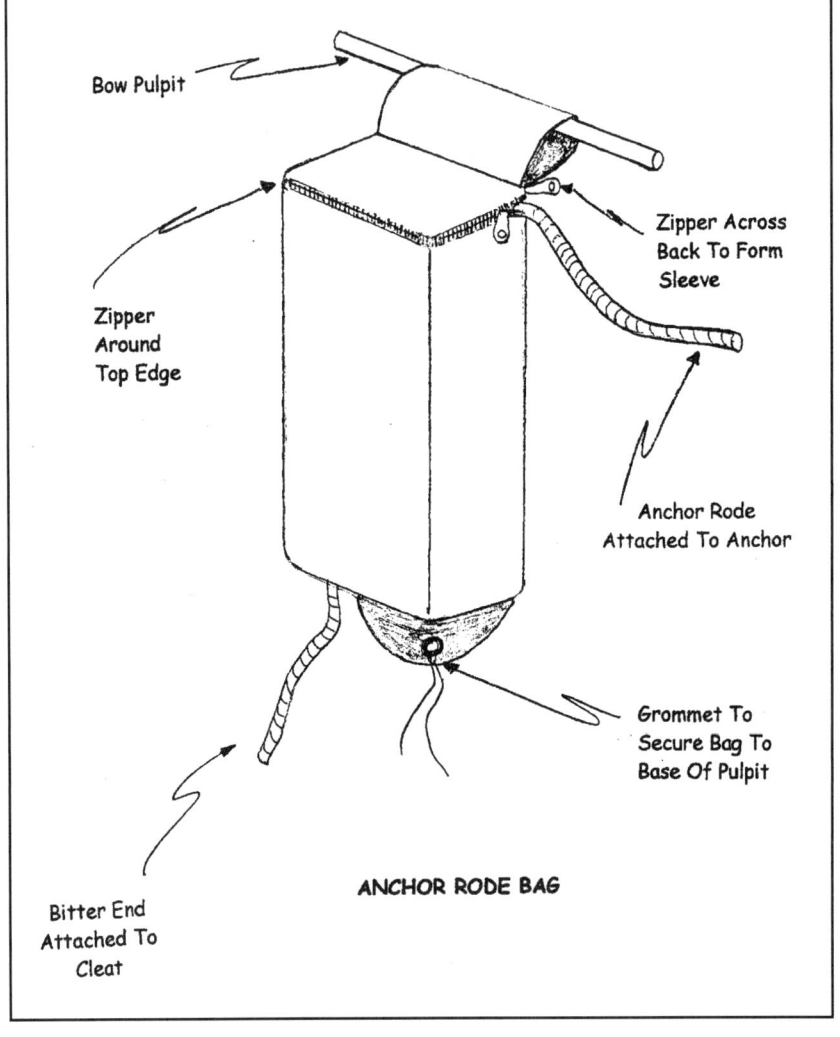

ANCHOR RODE BAG

33. ANCHOR RODE BAG

Once the pattern was complete, I took it to the local canvas shop and had it fabricated out of material matching my sail cover. In operation, I situate the bag close to the anchor, loop the sleeve around the bow pulpit's top rail, zipper it, and tie the bag's bottom to the pulpit's base. From the inside of the bag, I pass the bitter end of the rode through one of the grommets in the bag's bottom and secure it to a cleat. I then flake the rode into the bag and zipper the lid closed, leaving a short length of rode attached to the anchor to complete the system.

Having my ground tackle stored in this manner meets all the goals I established for easy access, protection, and discrete storage out of the way when not in use. By the way, using a #20 paper bag as a pattern provided more than enough room for the 150' of rode. I found the extra space to be a handy place to store gloves used to deploy and retrieve the anchor.

CHAPTER 34

MARKING THE ANCHOR RODE

It seemed that every time we anchored, the First Mate lamented that it was difficult to determine just how much rode had been paid out. Because of this, the accuracy in achieving the desired scope was often a by-guess-and-by-golly situation.

In order to eliminate this unknown before we dropped the hook again, we needed to develop a way to mark our anchor rode. What we came up with is a sailor's dream—uncomplicated, inexpensive, and accurate . . . plastic cable ties.

These simple, infinitely adjustable, self-locking nylon strips are easy to use, come in a variety of colors including fluorescent, are inexpensive (I bought a 1,200 piece assortment for under $5.00) and are downright tenacious in their grip.

Aboard *Splash* we have several anchors and three combination chain and rope rodes. Two of these are marked at 25-feet intervals using a three-color system, which is favored by the First Mate. Green is used at 25 feet and 50 feet, yellow at 75 feet and 100 feet, while red marks 125 feet and 150 feet. The first of each color is noted by the presence of one tie and the second by two ties.

Displaying a more nautical flare, the third rode, which is primarily a second backup and is sometimes used by the skipper as a stern anchor line, is calibrated every 30 feet in fathoms. Two colors are used, yellow for 5 fathoms and blue for 10.

While it may seem odd or even potentially confusing to employ two different systems on the same boat, we have yet to experience any problems or mix-ups. Eventually, we will most likely settle on one system we both feel comfortable with.

In actuality, we are using that third rode to experiment with the system's versatility, employing multiple colors and marking the rode in feet, meters, yards, and so forth. In our experiments, we have found that the cable ties work equally well on chain, twisted rope, and braided rope. Also, fluorescent ties are more easily seen in the dark.

While we don't have a windlass but rely on the Armstrong method of retrieval, we suspect that these plastic wonders will pass through a windlass without difficulty.

Having our anchor rodes essentially calibrated has taken some guesswork out of anchoring and has made it a little easier and less confusing. And as Martha Stewart would say, "That's a good thing."

CHAPTER 35

NORTH COAST PICK-UP BUOY

North Coast (Great Lakes) sailors can count on two distinct major seasons: sailing and snowing. The remaining two minor seasons are commissioning and decommissioning. One day I was experiencing the latter of the two major seasons, while clearing snow off my O'Day 222 (which was "moored" on her trailer in my backyard). To take my mind off the task at hand, I was mentally going down my sailing to-do list when I came to item #10: replace mooring pick-up buoy. At the same time, I mumbled to myself, "Wouldn't it be nice to have a handle on it like the one on this snow shovel?" As if on cue, a loud crack filled the air. Not paying full attention, I had wedged the snow shovel between a roller and the trailer frame and inadvertently (or maybe subconsciously) twisted and broken it. I now had the bright red handle I would need for my new mooring pick-up buoy. Off to the workshop I went, hoping that the unshoveled snow would melt by commissioning season.

The construction of my North Coast pick-up buoy is relatively simple and straightforward. The major components consist of a six-foot length of ½" PVC pipe, a two-foot piece of swim "noodle" with a hole through the center, a six-inch section of ½" wooden dowel, a galvanized eye bolt with wood screw end, and of course, the snow shovel handle. Fastening requires a small amount of epoxy and a couple of 1½" or 2" stainless steel machine screws with locking nuts.

To assemble, first slide the swim noodle onto the 6' length of PVC pipe. The noodle's exact location will ultimately depend on the weight of your mooring chain. This can easily be determined at the dock, where final adjustment/assembly can also be made. For instance, if you are using line instead of chain, it may be necessary to fill the lower third of pipe with BBs or add 3–4 links of heavy chain to the bottom eye. In either case, the goal is to have the pick-up buoy float straight out of the water.

Next, drill a hole into the end of a 3" piece of wooden dowel. After screwing the eyebolt into the hole, insert the dowel into the lower end of the PVC pipe, approximately ½" past flush. Use a 1½" stainless steel screw and nut to secure it in place. Fill the ½" space with epoxy, thus creating a watertight seal. At this point in the assembly process you may want to test out the buoy. If, after sliding the noodle up/down, the buoy does not float vertically when attached to the mooring line/chain, this is the time to add the links of chain or pour BBs down the pipe. If you use BBs, once the desired amount has been added, pour some epoxy down the pipe to secure them in place. Finally, insert the other 3" piece of dowel into the top of the pipe, sealing it with epoxy. This time use a stainless steel screw and nut to fasten the snow shovel handle through both the pipe and wooden plug.

Just as the Riviera has its Mediterranean mooring and the Caribbean its Bahamian anchoring, we Great Lakes sailors now have our North Coast pick-up buoy.

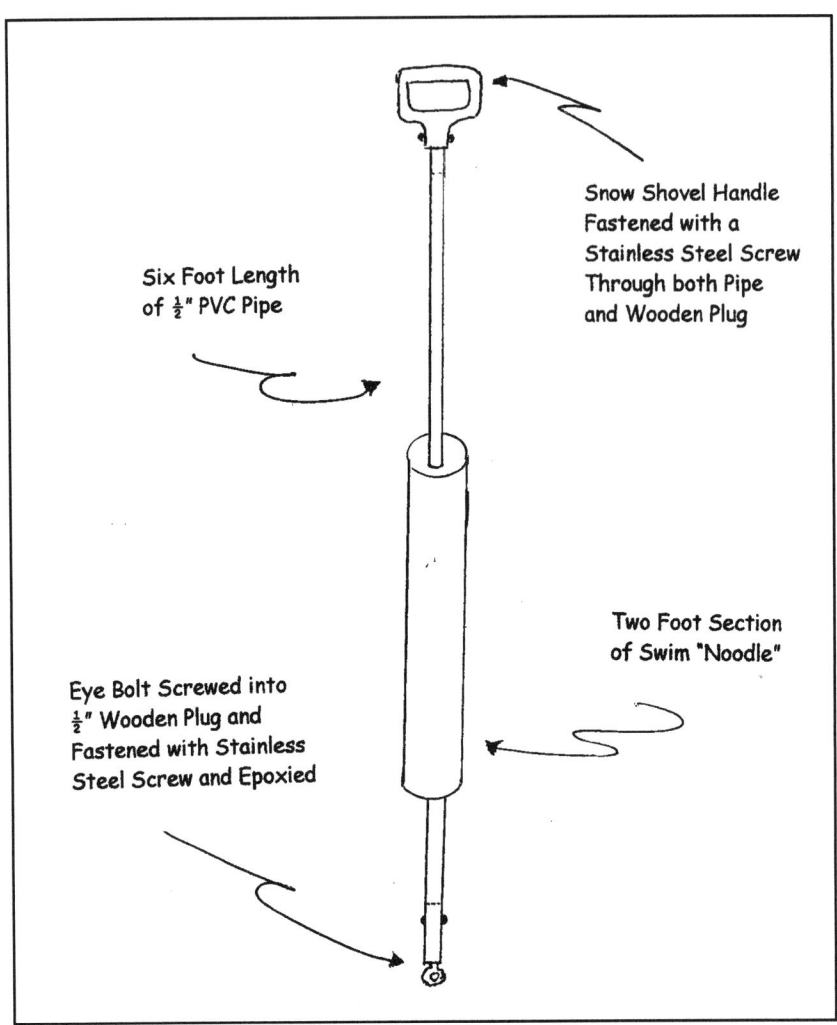

"North Coast" mooring pick-up buoy

SECTION VIII

LAUNCHING AND RETRIEVAL

Backing your trailer down a ramp to launch or even retrieve your boat can be intimidating. Patience and, above all, practice (trial and error) are required. Even though there are a number of techniques and pointers that seasoned trailer sailors may offer, none is better than the lessons experience will inevitably teach.

CHAPTER 36

LAUNCHING AND RETRIEVAL

Just as docking is often used as a measure of a sailor's ability to handle his/her boat in tight quarters, so is launching and retrieval a measure of a trailer sailor's technique. The key to a successful performance at the launch ramp is having a plan and executing that plan cautiously.

Don't monopolize space and time at the ramp. Prepare your trailer sailer for launching in a nearby parking area. This includes raising the mast, bending on the sails, preparing docking lines, and loading the gear aboard. Before stepping the mast, take a good look around. Be sure to check for overhead power lines, especially between the parking area and the ramp. With everything secure and the boat ready for launching, take a walk down to the ramp and assess the situation. Things to check out include the water depth, wind direction, current, and condition of the ramp. Don't be in a hurry. Watch how other sailors are launching their boats. If they seem to be doing something you don't understand, ask them. They may be aware of something that will help you in launching your boat.

LAUNCHING

Before you back down the ramp, make one last prelaunch check. Things to do include disconnecting the trailer lights, making sure the centerboard is up and secure, and installing the drain plug. Here's where a checklist comes in handy.

Two things that you need to be aware of when backing a trailer are: 1) You are not *steering* the trailer; you are pushing it around with your tow vehicle, and the pivot point is at the trailer ball. 2) Grip the steering wheel at the bottom or six o'clock position. Moving your hand to the right, the trailer will go to the right and vice versa.

With a crewmember walking alongside the boat, back the trailer slowly down the ramp. Instead of shouting directions/instructions, communicate via hand signals. In order to avoid any confusion, go over these hand signals before getting to the ramp.

Once you've reached the point that the boat can be launched, with the rear tires and exhaust out of the water, put the transmission in park, set the parking brake, and chock the rear tires.

As skipper, climb aboard the trailer, disconnect the trailer winch line from the bow eye, and push the boat towards the water. While you're freeing the boat from the trailer, your crew should be using lines that had been affixed to the bow and stern to maneuver the boat clear of the ramp and to a nearby dock or beach.

Once the boat has been launched and is under the control of the crew, leave the launch ramp. Don't forget to take the wheel chocks. If you have launched in salt water, hose off the trailer with fresh water.

RETRIEVAL

Since the trailer is now empty, which makes for good visibility, only one person is usually needed to back it down the ramp. Secure the tow vehicle as was done for launching.

Oftentimes with the trailer completely submerged it is difficult for the crew on board the boat to make a proper approach. Guide-ons, in the form of tall poles or flags attached to the rear corners of the trailer, will give the crew something to aim between. Even a single pole centered at the winch will be helpful.

While the skipper is dealing with the trailer and tow vehicle, the crew is securing the boat and its gear and attaching bow and stern lines. With the sails lowered, the crew should slowly approach the trailer, bow first. The skipper or possibly another crewmember, standing on the trailer or in the water, should meet the boat and connect the winch line to the bow eye. Once the boat is partially on the trailer and centered (it may be necessary to use the bow and stern lines to adjust the boat), winch the boat forward. Secure the boat in place and slowly drive up the ramp to the parking area. Derig the boat and prepare it and the trailer for road travel. Here's another place where a checklist can make things easier.

CHAPTER 37

KISS: KEEP IT SIMPLE, SAILOR!

The versatility of trailersailing affords one the opportunity to enjoy a variety of diverse sailing grounds. In order to take advantage of this versatility, all one needs to do is hitch the boat to the tow vehicle and drive there. However, sailing to windward at 55 miles per hour has its challenges, both on the road and at the launch ramp.

MAKING FAST FOR THE FAST LANE

One of the biggest advantages to trailersailing is that you are not limited to one sailing area in a single sailing season, but rather can experience a cornucopia of sailing destinations, compliments of our extensive highway system.

In order to achieve this enviable versatility, the mast must be unstepped, gear properly secured, and rigging made fast for the ensuing road trip. While a boat's rigging is designed to withstand the various stresses of sailing, its ability to cope with the stresses of highway speeds is definitely challenged. Running rigging can be easily removed and stowed. However, it's the standing rigging, the stainless steel wire shrouds/stays that can be damaged or even cause damage to your craft, if not properly prepared for high speed, highway travel. Like running rigging, standing rigging can also be removed and stowed. Nevertheless, this process is more involved and basically equates to: the more rigging removed = the more time spent rerigging + the less time spent sailing. Not a balanced equation!

There are numerous methods for securing rigging for transit, and I've tried most of them with various degrees of success. Using short lengths of line or "small stuff" is nautical, but often results in slippage and the unrestrained flapping of loose ends. Also, if one is not adept at knot tying, the resultant jumble looks like a Boy Scout gone berserk. Store-bought clip, buckle, or Velcro-type ties are just an expensive alternative to rope and in actual practice don't work as well. Tape (riggers, electrical, duct, and the like) works very well and is both quick and easy to apply and remove. However, it more often than not results in leaving behind a sticky adhesive residue. The method that I found to be foolproof is...cable ties.

These simple, adjustable, nylon, self-locking strips are easy to use, come in a variety of lengths, are inexpensive (I bought a 1,200 piece assortment for under $5.00), and are downright tenacious in their holding power.

If you've ever done any electrical work aboard, you know how handy these little gems are at keeping wiring in shipshape fashion. In addition to their intended electrical use, cable ties are excellent in securing all types of rigging for highway transport. The beauty is in their simplicity and versatility.

To prevent rigging from slapping, getting caught on something, or coming loose and being damaged or causing damage, use cable ties to secure it to the mast, lifelines, or even to itself. Then, once you've reached your destination, remove the cable ties quickly and easily with a mere snip of your wire cutters or slice of your pocketknife.

Once you've tried them, you'll agree that nothing beats cable ties for securing your rigging for a high speed, interstate experience.

37. KEEP IT SIMPLE, SAILOR!

NO LEAPING REQUIRED

Stepping the mast of a trailerable sailboat is one of the least glamorous of the necessary tasks. Over the years, trailer sailors around the globe have spent countless hours and devoted vast quantities of gray matter in trying to devise the easiest, quickest, and most painless way to overcome this common dilemma. To date, no definitive technique (other than having someone else step the mast for you) has yet been developed.

Over the years, I've witnessed and/or used various configurations of gin poles, A-frames, stainless steel wire or rope bridles, block and tackle, numerous trailer modifications, and even springs to get the job done. Other than personal preferences, most all of the techniques have yielded successful results. However, the one characteristic that most all of them share is the addition of some sort of permanent or semipermanent rigging and/or the addition of another piece of single-use hardware that has to be stowed or carted around. (Excuse me if I digress here a moment. While I believe in taking my sailing seriously and have outfitted our 22-foot trailer sailer to a point that could possibly make a few of its larger bluewater cousins envious, I'd rather not add anything else that might cause the First Mate to mutiny. And quite frankly, I'm not too excited myself about complicating the rigging. Therefore, I set out looking for a way to make mast stepping easier, using only what I normally have onboard.)

You've probably heard the expression, "One can't see the forest for the trees." Well, it turned out to be just that. All the elements were already in place; they just had to be used differently or replaced with a more ambidextrous item.

In its transport position, the mast has all stays attached, except for the headstay, and is supported at three points. The bow pulpit serves as the forward support. Here the base of the mast is secured for travel with Dacron webbing. Amidships, the mid portion of the spar rests on a wooden cradle that is mounted over the tabernacle. At the stern, the top of the mast is tied to a mast crutch that is mounted to the gudgeons during transport. It is this mast crutch, or more correctly its adjustable replacement version, that is the key to my use-whatever's-aboard mast stepping system.

In the past, when I needed to step the mast, I'd slide the mast aft while it rested on the mast crutch. Once the base was at the tabernacle, I'd pin it in place. At this point, I'd attach the jib halyard shackle to the tack fitting at the boat's bow, run the other end of the line through the jib downhaul block, located at the stemhead fitting, and back to a winch. The mast was now near parallel to the ground and ready for stepping. With the First Mate operating the winch, I'd stand in the cockpit and raise the mast over my head and begin to walk it up. Early on in the process, I'd have to make a leap from the cockpit onto the coach roof, where I would guide the mast to its upright position. While this technique had served us for many years, it was that infamous leap and the associated lack of lateral support for the mast that often made things interesting. Also, my initial efforts went entirely into getting the mast from an almost parallel position to about 30 degrees, before the winch could do any of the work.

To dramatically improve the situation, I replaced the fixed mast crutch with an adjustable one. I fabricated the adjustable crutch using the original 1½-inch outside diameter (OD) crutch pipe minus the V-rest. To the V-rest I welded a 6-foot length of 1¼-inch OD pipe that easily slides up and down inside the 1½-inch pipe, which has an inside diameter (ID) of 1⅜ inches. Matching ⅜-inch holes were drilled through the pipes, one in the transport position and another in the extended position. To secure the pipes in either position, I use a ⅜-inch hitch pin.

Now when I go to step the mast, I first extend the mast crutch to its full height of approximately 8 feet. I then slide the mast aft, pin it to the tabernacle, and attach and route the jib halyard. Instead of the mast starting out near parallel, it's close to 30 degrees. I am now able to start from on top of the coach roof, letting the winch do most of the work with me there to guide the mast into place. Once I attach the headstay, the mast crutch is lowered and stowed in the tow vehicle as always.

By the way, performing the process in reverse beats lowering the mast the old Armstrong way hands down. Also, much to the disappointment of onlookers, no leaping is required.

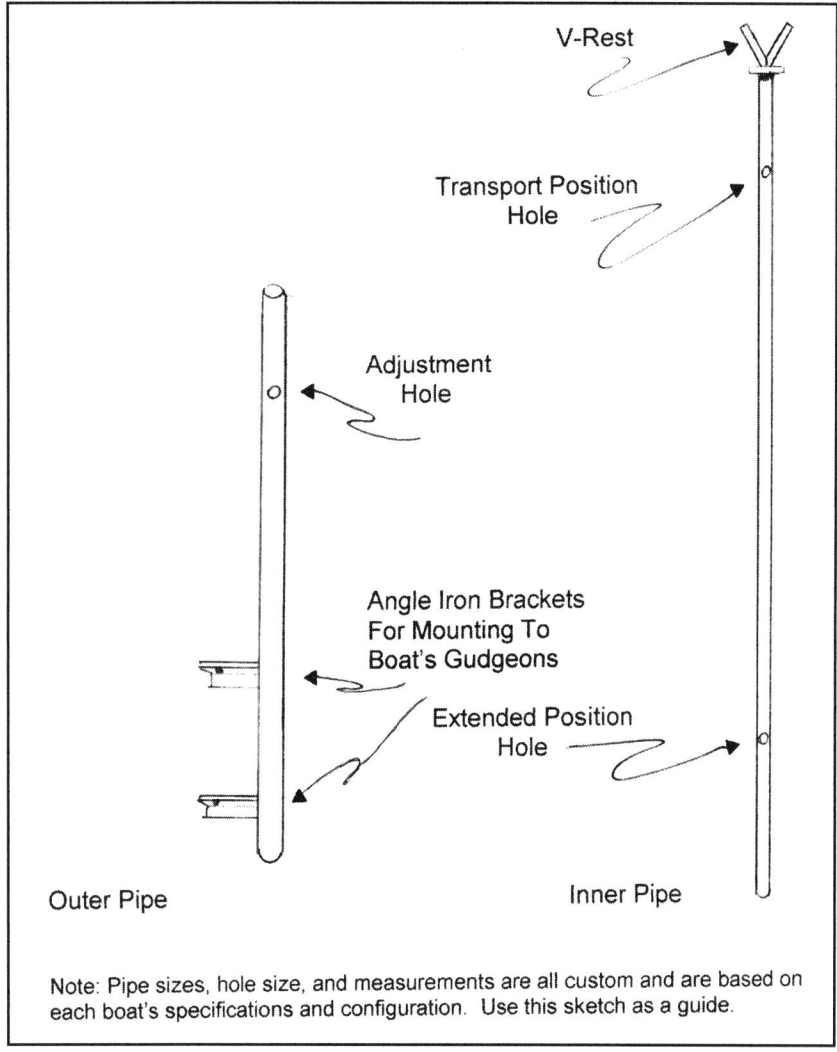

NO LEAPING IS REQUIRED IF YOU USE AN ADJUSTABLE MAST CRUTCH.

WHEEL CHOCKS

One of the most vivid recollections of my childhood is of a boat launching at a local public ramp. I remember it as though it were yesterday.

A young man and his attractive girlfriend arrived in his new convertible, with the top down, pulling a sleek Thistle sailboat on a trailer. While he was launching the boat single-handedly, his swimsuited girlfriend stood around attracting attention and probably distracting him. Not only did he launch his boat, but the trailer, along with the convertible in tow, followed. No amount of applied engine horsepower could stop the backward slide. We all watched helplessly as the rear seat, followed by the front, filled with water. Fortunately the ramp was shallow and the car eventually settled with the water gently lapping against the lower portion of the dashboard. It took three tow trucks and a complicated block and tackle arrangement to extract boat, trailer, and convertible from the lake.

I don't know if the brakes failed or weren't set properly, or if the algae on the ramp didn't afford enough friction to hold car and trailer in place. What I do know is that the wheels of the convertible weren't chocked.

Having this vivid recollection and being a trailer sailor, chocking my tow vehicle's wheels is standard procedure. During these visits to the launch ramp it seems that there's a laundry list of things to do, not to do, be aware of, watch out for, et cetera. While chocking wheels is one of the first, unchocking is one of the last and is sometimes overlooked—that is, until they're run over by the trailer, are last seen floating out into the lake, or are left behind on the ramp.

To help remind me to remove the wheel chocks, instead of tying a string around my finger, I've fashioned a line onto each chock. I can attach the other end of the line to my bumper or can close it in a door. Now when I pull away from the ramp, the now tethered chocks follow along. Once at the parking area I can complete my derigging, reconnect my trailer lights, and stow the wheel chocks. Another benefit of having the wheel chocks attached in this manner is that they afford anti-rollback protection up until the moment I pull away from the ramp.

TONGUE EXTENDER

With its shoal draft keel/centerboard combination, my trailer sailer draws only 22 inches. However, if I want to float it off or onto its trailer, I need approximately 3 feet of water. This is because the trailer raises the boat an additional 14 inches. Normally, this is not a problem. Proper scouting of the launch ramp combined with the fact that my trailer has rollers instead of bunks, usually overcomes any potential launch ramp perils. With a push/pull effort, I can roll the boat on/off in water around 2 feet. However, in the past 3 years, below-normal precipitation in my sailing grounds has left many lake levels, including the Great Lakes, well below their norms.

After struggling to retrieve my boat on two occasions and witnessing the towing eye of one boat being unceremoniously pulled out while the owner was attempting to winch it onto its trailer, I vowed to do something to improve my launching/retrieval ability. If I could get the boat/trailer farther out into deeper water, my problem would be solved. Unfortunately, my tow vehicle wasn't equipped for submarine service, so what I needed was a tongue extender.

Over the years, I have seen all manners and configurations of tongue extenders and associated trailer modifications. Having benefited from this, I elected to follow the KISS principle...keep it simple, sailor! In selecting my materials, I made certain that all were off-the-shelf and commonly available.

The end result is a 12-foot length of 2½-inch x 2½-inch square steel box, with a coupler bolted to one end and a ¾-inch hole drilled horizontally through the other. Four feet from the end with the hole, a hitch ball is welded in place. To make handling easier, two handles are welded to the top of the 12-foot extension, one at 5 feet from the end with the hole and another at 7 feet. Modifications to the trailer are minimal. Using two 6-inch lengths of ½-inch by 2-inch flat stock, one pair of the trailer's brackets now extends 2 inches below the tongue. A ¾-inch hole drilled horizontally through both straps, mates with the hole in the tongue extender. To guide the extender into place, a pair of 10-inch-long ½-inch x 1-inch bars is fastened with three 4½-inch bolts just behind the trailer's hitch, forming a sort of box.

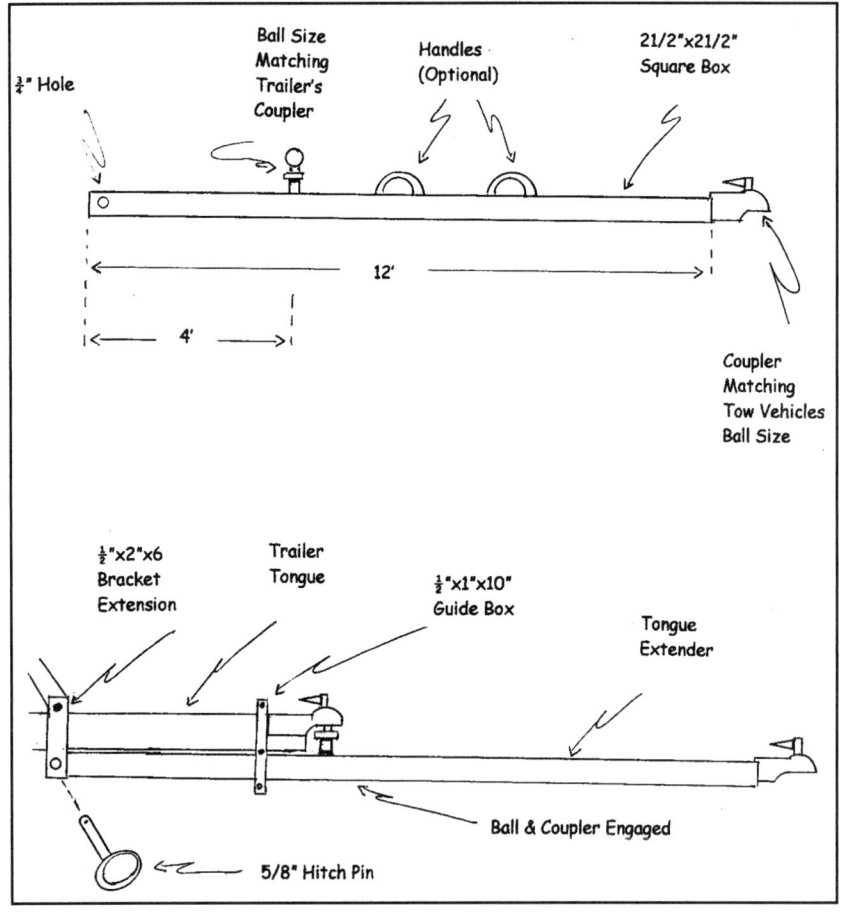

A TONGUE EXTENDER MAKES SHALLOW WATER
LAUNCHING AND RETRIEVAL EASY.

In operation, the tongue extender is slid through the trailer tongue's new guide box and back until the hole in the extender matches with the holes in the newly lengthened trailer bracket. Once this has been achieved, a ⅝-inch hitch pin is inserted and clipped into place. The extension is then lifted up by its handles, thus engaging the ball on the extension with the trailer's coupler. Once the trailer's coupler is locked, the extension's coupler is connected to the tow vehicle's ball. With the wheel jack raised, the extension is ready for use. For stowage, I simply bungee the tongue extender beneath the boat to the trailer's frame, thus keeping it simple, sailor.

FLAG GUIDE-ONS

At a boat show I overheard a salesman tell a prospective buyer, "Retrieving a trailerable sailboat is easy. It's just like launching one, only in reverse with a few minor changes. Simply run the boat up onto the trailer, hook onto the winch, pull the boat the rest of the way on, and drive up the ramp." After what seemed to be almost a minute's pause, the salesman casually added, "Oh yeah, make real sure that the boat's centered on the trailer."

While what the salesman said was loosely true, the offhanded comment or caveat regarding the proper centering of the boat on its trailer is key to a successful retrieval and highway travel. This is especially important for a boat having any sort of keel. A keel increases the boat's draft and weight, compared to a sailboat with a centerboard or daggerboard, and necessitates that the trailer be submerged, often to the point where only its winch will be above water. Having a single point at which to aim can make proper centering very difficult. Guide-ons, installed near the trailer's rear corners, provide a lane to sail in and make centering the boat on the trailer much easier.

Store-bought trailer guide-ons cost between $65.00 and $85.00 dollars. They are not much more than lengths of PVC tubing that are rigidly bolted to the trailer and extend several feet above the water.

To me, the idea of something "rigid" combined with crosswinds, waves, wakes, and/or piloting errors conjures up all sorts of potential catastrophes, from broken guide-ons to boat damage. A trip to the local discount department store provided me with a better, safer and, best of all, cheaper set of trailer guide-ons. For only $10.89 I purchased two six-foot, bicycle safety flags and all the necessary hardware (nuts, bolts, and washers) to make my own custom trailer guide-ons.

The rear mounting brackets that hold my trailer's fenders extend ever so slightly past the maximum beam of my boat. Here I drilled a hole in each one, and using a bolt, washer, and wing nut combination, installed my new trailer guide-on flags. The wing nut arrangement allows me to install the flags only when needed. Realizing that each trailer/boat configuration is different, I checked out the trailer/boat combos at my sailing club. Most of the over 50 trailers present afforded a similar means to attach these guide-on flags. In the worst instance, the addition of two short lengths of perforated steel angle brought the mounting points out to the desired width.

RETRIEVAL BELT

While my tongue extender does the trick in launching my boat and works well 80 percent of the time during retrieving it, to cover the remaining 20 percent I needed to pay a visit to my local discount auto parts store.

Before I did that it was necessary that I measure the perimeter of my boat. Starting at the bow, I secured my tape measure to the towing eye and, maintaining that level, extended my tape aft, around the stern, and then forward to where I began. The tape read 50 feet. At the auto parts store I found a variety of heavy duty vehicle recovery straps. These straps, with pull loops on each end, are constructed of nylon webbing; they come in several widths, lengths, and capacities. To fulfill my requirements I purchased two belts, one 20 feet long and one 30 feet in length. When looped together, they give me a 50-foot belt. Both are 2 inches wide and have a rated capacity of 18,000 pounds, more than adequate to handle my 2,200-pound trailer sailer.

When needed, prior to retrieval I wrap the belt around the hull of the boat. To keep it from sliding down into the water, I loosely suspend the belt from stanchions, cleats, or other deck fittings by means of light line. At the bow I connect my winch to the belt loops, not the towing eye, and begin winching the boat onto the trailer. Instead of putting all the strain on the small towing eye and surrounding area, it's now spread out around the entire boat. It works great!

SECTION IX

DON'T OVERLOOK THE DETAILS

We've all heard the expression, the devil's in the details. While I'm not exactly sure what the author of that phrase meant, I do know that if one overlooks an obvious yet seemingly unimportant item when sailing a small craft, it can often lead to undesirable, even catastrophic consequences. Don't forget to install the drain plug *before* launching; keep an eye on the weather; know how long, tall, and deep your craft is; and take the time to use a checklist.

CHAPTER 38

WEATHER 101

Since the beginning of time, the one factor that has always dramatically affected the performance, comfort, and safety of a sailboat has been weather. Sailors can observe, record, and plot weather; however, unlike most other variables that impact one's sailing, the best one can normally hope for is to attempt to understand it.

Do not despair. Armed with a knowledge of basic weather phenomena, along with a few tools, even the most casual sailor can recognize several common situations heralding weather changes.

Everyday changes in weather, from relaxed, tranquil seas to the most violent storms, are caused by the interaction of different air masses. These air masses, typically warm and cool, are moved around the earth by wind. The leading edge or boundary between two different air masses is called a front.

FRONTS, BOTH WARM AND COLD

A warm front forms when a warm air mass moves into contact with a cold air mass. This warm air gradually rises over the cold air and begins to cool. Moisture contained in the warm air begins to condense and form clouds.

38. WEATHER 101

The first clouds to appear, well ahead of the actual warm front, are typically delicate, wispy strands of cirrus. This high-level cloud is normally followed by layers of middle and lower-level stratiform-type clouds, which are usually thick and cover a large area. They are the ones that produce widespread precipitation, which may be accompanied by fairly strong winds. Weather of this type may last 24 hours or more, depending upon the rate at which the front is moving.

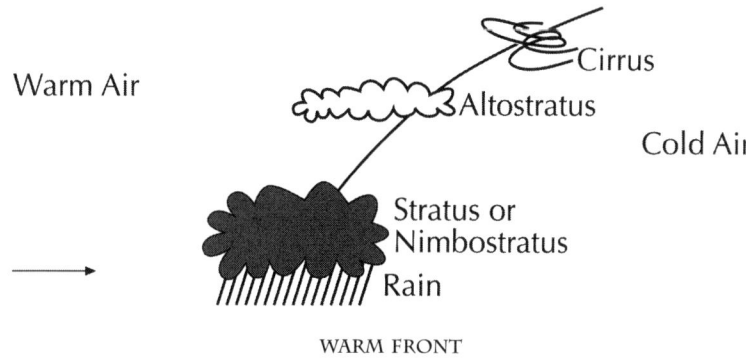

WARM FRONT

Generally associated with low pressure systems, cold fronts tend to produce more volatile weather than do warm fronts. A cold front forms when a cold air mass moves into an area of warm air. As a result of this contact, the warm air mass, which is less dense, is forced sharply up and somewhat over the cold air mass. This action creates instability as well as very powerful convection.

Very large cumulus clouds and even the king of clouds, cumulonimbus, may develop, triggering storms along the entire front. Also, an area of low pressure is created, which strengthens the localized winds. The rain showers will be heaviest and the winds strongest along the front. As the front passes, additional showers may develop as clouds form in its wake. The showers are generally short-lived, with dry spells between showers usually lasting longer than the showers themselves.

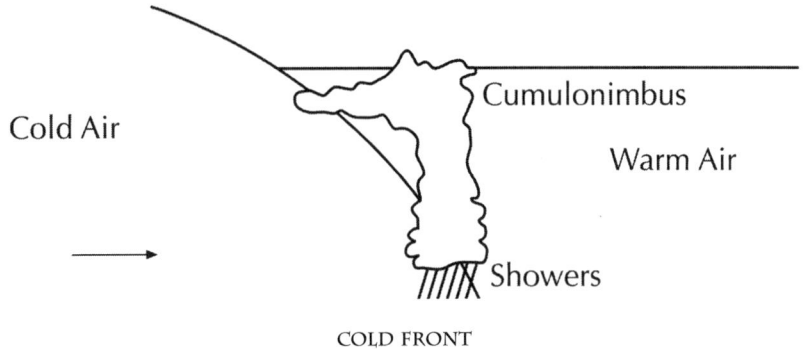

COLD FRONT

PRESSURE, BOTH LOW AND HIGH

Air is composed of billions of molecules in constant movement and collision with each other. These molecular collisions are known as air pressure.

When an air mass is warmed, it expands and rises. This expansion reduces the number of molecular collisions. As a result, an area of low pressure is created. Conversely, as air is cooled, it becomes more dense, causing the air molecules to collide more often. This dense air sinks back to earth and results in an area of high pressure. Nature constantly works to restore equilibrium: consequently, air moves from high pressure areas to those of low pressure. This movement from high to low *(always in the same direction)* is what we know as wind.

Expanding these two basic principles, as air rises and creates an area of low air pressure, water vapor in the air begins to condense and form clouds. Cooler, sinking air generally indicates no condensation can take place and the resultant high pressure area usually gives rise to clear skies. Fluctuations in air pressure can often indicate pending weather changes. For example, rapidly falling air pressure indicates that a low pressure system is approaching, which may be accompanied by rain.

While localized high and low pressures can affect weather in a small geographical area, large areas of high or low pressure, called systems, can be responsible for more widespread atmospheric changes, (i.e. brief afternoon showers vs. hurricane).

A large weather phenomenon in which air pressure decreases towards its center is called a low pressure system. It is usually the result of a warm air mass being forced upward by colder air, such as occurs in the formation of a cold front. Low pressure systems are usually associated with unstable weather conditions.

As the warm air rises and pressure falls, more and more air is drawn into the system. This movement of air results in strong winds, which blow counterclockwise *(in the northern hemisphere)* around a low.

In a high pressure system, cool dense air sinks to the earth and the resultant winds rotate clockwise *(in the northern hemisphere)* around the high. Highs are normally associated with stable conditions and clear skies.

Knowing these established wind rotation relationships, one can then determine where winds will be coming from and where they may be shifting to. For example, if a high is located to the west of a given position, the winds will be blowing generally from the NW-N. Conversely, if it's a low to the west, the winds will most likely be coming from the S-SW. Should a system then track to the north of that same given position, anticipate the wind to shift from a northerly to easterly direction with a high and from a southerly to westerly direction with a low.

WEATHER WATCHER'S TOOL BOX

In addition to a basic understanding of common weather phenomena, a sailor needs a few simple tools on board with which to measure and record his/her atmospheric observations. They include:

- A barometer, preferably one with an adjustable reference hand, with which to measure air pressure, as well as to determine a stable, rising, or falling trend.
- A thermometer, with which to measure air temperature.
- Something to measure wind direction: a Windex or telltales and a compass or a bona fide wind vane.
- An anemometer and/or Beaufort Scale to measure or estimate wind speed.
- A cloud chart, with which to identify weather-heralding clouds (following section).
- Ship's log or notebook, in which to record weather observations.

With these half dozen items, a sailor instantly becomes a fairly well equipped weather observation/forecasting center. However, one of the most important things that a sailor needs to constantly remember is that one or two or even three consecutive observations do not make for an accurate forecast. Individual observations are mere snapshots of a greater picture. Weather is dynamic and is always changing, much like a motion picture that shows scene after scene after scene. An accurate forecast is based on what has happened, what has been happening, and what is happening, as well as an abundance of cause-and-effect historical data.

One of the most significant and helpful tools in a sailor's weather forecasting arsenal is a cloud identification chart. This is a high powered cause-and-effect, or more correctly expressed, cause-and-anticipated-effect tool.

38. WEATHER 101

HEAVENLY BODIES: CLOUDS

Simply stated, when condensation takes place above the earth's surface, clouds form. Normally, air temperature decreases with increasing height. Therefore, clouds that form at high levels tend to be made of ice crystals, while those forming at the lowest levels normally consist of water droplets. Middle level clouds may be composed of a mixture of water droplets and ice crystals, as well as super cooled water droplets. The exact type of cloud depends upon such factors as the amount of moisture in the air, the amount of uplift, and the degree of atmospheric stability.

High level clouds form above 16,500 feet. They are called cirrus or have the prefix cirro-. Middle clouds occur between 6,500 feet and 16,500 feet and their name is usually prefixed with alto-. Low clouds form below 6,500 feet and have no prefix. They have their own names, such as cumulus and stratus. There is also that exception, cumulonimbus, which inhabits all three levels of the atmosphere. It is included with low level cumuliform-type clouds because it develops out of such formations.

The sky can be embellished with over 100 cloud varieties or combinations thereof, making for endless possibilities and a host of atmospheric events. In this section, this vast array of clouds has been distilled down to fewer than a dozen "predicting" clouds.

CUMULUS (HUMILIS)
"WOOLY FLEECES DECK THE HEAVENLY WAY,
MAKE SURE NO RAIN WILL MAR THE DAY." *

Cumulus clouds (above and facing page) usually appear in the late morning or early afternoon. They develop as the result of weak, localized convection, in which surface air, in contact with the sun-warmed earth, warms up and rises into the atmosphere. In the cool upper environment, water vapor in the once warm air condenses and a cloud is formed. Cumulus resemble small cotton balls that have small rounded tops and flat bases at around the 2,000 foot level. These clouds are often referred to as fair weather cumulus and normally indicate no immediate change in weather. The winds associated with them are usually light to moderate, with daytime readings of 4-10 knots and 1-6 knots at night. Temperatures will be highest in early afternoon and coolest at dawn. The barometric pressure will normally be steady or may rise slowly. While this form of cumulus is associated with fair weather, should it continue to build rapidly, you may want to be prepared to reduce sail area.

38. WEATHER 101

CUMULUS (MEDIOCRIS)
STILL A FAIR WEATHER CLOUD; THIS PHASE OF CUMULUS
IS OFTEN A TRANSITION STAGE BETWEEN THE LESSER HUMILIS
AND THE MORE DEVELOPED CONGESTUS STAGE.

CUMULUS (CONGESTUS) "A ROUND-TOPPED CLOUD,
WITH FLATTENED BASE, CARRIES RAINFALL IN ITS FACE." *

This advanced form of cumulus (congestus, preceding page) is taller than it is wide and its development is associated with atmospheric instability, in which the temperature of the surrounding air drops more rapidly with height than is normal. At this stage of advancement, this form of cumulus is capable of generating heavy and prolonged showers. If the winds are blowing from the SW to NW, precipitation and gusty winds or only wind squalls are likely in 4-8 hours. Should the cloud become darker, it may grow into cumulonimbus. Time of day is a deciding factor. If cumulus is the tallest cloud in the sky by late afternoon, it is unlikely that it will progress to cumulonimbus. However, if color darkens and vertical development increases in the early afternoon, expect squalls within 1-3 hours.

STRATOCUMULUS FORMED FROM THE SPREADING OUT OF CUMULUS.

Stratocumulus (above and facing page) typically forms when stable layers in the atmosphere retard the vertical development of cumuliform clouds and channel it horizontally. Consequently, stratocumulus and cumulus are frequently seen together in the same sky. Stratocumulus is usually white or somewhat gray in color and forms in patches, sheets, or layers. It has a ragged appearance along its upper surface, with well-defined, flattish bases, developing between 2,000 feet and 6,500 feet. It is commonly observed in conjunction with stable high pressure areas and normally is an indicator of no change in weather type. Winds associated with this low cloud are normally light to moderate, with daytime readings 4-10 knots and 1-6 knots at night. Relatively warm temperatures and little change in pressure are usually experienced.

STRATOCUMULUS (UNDULATUS)
NOT FORMED BY THE SPREADING OUT OF CUMULUS.

Stratus clouds (next page) are generally very low (0-6,500 feet) in the sky. They are usually a gray layer with a fairly uniform base and result in overcast conditions. Stratus clouds often form when a mass of warm, moist air rises over the surface of a warm front. Since these clouds normally cover a wide area, any precipitation tends to be widespread and relatively long lasting. Stratus that give rise to significant precipitation are known as Nimbostratus. Winds from the NE to S may bring heavy rains, while winds from other directions may only bring light drizzle or just an overcast sky. The visibility with low-lying stratus may be ½–2 miles, the temperature normally steady with high humidity, and the pressure also steady or possibly falling.

STRATUS
"WHEN MIST COMES FROM HILL, THEN THE WEATHER IT DOTH SPILL;
WHEN THE MIST COMES FROM THE SEA, THEN GOOD WEATHER WILL IT BE." *

Cumulonimbus (facing page) is a heavy and dense cloud with considerable vertical extent. While its base is around 2,000 feet, its top routinely reaches to 30,000 feet and, upon occasion, as high as 60,000 feet. It is often referred to as the king of clouds. The formation of cumulonimbus can begin early in the morning as simple cumulus. In order for this to occur, powerful convection must combine with atmospheric instability. This combination produces vigorous updrafts that force the cloud up into the highest levels of the troposphere. Distant cumulonimbus clouds often show an anvil-shaped cirroform top.

If cumulonimbus clouds are present, especially if the winds are coming from the SW–N, batten down hatches, stow loose items,

38. WEATHER 101

CUMULONIMBUS
"WHEN MOUNTAINS AND CLIFFS IN CLOUDS APPEAR,
SUDDEN AND VIOLENT SHOWERS ARE NEAR." *

reduce sail, and don foul weather gear. If close to sheltered waters, head for them. Winds of 18–28 knots, with gusts up to 40–60 knots can be anticipated, along with thunder and lightning, heavy showers, and possibly hail. Unlike the long lasting, widespread rain associated with stratiform-type clouds, these showers will be localized and may last only minutes. In the storm cell, a large temperature drop will be experienced, as well as poor visibility (half a mile or less).

ALTOSTRATUS
WHEN THIN, THE SUN CAN BE SEEN VAGUELY;
IF THICK, THE SUN MAY BE BLOCKED OUT COMPLETELY.

38. WEATHER 101

Altostratus (facing page and below) is a middle level, featureless cloud, ranging from a thin veil to a dense gray mantle. As a middle cloud its base is at around 6,500 feet. It can be an extensive cloud deck and may extend over hundreds of square miles. Altostratus is formed by the lifting and condensation of a large air mass over the top of a warm front.

At a minimum, it produces an overcast sky. However, if sufficiently thick it becomes the forerunner of nimbostratus, which produces widespread, steady rain, especially if the winds are steady from the NE to S. This cloud is an indicator of moderate deterioration of weather conditions. At its worst, it can bring winds of 15-20 knots, cooler temperatures, and a falling barometer.

ALTOSTATUS
WHEN THICK, THE SUN MAY BE BLOCKED OUT COMPLETELY.

Altocumulus (below, facing page, and following page) is a middle cloud, which most commonly occurs in the form of a layer of cloudlets that are fairly regularly arraigned. It is formed by the lifting of an air mass, followed by condensation combined with instability. Altocumulus is normally a sign of fair weather and possibly just an overcast sky. However, if altocumulus thickens to more of a washboard appearance, light rain, heralding an approaching front, is likely in 16–24 hours. This can be anticipated if the winds are steady from NE to S.

ALTOCUMULUS (FLOCCUS) RESEMBLES A FLOCK OF SHEEP
STANDING CLOSE TOGETHER IN A SKY PASTURE.

38. WEATHER 101

WHEN ALTOCUMULUS THICKENS TO MORE OF A WASHBOARD APPEARANCE, LIGHT RAIN IS LIKELY IN 16-24 HOURS.

ALTOCUMULUS (UNDULATUS) NORMALLY RESULTS FROM WIND SHEAR AND OFTEN RESEMBLES RIPPLES ON THE SURFACE OF A POND.

IX: DON'T OVERLOOK THE DETAILS

ALTOCUMULUS FORMATIONS ARE OFTEN MORE DISTINCT
AND DRAMATIC AT SUNRISE AND SUNSET.

CIRRUS
"MARE'S TAILS, LEAVE SHORT SAILS." * (FORECAST: GOOD WEATHER,
PERHAPS THE APPROACH OF A WARM FRONT.)

38. WEATHER 101

CIRRUS

This high level cloud (below on facing page, also above) appears as delicate, wispy strands that often stretch across the sky. Its base is at 16,500 feet and its presence indicates moisture at high levels. Cirrus is the highest of all clouds and is composed of ice crystals.

There's a fine day in store if the winds are W to N and the cloud is isolated or very wispy in appearance. Visibility will be 10+ miles with light to moderate winds of 5–15 knots and a barometer showing little change.

More often than not, cirrus clouds form in the leading edge of a frontal system. Precipitation within 24–48 hours is likely, especially if the cloud changes to cirrostratus or cirrocumulus or if the winds are from the NE to S.

Cirrostratus (below) is a high, even layered cloud that can cover a wide area of the sky. It is formed by the saturation of a large air mass at high levels.

A darkening and thickening of the cloud layer may indicate the approach of a frontal system. Expect precipitation in 24-48 hours if the winds are steady from the NE to S, or sooner if SE to E. Watch the rate of barometric pressure fall, as another indicator of how soon to expect the rain. The faster the pressure falls, the sooner you can expect the rain.

CIRROSTRATUS
"IF CLOUDS LOOK AS IF SCRATCHED BY A HEN,
GET READY TO REEF YOUR TOPSAILS THEN." *

Cirrocumulus (facing page), like cirrostratus, forms because of the saturation of a large air mass at high levels. However, unlike cirrostratus, instability at cloud level gives cirrocumulus its cumuliform appearance. It can stretch for hundreds of miles across the sky, often appearing as a fine rippled pattern, said to resemble the scales of a fish.

38. WEATHER 101

CIRROCUMULUS
"MACKEREL SKY, MACKEREL SKY, NOT LONG WET, NOT LONG DRY." *

As the old mariner's saying goes, "Mackerel sky, mackerel sky, not long wet, not long dry," cirrocumulus is an indication of an approaching frontal system. Precipitation is likely in 12–18 hours, especially if the winds are NE to S.

CIRROCUMULUS

CONTRAILS BEING FORMED.

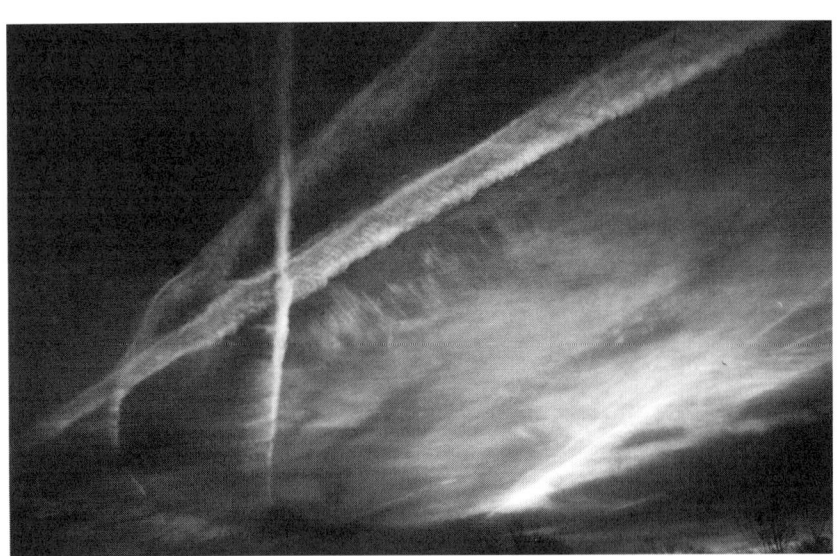

"OLD" CONTRAILS MIXED IN WITH CIRRUS.

38. WEATHER 101

Aircraft operating at high levels (>16,500 feet) emit water droplets from their exhausts. Since the air temperature at these levels is normally well below freezing, these water droplets form ice crystals and create an artificial cloud. The term contrails is an abbrevation for these condensation trails. (See illustrations, facing page.)

If the surrounding air contains little moisture, the contrails will be short lived and invisible from earth. However, if the surrounding air is close to saturation, the contrails will be much more noticeable and can last for ¾ hour or more. It is these long lasting contrails that indicate an approaching frontal system.

SUMMING IT UP

When the sky overhead has a certain look, quite often a sequence of atmospheric events or "weather" follows. However, there is nothing certain about it. Sometimes the weather suggested by the look of the sky will develop true to form, sometimes not. Remember, weather is affected by a myriad of things including seasonal factors and local topography, as well as an error in timing. If bad weather is anticipated, it's better to assume it will arrive sooner than expected rather than later, especially if you're on the water.

* Ancient mariner weather proverbs

CHAPTER 39

A PROPER WINTER COVER
(AND I DON'T MEAN SNOW)

October on the north coast (Great Lakes), or for that matter anywhere north of the 38th parallel, means taking the boat out of the water and preparing it for cold storage. Over the years, I've determined that a significant portion of the pleasure I experience when my boat is released from its winter cocoon in the spring, is directly proportionate to how well I've prepared it in the fall. In addition to the washing, waxing, lubricating, repairing, inspecting, etc., the one aspect of winter storage that affords the greatest impact is the boat's winter cover.

As an owner of a 22-foot trailersailer, I have a distinct advantage over owners of much larger and less trailerable craft, in that I can easily transport my boat home. There I can perform the required fall ablutions, benefiting from the convenience of my workshop's tools and supplies. Once the fall decommissioning is complete, it's time to cover the boat for its long winter's rest. It is at this phase in the winterizing process that boats of all sizes can benefit from a proper winter cover, regardless of whether they're on the hard at the marina or parked in the driveway.

First, I unstep the mast and support it horizontally at three locations on the boat. The bow pulpit serves as the forward support. Amidships, the mid portion of the spar rests on a wooden cradle mounted over the tabernacle. This avoids any swayback or bending to the mast. At the stern, the top of the mast rests on a mast crutch that is pinned to the boat's gudgeons. In this fashion, the mast serves as the backbone support for the winter cover. Since it's almost 27 feet long, the mast overhangs both the bow and stern and allows for excess tarp at both ends. This insures a complete coverage of the entire boat.

I also remove the stanchions and lifelines. Stanchions are potential tarp tearers that, if allowed to remain, must be heavily padded. With them gone, into each vacant stanchion base I insert one end of a ¾-inch PVC water pipe. The pipe is then bent over the mast, where it is supported, and the other end is inserted into the opposite side's empty stanchion base. The finished product resembles the hoops of a covered wagon.

To maintain this rounded and smooth form on which the tarp will rest, I pad all potential sharp spots with closed cell foam. This includes the tangs, cleats, steaming light, and other mast fittings, as well as any protruding fixtures on the boat itself. I purchased the closed cell foam at the Army/Navy store, in the form of a surplus 2-feet by 7-feet sleeping pad. The pieces that I need are cut to size and held in place with duct tape. I use the same PVC water pipe and closed cell foam pieces year after year; only the duct tape is replaced. By the way, no tape touches any part of the boat or the mast.

The winter cover is draped over the entire boat, with the bulk of the tarp's excess drawn to the stern. Starting under the bow of the boat and working my way to the stern, I weave a line back and forth through the tarp's grommets, much as one would do with shoes and shoelaces. The bow end of the tarp is closed with a combination of lacing the grommets together and using spring hand clamps. The excess tarp at the stern is rolled together and held in place with a series of spring hand clamps. Should I need to go aboard during the winter months, removing a few clamps is a lot easier than trying to untie line using cold fingers.

For the cover, I chose a 24-feet by 30-feet reinforced poly tarp, silver on one side and black on the other. By facing the silver side outward, greater reflectivity and UV resistance is achieved, while underneath, the environment is cool and airy. Also, the tarp is sized to cover the boat not only from stem to stern, but also from waterline to waterline, leaving only last season's bottom paint exposed to the elements. The tarp is on its sixth season and is holding up very well.

I found that a careful fall lay-up, with emphasis on a proper winter cover, is like getting a head start on next year's spring commissioning.

WITH PVC PIPES SPANNING THE BOAT'S BEAM
FROM STANCHION BASE TO OPPOSITE STANCHION BASE
AND ALL POTENTIAL SHARP SPOTS COVERED WITH CLOSED CELL FOAM PADDING,
THE BOAT IS READY FOR THE TARP COVERING.

CHAPTER 40

PASSING SAFELY BENEATH

I know the height of my mast from waterline to the tip of my antenna; however, this one piece of information is of little use in instances where a bridge's height and possibly a tidal rise is unknown or not readily available. Here's a technique that can be used to ensure safe mast clearance.

At your convenience, locate a sailboat whose mast height is considerably greater than that of your boat's. Position your boat about 100 yards from this taller craft. While in your cockpit, stand at your normal steering position. Line up the taller boat's mast with your own. Using a contrasting color tape, have a member of your crew mark your mast where the other boat's waterline and masthead come. These are your guide marks.

Now, when you are 100 yards or a bit farther (never closer) from a bridge, position your guide marks under the bridge. If they fit under the bridge easily, you should be able to pass beneath it with a margin to spare.

The following points must be stressed:
1. The judging distances must never be less than 100 yards.
If you are unsure or uncomfortable, this distance will give you sufficient maneuvering room, even under less than ideal conditions.
2. This method is only reliable if the eye height is the same. These are *your* guide marks. They cannot be used by other crewmembers, especially ones of different heights.

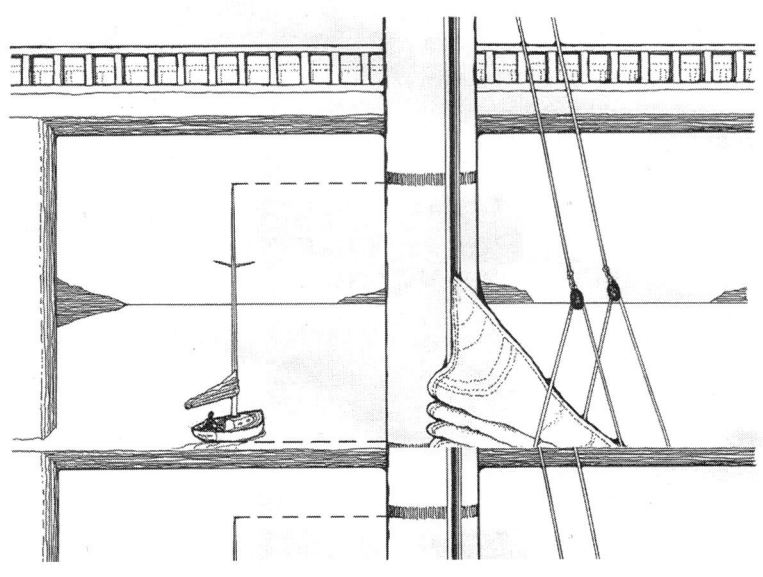

**USING GUIDE MARKS TO DETERMINE
IF YOU'LL SAFELY PASS BENEATH AN OVERHEAD OBSTRUCTION.**

CHAPTER 41

CHECKLISTS

I don't know about you, but I enjoy trivia and somewhat pride myself in mentally warehousing innumerable disjointed facts and recalling them at will. (My wife once said that my brain is becoming a compendium of useless information, such as knowing the name of the Lone Ranger's nephew's horse. Well, that's her opinion!)

However, when it comes to some of the aspects of my sailboat, I don't rely entirely on my memory; I use checklists. This way I ensure that everything that needs to be done is done. Also, as a trailersailor, I have the additional tasks/responsibilities of launching, retrieval, a trailer, and a tow vehicle. Checklists make life a lot easier for both skipper and crew.

The following checklists have been developed over time and address a variety of sailing related tasks. They are by no means complete, owing to the fact that not all boats, trailers, sailing grounds, etc. are the same. More importantly, each skipper has his/her own way of doing things. Therefore, use these checklists as a guide, and massage them into a customized/personalized form.

While it is always a good idea to check the tow vehicle, boat trailer, and sailboat just minutes before leaving, some things should be done the day before departure. Then if a deficiency is found, there is time to take corrective actions. In any event, double-checking never hurts. The following predeparture checklists will help you to ensure safety and security of your towing rig, as well as to minimize any on-the-road problems.

TRAILER PREDEPARTURE CHECKLIST
- ❏ tire pressure
- ❏ wheel bearing grease
- ❏ lug nut tightness
- ❏ spare tire pressure
- ❏ ball greased
- ❏ trailer to tow vehicle connection solid
- ❏ coupler locked
- ❏ electrical connection made
- ❏ brake-away cable, if equipped with brakes
- ❏ heavy duty flasher installed
- ❏ trailer brake, turn signal, and running lights working
- ❏ safety chains attached and crossed
- ❏ tongue jack up and locked
- ❏ boat secured at bow
- ❏ winch locked
- ❏ boat tie-downs secure
- ❏ centerboard down and resting on cross-member
- ❏ rigging, boom, and mast secured
- ❏ all gear aboard properly stowed
- ❏ motor removed or secured for trailering
- ❏ rudder removed or secured for trailering
- ❏ license plate on and registration valid

TOW VEHICLE PREDEPARTURE CHECKLIST
- ❏ fluid levels
- ❏ engine oil
- ❏ transmission
- ❏ battery electrolyte
- ❏ power steering
- ❏ brake fluid
- ❏ radiator

- ❑ windshield washer
- ❑ condition of radiator hoses and cap
- ❑ battery terminals corrosion-free and tight
- ❑ fan belt tension and condition
- ❑ air filter
- ❑ tire pressure and condition
- ❑ heavy duty flasher
- ❑ brake, turn signal, running lights
- ❑ fuel level
- ❑ ball matches trailer hitch

EMERGENCY TRAILERING EQUIPMENT CHECKLIST
- ❑ trailer jack
- ❑ lug wrench for trailer lug nuts
- ❑ trailer spare tire
- ❑ spare pair of wheel bearings
- ❑ wheel bearing grease
- ❑ tire pressure gauge
- ❑ wheel chocks
- ❑ spare light bulbs
- ❑ spare fuses
- ❑ duct tape
- ❑ spare line and tiedowns
- ❑ assortment of tools
- ❑ flashlight
- ❑ breakdown triangles/flares

When towing a sailboat and trailer, be sensitive to any unusual sounds or handling characteristics you may encounter. Should something alert you, pull over to the side of the road, stop immediately, and check it out. Additionally, periodic on-the-road checks of your towing rig should be made at hourly intervals. The following checklist highlights those major items that can potentially cause you on-the-road problems, if not periodically addressed and maintained in proper order.

ON-THE-ROAD CHECKLIST
- ❑ wheel bearing temperature
- ❑ slacked-off lug bolts
- ❑ tire pressure
- ❑ brake, turn signal, and running lights
- ❑ security of boat tie-downs
- ❑ security of rigging, boom, and mast

Do everything you can to ready your craft for launching *before* moving to the launch ramp. Especially with a sailboat, you have some work that needs to be done before you're ready to launch. There's no point in holding up others while you accomplish it. The following checklist will help you address those prelaunch activities.

PRELAUNCH CHECKLIST
- ❑ check for overhead obstructions
- ❑ remove and store travel cover
- ❑ undo all tie-downs, except winch/bow connection
- ❑ install drain plug
- ❑ step the mast
- ❑ attach boom
- ❑ bend on sails and secure (do not hoist)
- ❑ check to see that nothing protrudes from the boat to snag on the trailer frame.
- ❑ rudder off or in the up position
- ❑ centerboard up all the way and pennant made fast

41. CHECKLISTS

- ☐ motor up
- ☐ unplug tow vehicle to trailer electrical connection
- ☐ attach launch lines to bow and stern
- ☐ attach fenders
- ☐ assure all gear is on board and secured

Launching ramps come in all degrees of slope and condition. Look it over carefully before you back down. Also, familiarize yourself with the following checklist. Remember, your tow vehicle isn't waterproof.

LAUNCHING CHECKLIST
- ☐ man the launch lines
- ☐ slowly back down the ramp
- ☐ chock wheels of the tow vehicle
- ☐ stay in tow vehicle with foot on brake, engine on, ready to pull forward
  (if needed to launch: set parking brake, engine off, transmission in 'Park' if automatic, 'First' if manual)
- ☐ launch boat
- ☐ tie off boat to dock
- ☐ pull tow vehicle and trailer to parking area

Whether you sail from a trailer, slip, or mooring, it's always prudent to conduct a presail check. While the following checklist is by no means near complete, the four items it contains are often routinely neglected and should be incorporated into your own personalized presail checklist.

PRESAIL CHECKLIST
- ☐ obtain a weather report
- ☐ file a float plan (If the sail is going to be more than

a few hours, a float plan should be filed with the nearest harbor authority [not USGC], yacht club, friend, or relative. If trailering, leave a copy under the windshield of your tow vehicle.)
- ❑ check the bilge for water
- ❑ turn battery switch to On position

Before you set sail, you should familiarize all your guests with your boat and its safety equipment. The degree of detail you go into will depend upon several factors, including the guest's sailing experience, his/her familiarity with your boat, and the length of the cruise. Use the following checklists to brief your guests or new crewmembers.

GUEST BRIEFING CHECKLIST
- ❑ life jackets' location and fit each guest
- ❑ operation of engine
- ❑ sail handling
- ❑ how to operate radio
- ❑ location and operation of fire extinguisher
- ❑ location of first aid kit
- ❑ location of signaling equipment
- ❑ MOB procedures
- ❑ operation of head
- ❑ operation of stove
- ❑ potable water system's operation, capacity, and conservation
- ❑ location of electrical switches
- ❑ operation of battery switch
- ❑ anchoring techniques
- ❑ stowage
- ❑ sleeping arrangements

- ❏ safety harness
- ❏ watch schedule
- ❏ familiarize with checklists

OUTBOARD MOTOR OPERATION CHECKLIST

STARTING

- ❏ moor boat securely
- ❏ fuel tank full
- ❏ fuel line connected properly to both tank and motor
- ❏ fuel tank vent open
- ❏ gear shift in Neutral position
- ❏ turn throttle to Start position
- ❏ if electric start, battery fully charged
- ❏ pump primer bulb until firm
- ❏ pull out choke
- ❏ slowly pull starter cord until resistance is felt, THEN pull starter cord in short swift motion
  OR
  if electric start, turn battery switch to On position AND turn key to engage starter
- ❏ once engine engages, push choke in
  (if engine does not start, see troubleshooting section of your engine manual)
- ❏ check for cooling water discharge
  (if no discharge, turn off engine and check for fouled water intake)
- ❏ set throttle to Idle position

STOPPING

- ❏ gear shift in Neutral position
- ❏ turn throttle to Idle position
- ❏ push engine stop/kill button OR if electric start, turn key to Off.
  (if no button, pull choke all the way out)

REFUELING
- ☐ moor boat to fuel dock securely
- ☐ shut off engine
- ☐ make sure all passengers are ashore
- ☐ don't smoke
- ☐ extinguish all open flame
- ☐ close all portlights and hatches
- ☐ don't use electrical switches
- ☐ be sure you're pumping into fuel tank
- ☐ take portable tanks ashore
- ☐ ground the nozzle against filler pipe
- ☐ don't overfill the tank
- ☐ wipe up any spillage
- ☐ check for vapors before starting engine
- ☐ if onboard gasoline engine, turn on blower for 5 minutes
- ☐ start engine before re-embarking passengers

Before leaving your sailboat at its slip or mooring, go over those items that will help to ensure that your boat will be safe and secure in your absence.

POST-SAIL CHECKLIST
- ☐ turn off all electrical equipment (except bilge pump, which should be wired directly to the battery)
- ☐ turn battery switch to Off position
- ☐ stow all gear
- ☐ remove and stow or cover all sails
- ☐ secure halyards/running rigging
- ☐ secure tiller
- ☐ remove all trash for proper disposal
- ☐ remove all perishable foodstuffs

- ❏ secure all hatches and portlights
- ❏ make a list of items that need to be brought on board or attended to
- ❏ double-check all the dock/mooring lines
- ❏ wash the deck and cockpit
- ❏ lock the boat

Retrieval is basically the reverse of launching. Use the following checklist in this process. Also remember that pulling a boat and trailer up a wet ramp, especially if it's steep, is almost always harder than backing down the ramp. Therefore, once the boat's bow is secured to the trailer, use low gear and gently apply the gas.

RETRIEVAL CHECKLIST
- ❏ attach and man the launch lines
- ❏ raise the centerboard and secure it
- ❏ remove or raise the rudder into trailering position
- ❏ raise outboard motor
- ❏ connect winch cable to towing eye on boat
- ❏ pull/float boat onto the trailer
- ❏ lock winch, securing the boat to the trailer
- ❏ pull up ramp to the parking area
- ❏ lower centerboard
- ❏ remove and stow sails
- ❏ lower mast and secure it, boom, and rigging for travel
- ❏ remove or secure outboard motor for trailering
- ❏ secure all loose items
- ❏ remove drain plug
- ❏ tie-down boat fore and aft
- ❏ replace boat cover
- ❏ plug in tow vehicle to trailer electrical connection

With the sailing season over, it's time to store your sailboat for the off-season. At no time is there a greater opportunity to prevent problems than at lay-up. By using a checklist, you can just about guarantee that your spring commissioning will go off without a hitch.

LAY-UP CHECKLIST

BELOW DECKS

- ❏ remove sails, bedding, cushions, and spare cordage (clean, repair, dry, and store in warm, dry location.)
- ❏ remove electronics
- ❏ remove flashlights and equipment with dry cell batteries
- ❏ remove all foodstuffs
- ❏ drain potable water system or charge it with nontoxic antifreeze
- ❏ leave all cupboards and storage bins open
- ❏ remove all traces of water from the bilge
- ❏ clean and grease all seacocks and leave open
- ❏ remove and service Porta Potties OR flush, disinfect, and drain all heads
- ❏ clean, disinfect, and dry all surfaces (inside and out of storage areas also)

TOPSIDE

- ❏ inspect and clean all standing rigging (repair or renew as required)
- ❏ store loose shackles, swivels, clevis pins, etc. in a sealed container (prior to storage, spray them with light oil or dry lubricant)
- ❏ inspect and clean mast and boom (clean and lubricate all luff grooves, channels for slugs, and sheave boxes; repair as required.)
- ❏ check all fittings for tightness, corrosion, and operation

- ❑ inspect, clean, and repair all sails (after dry, loosely flake and store in warm dry location)
- ❑ remove all running rigging
- ❑ inspect, repair, and replace running rigging as required
- ❑ wash and dry all running rigging before storage
- ❑ clean and service all winches

BATTERY
- ❑ top off electrolyte with distilled water
- ❑ clean battery terminals of any corrosion products
- ❑ charge battery fully
- ❑ during storage, periodically charge battery (better yet, float charge)

TRAILER
- ❑ inspect and repack wheel bearings
- ❑ block up trailer frame taking weight off of tires and springs
- ❑ cover tires to protect from UV

OUTBOARD MOTOR
- ❑ follow manufacturer's lay-up procedures
- ❑ empty all gasoline from auxiliary tank and store dry

look at your winter-lay up checklist from last year; you'll need to undo some of those items during spring commissioning.

SPRING COMMISSIONING CHECKLIST
- ❑ lubricate seacocks
- ❑ close all seacocks that were opened in the fall
- ❑ inspect all hoses and hose clamps
- ❑ inspect fire extinguisher
- ❑ inspect flares and check expiration date
- ❑ inspect bilge pump and float switch
- ❑ drain and flush potable water system: if laid-up, with

nontoxic antifreeze; if laid-up dry, flush with baking soda and water to freshen
❑ check electrolyte and charge levels of battery before reinstalling

No matter how comprehensive the checklist, if you don't use it, chances are that something will be missed. While sailing is not rocket science, it is analogous to flying. Pilots use checklists all the time to ensure a safe and efficient flight. Why not adapt and benefit from this low tech yet almost foolproof technique? (By the way, the Lone Ranger's nephew's horse's name is Victor.)

APPENDIX

Manufacturers and their trailerable sailboats currently in production:

Arey's Pond Boat Yard
P.O. Box 222
So. Orleans, MA 02662
508-255-0994
www.areyspondboatyard.com
catboat@cape.com
Catboats 12, 14, 16, & 20', 18' Daysailer

Cape Cod Shipbuilding Co.
P.O. Box 152
7 Narrows Rd.
Wareham, MA 02571-0152
508-295-3550
www.capecodshipbuilding.com
info@capecodshipbuilding.com
 9' MK Dinghy to 23' Marlin & several other in between

Catalina Yachts
21200 Victory Boulevard
Woodland Hills, CA 91367
818-884-7700
www.catalinayachts.com
Daysailers and Pocket Cruisers 8' to 25'

Corsair Marine
150 Reed Court
Chula Vista, CA 91911
619-585-3005
877-FAST TRI
www.corsairmarine.com
Trimarans

General Boats
114 Midway Drive
Edenton, NC 27932
252-482-4372
www.rhodes22.com
wwrhodes@rhodes22.com
Rhodes 22

Hake Yachts
4550 SE Hampton Court
Stuart, FL 34997
772-287-3200
www.seawardyachts.com
Seaward 26RK & 32RK

Hobie Cat Company
4925 Oceanside Blvd.
Oceanside, CA 92056
www.hobiecat.com
info@hobiecat.com
Catamarans

Hunter Marine Corp.
Route 441
P.O. Box 1030
Alachua, FL 32616
386-462-3077
800-771-5556
www.huntermarine.com
info@huntermarine.com
Daysailers 9'-21' 7 Pocket Cruisers 25'-27'

Hutchins Company, Inc.
1195 Kapp Dr.
Clearwater, FL 33765
727-443-4408
www.com-pacyachts.com
info@com-pacyachts.com
Picnic/Sun/Horizon Cats, Legacy, Eclipse, Com Pac 23/IV & 25

International Marine
922 W. Hyde Park Blvd
Inglewood, CA 90302
800-433-4080
www.imsailboats.com
www.wwpotter.com
West Wright Potter 15 & 19, Sanibel 18

Legnos Boat Building Company, Inc.
973 North Road
Route 117
Groton, CT 06340
203-446-8058
Peter Legnos
Mystic 20

MacGregor Yacht Corp
1631 Placentia
Costa Mesa, CA 92627
949-642-6830
www.macgregor26.com
MacGregor 26

Marine Concepts
243 Anclote Rd.
Tarpon Springs, FL 34689
800-881-1525
www.marine-concepts.com
Sea Pearl

Marshall Catboats
Box P-266
South Dartmouth, MA 02748
508-994-0414
www.marshallcat.com
Marshall Cat 15, 18, & 22, Sanderling

Nimble Boats, Inc
1618 S. 51st St.
Tampa, FL 33619
813-247-2770
813-601-8101
www.nimbleboat.net
info@nimbleboat.net
Peep Hen, Mud Hen, Nimble 20, Nimble 24, Kodiak, Wanderer

Precision Boat Works
1511 18th Ave. Drive East
Palmetto, FL 34221
941-722-6601
www.precisionboatworks.com
Precision 15, 165, 18, 185, 21, 23, & 28

Skimmer Boats
A Division of Creative Marine Products
243 John R. Junkin Dr.
P.O. Box 2121
Natchez, Mississippi
800-824-0355
www.creativemarine.com/skimmer/about.html
Skimmer 25

During the "Age of Trailer sailers" (the 70s and early 80s), there were numerous companies producing trailerable sailboats. Most of those that are no longer with us succumbed to a variety of business related issues, not necessarily problems with product quality.

Hundreds of their seaworthy craft are still being enjoyed today; many can be obtained quite reasonably. Three good sources for information on previously experienced trailer sailers are:

www.trailer sailer.com
www.goodoldboat.com
www.smallcraftadvisor.com